first nations food companion

This book was created on the traditional lands of the Ngadjuri, Kaurna, Cammeraygal, Gadigal, Wangal, Kuringgai, Wurundjeri and Boon Wurrung people. We pay our respects to their elders past, present and future. Sovereignty was never ceded.

Dedicated to our sons. All the work, before you and beyond, by your mama and dadda, is for you. For your Yarta (Country), your story, your culture, your future.

Murdoch Books will donate $1 from the sale of each copy of this book to the Indigenous Literacy Foundation.

How to
buy, grow,
cook and eat
Indigenous
Australian
ingredients

first nations food companion

DAMIEN COULTHARD | REBECCA SULLIVAN

murdoch books
Sydney | London

Foreword by Ngarrpadla Daphne Paringangki Rickett

(Aunty Daphne River Woman Rickett)

I am a proud Kaurna, Ngarrindjeri, Latji Latji woman born in the Riverland region of South Australia. I am the sixth child of thirteen children, a mother of two, grandmother to seven and great-grandmother to three. I am an Elder of the Southern Kaurna Community, where I have lived and spent most of my life in an urban settlement.

Over the last 25 years, my passion for Australian native bush foods and how to use them has grown. I am reclaiming my Culture and expanding the knowledge about the native plants and animals my Ancestors used in everyday life. Working alongside other people — my friends who are chefs, plant growers, environmentalists, and many others with a passion for bush foods — has given me the opportunity to further develop my expertise. I have spent many years travelling the Countries of our land and sharing the knowledge I have gathered along the way.

Recent times have seen a resurgence in the use of native plants in contemporary cooking, and when the opportunity came to work with Damien and Rebecca on the creation of this book, I was very excited. It has been a pleasure working with them and supporting them with this important work.

During the process of making the book, I was proud to share my Culture and I enjoyed cooking many of the exciting new dishes found in these pages. I was exposed to a modern world of cooking with the native plants that are found all over Australia and was introduced to dynamic recipes with a wide range of flavours. It was a privilege and an honour to be involved in this process, creating meals using a wide variety of herbs and ingredients that are delicious to the palate.

Damien and I shared the stories of our people, and what it was like growing up in different eras and on different Country. It was an eye-opener to listen to how Damien grew up with his people, learning and sharing Culture. This experience enhanced my passion for cooking with bush foods even more than I expected.

The information and recipes in this book will help readers understand more about my culture and other First Nations cultures through cooking and enjoying meals with friends and family. Sharing this Traditional knowledge offers us an opportunity to further heal the past.

I congratulate Damien and Rebecca for promoting Aboriginal Cultures through native plants and animals as food in a modern world. My hope is that people reading this book will be immersed in a new world of cooking and discover the richness and diversity of Australian native plants found in their own backyard.

Foreword by Bruce Pascoe, author of *Dark Emu*

(Uncle Bruce Pascoe, Yuin man)

This book provides an important opportunity for Australia to contemplate the full 100,000 years of Australian history and the brilliance of Aboriginal land use and sustainability. Acceptance of those truths brings Australians — black and white — closer to our history and geography, and more in tune with the reality of our location without the need to justify the theft of the land. That understanding will produce a maturity and generosity in the country that has been lacking.

The exploration of Aboriginal and Torres Strait Islander botanical and culinary knowledge is not only relevant to our health and of interest for the flavours it helps us generate from our kitchens, but it also invites Australia to contemplate the use of our land and climate. These plants are Australian; they thrive in the Australian climate and soils, so don't require the coddling and artificial support of plants imported from other countries.

Ploughing and irrigation have reduced some Australian agricultural districts to salty deserts. Engineers can organise the relocation of soil and fertility, but seem incapable of reversing salinity, empty rivers and environmental degradation. Growing Australian plants and eating soft-footed animals, however, goes a long way towards rectifying the destruction of Australian soils, whose fertility has been plummeting for more than 200 years.

Eating less meat will also be a good thing for the planet in general. Our diets, being so meat-orientated, create a burden for the planet that is unsustainable. Enthusiastic meat-eaters like me need to find alternatives. This *First Nations Food Companion* is our chance to adopt a more sustainable diet.

Enthusiasm for our food still has one more requirement: Aboriginal people have to be involved in the agricultural economy or it becomes just one more dispossession. You cannot eat our food if you can't swallow our history.

Gubinge
(Kakadu plum, page 30)

Contents

First flavours	9
The ultimate in local food	10
How this book works	13
Ingredients guide	15
Stock your pantry	56
First Nations flavour wheel	58
Spice	63
Herbal	85
Nutty	105
Fruity	123
Medicine garden	135
Floral	143
Citrusy	173
Marine	195
Earthy	203
Tips on preserving	232
Stockists	234
Featured artists	236
Acknowledgements	238
Index	240

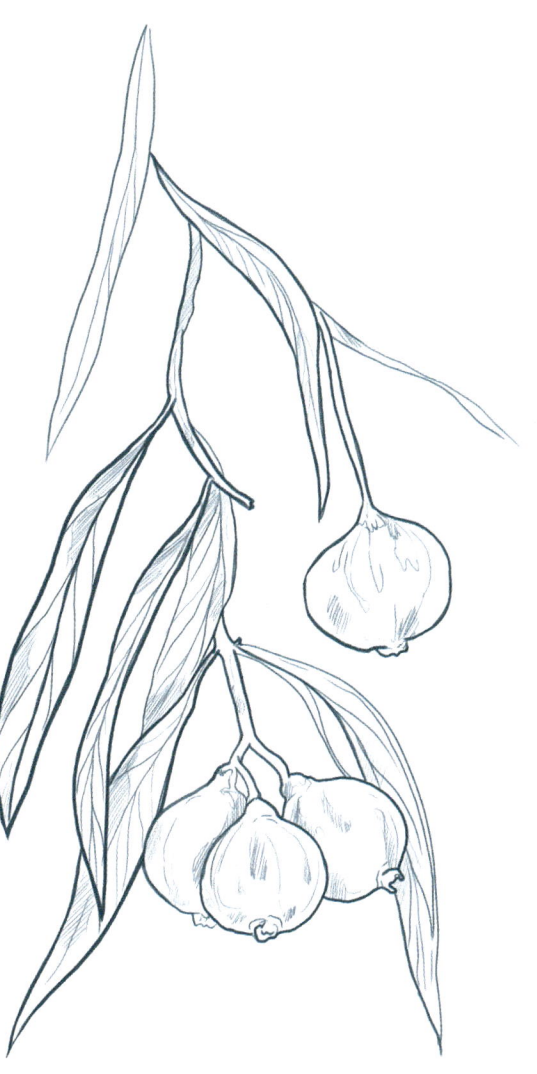

First flavours

There is nothing better than seeing the excitement and happiness on a child's face when they are greeted with food. Our son Mallee is a willing consumer of all foods, especially First Nations foods, and he's always happy to discover a new or unfamiliar flavour.

From an early age, Mallee's introduction to native foods has been an open lunchbox. My parents and family share harvested foods from Country, and when we receive a new package from a harvester, grower or farmer, Mallee is almost always the first to try. Muntries and quandongs, eaten handfuls at a time, are his favourite. With every handful comes an opportunity to share stories through a First Nations lens. It's this sense of adventure, discovery and wonder that we hope to share with you in this book.

The *First Nations Food Companion* is an opportunity for all people, young and old, from all backgrounds, to taste the flavours of the oldest living, continuous culture in the world. If we approach it with open arms and an open mind, like Mallee we have the opportunity to learn the provenance of each native species that has been enriched by ancient soils and carefully cultivated by traditional owners guided by complex knowledge systems. Celebrating First Nations peoples, their voices and resources, is an integral part of achieving our aspirations. The restoration of cultural practices reflective of complex kinship associations, strengthening the co-culture community relationships and the healing of Country are at the heart of restoring and reclaiming First Nations knowledge and creating a sustainable native foods industry that functions with integrity.

We can all play a role in supporting and strengthening our communities through First Nations foods. This can be as simple as sitting with Elders as equals, and listening respectfully with your heart. There is so much to be learnt from our knowledge keepers. Our ancient lands hold vast amounts of information, with interwoven histories shared over millennia that map our continent.

So, how do we find out more? By forging respectful, genuine and authentic relationships, engaging in experiences on Country outside of Reconciliation Week or NAIDOC week and listening with the intent to learn. By being open to feeling uncomfortable and challenged, by engaging in conversations and, most importantly, by taking responsibility for your own journey by supporting Aboriginal-led businesses and non-Aboriginal businesses operating with integrity and authenticity.

Over the past decade there has been a rapid growth in the native foods industry: First Nations foods are now front and centre at gin distilleries, featured on menus at local cafés and top restaurants in most major cities. Native botanicals that have provided health and wellness for diverse nations over many generations are new-but-old flavours for some. It is exciting to see Aboriginal and non-Aboriginal businesses celebrating cultural heritage through their chosen products, but many native species featured in this book are significant to their place and community, and it's important that this cultural and intellectual property remains with traditional owners.

As I get older, learning more about my culture has become a matter of urgency. Across Australia, Aboriginal languages are at great risk, with some already on the brink of no return and many extinct. As we lose languages, we also lose histories and family heritage; important knowledge systems left to sleep in the land. I see our foods as an equally important element of these systems.

Thank you for opening your hearts and minds to learning more about our rich cultures and amazing First Nations foods.

Damien Coulthard

The ultimate in local food

My journey into the First Nations food industry came about in 2013, when I first met Damien. As an advocate of local food my entire career, it soon became clear after meeting Damien how much I had left out of what 'local' really meant. How could I possibly be an advocate of local foods if I had never tried lemon myrtle or wattleseed?

When we reach adulthood, we think that it is near-impossible to try anything new or discover any foods that will challenge us. But even if you are a seasoned chef, or are familiar with some of these flavours, I can guarantee that there are First Nations foods you will find new, exciting and wonderful. My first experiences of many of these foods felt like being a child eating things for the first time. Of course, many First Nations foods no longer exist, after centuries of colonisation and destruction of traditional lands, but there are still more than 6500 of these foods all around Australia that are as local as it gets, as well as being nutritious and absolutely delicious.

In 2014 Damien and I created Warndu, an ethical lifestyle brand championing native foods. Our mission was to regenerate community, culture, tradition, health, seas and soils. Soon after this we decided it was time to properly live out our values around sustainable food and fulfil our desire to grow these foods, so they could be more widely shared, understood and enjoyed. We bought a property of 96 acres on Ngadjuri Country, in the Clare Valley, where we live off-grid in a straw-bale house surrounded by native forest. It's here that we continue to grow our brand, grow our foods, and learn about these amazing native plants each and every day.

We are still learning, and always will be. These are the oldest foods eaten — but also the newest foods, in the sense that they are finally getting the attention they deserve. For some of them, we still don't know for sure their Indigenous names or on whose Country they originated. Yet these foods are so important from environmental, cultural and health perspectives — they are absolutely not just a 'foodie trend'. They are medicine, story and reconciliation. And they present potential climate-resilience solutions for this overfarmed and arid continent.

Having been immersed in the Indigenous foods industry for more than eight years, I have seen it grow steadily, and demand is now consistently outweighing supply. As an industry, we still have many issues to overcome, in particular ensuring that the intellectual property of these foods remains with First Nations people, plus an array of frustrating certification issues and supply-chain challenges. Even so, the growth, positivity and support from new consumers who are keen to learn along with us gives us the warm-fuzzies every day.

While growth is magnificent news for any industry, the particular challenges faced by the native foods industry mean that supply is not as consistent as we are used to in modern-day supermarkets. But if we all continue to work together, with the goal of growing the industry, we are confident that soon enough all the ingredients in this book will be available as part of every Australian's weekly shop.

Rebecca Sullivan

How this book works: ingredients, flavours, recipes

The first part of this book is our generously detailed, but not exhaustive, ingredients guide, devoted to edible and accessible native plants. For the most part, the plants we focus on in this section are available to buy in frozen or dried forms, though some are available fresh. The chapter also includes a mini encyclopaedia of native foods you can grow at home, where suitable and culturally appropriate. Whether you have a little balcony or live on an extensive plot, these growing tips are tried and tested by us, and we highly recommend giving them a go.

This book is both for beginners to First Nations foods, and for those who already have a grasp of the bounty of Australian native plants and produce and are seeking to expand their understanding and palate. So after our ingredients guide, a great place to start 'thinking' with your tastebuds is our handy First Nations flavour wheel (page 58), which visualises what these native ingredients can offer in the kitchen. Once you're familiar with the flavours, dive into the recipes.

These chapters champion common native ingredients and are handily organised by flavour: Spice, Herbal, Nutty, Fruity, Floral, Citrusy, Marine and Earthy, along with a medicine garden chapter of recipes for herbal remedies. For the purposes of this book, we have focused on recipes made with ingredients that are readily available, and we have included details of some of the many wonderful stockists where you can find First Nations foods (page 234) both in store and online. For instances when you can't get a particular ingredient, or your plant is not yet in season, we have added a handy substitution guide to each recipe so you can swap in everyday supermarket ingredients where needed.

We encourage you to experiment, substitute, try, taste — and most of all, have fun!

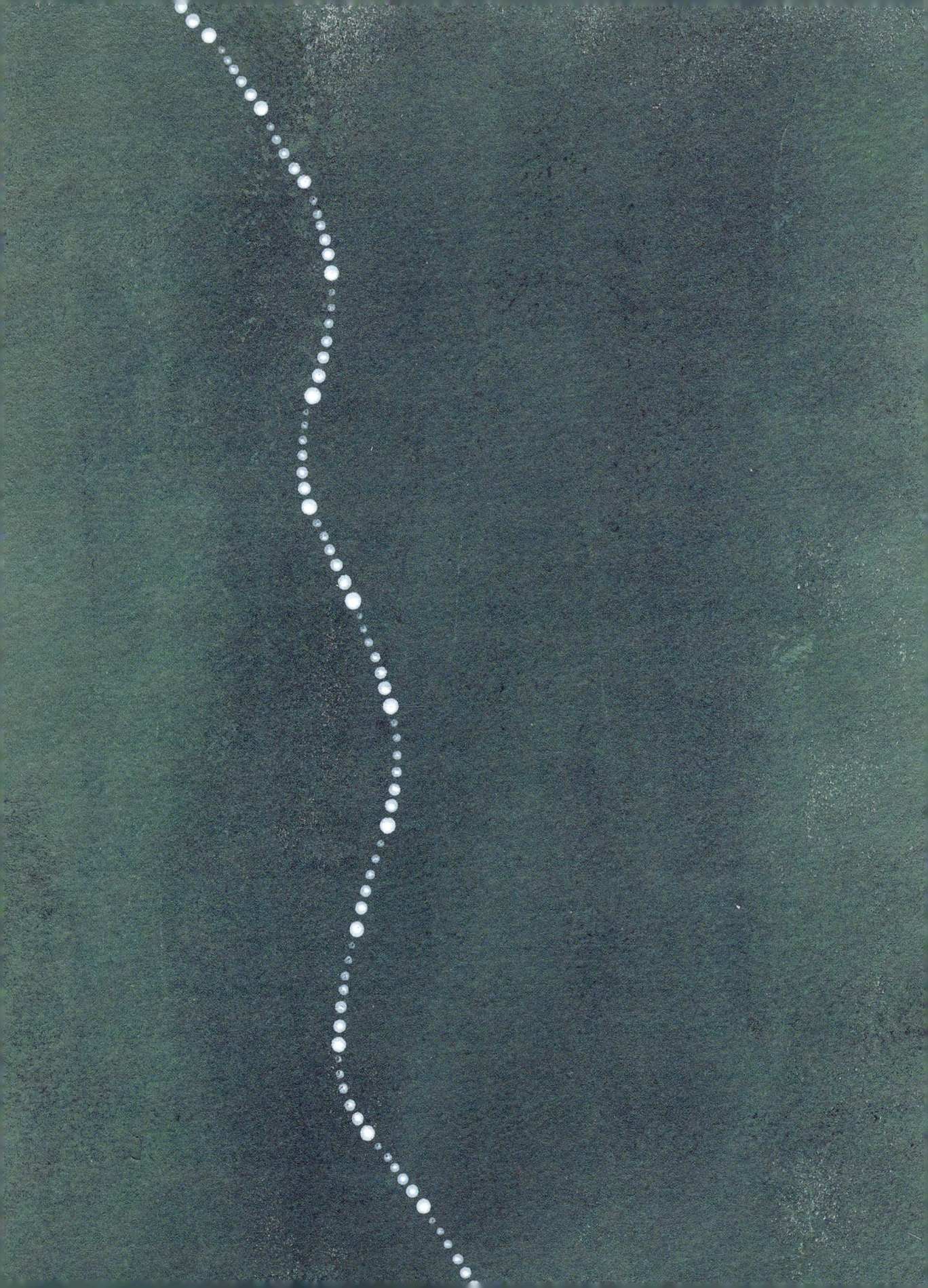

ingredients guide

Ingredients guide

The native foods in this culinary and planting guide have traditionally been used and eaten by First Nations peoples for tens of thousands of years. Due to the devastating impacts of colonisation, knowledge of many plants has been lost. Likewise, many Language names for known plants have been lost, or at least couldn't be found after consulting with many Elders, colleagues and experts. For example, pepperberry (page 40) is quite well-known and easy to find, but has no known name in Palawa kani (the collective name for reconstructed Tasmanian language groups). On the other hand, some plants have many known names, as these can differ between regions and Language groups. This guide is organised in alphabetical order by English name, but leads with the Aboriginal Language name where available.

This is a guide to the foods of many First Nations, not just the ones near us. We've tried to highlight the most commonly known names for ingredients, or the names relevant to the places where particular plants are endemic and tend to grow. However, this guide cannot be, and does not aim to be, comprehensive or authoritative — we prefer to think of it as a living, growing repository of knowledge, hopefully with some practical and delicious uses. We hope it will encourage you to engage more meaningfully with First Nations foods, and hopefully will bring enough attention to these ingredients that it draws out further Indigenous knowledge and brings it into new use. We hope to update and revise this guide for future editions, so please get in touch through our website (warndu.com) if you know something we don't.

General note on foraging: Where culturally appropriate, this directory also shares how to pick or forage plants. When doing so, it is essential to check the identity of any plant at least three times before picking, to make sure it is an edible species. Always ask permission if you're on someone else's property, and avoid major roadways due to potential pollutants. Most importantly, be respectful, both culturally and environmentally. Always take only what you need, and leave plenty behind for the birds and the bees.

Wurrganyga | Anise myrtle | *Syzygium anisatum*

Known as wurrganyga in Gumbaynggir (mid-north coast NSW), anise myrtle is a native rainforest plant whose leaves have a strong liquorice or aniseed flavour. Also known as ringwood and creeping myoporum, anise myrtle grows along the streams and lower slopes of the subtropical rainforests of northern New South Wales, around the Bellingen and Nambucca valleys. It is not only a wonderful addition to cooking; the leaf used as tea is a powerful digestive and great for stomach aches.

USE: Anywhere you want the flavour of fennel or liquorice (or, anise, of course). Dried or fresh leaves will impart flavour to sweet and savoury dishes. Ground leaves can be cooked or sprinkled on raw.
BUY: Fresh or dried.
PICK/FORAGE: Pick young, fresh leaves any time of year. More mature leaves are best for drying and infusions.
STORE: In the fridge or freezer. If dried, in an airtight container.

GROW: Anise myrtle prefers well-drained, nutrient-rich soil with morning sun and some shade. We have had huge success growing anise myrtle in pots. Established plants are relatively hardy and will tolerate dry weather.
- Best in morning sun
- Tolerates sandy soil and drought; keep well watered when flowering
- Good in gaps, hedges and screens
- Biodiversity habitat

First Nations Food Companion

Djarduk | Bush apple | *Syzygium forte*

These apples, known as djarduk in Arnhem Land (north-eastern NT), are about the size of a small tennis ball and have a really huge seed in them. The fruit itself, which comes in a range of scarlet colours, is soft and tart. We love them sliced fresh into salads or just eaten like you would an apple (but navigating the seed). They can also be frozen whole for later use, or dehydrated. Also known as lady apple and wild apple, they have stunning rose-petal smell and flavour.

USE: Fresh or cooked, as you would apples or nashi. Dried, they're a great snack for kids.
BUY: Online, fresh or frozen. Occasionally found at specialty shops in the right regions.
PICK/FORAGE: You need to be able to climb a tree safely to forage for this one, but you are unlikely to find it on non-traditional-owned land, so best to buy it.
STORE: In the fridge or freezer, or dried in an airtight container.
GROW: Loves warm, tropical parts of Australia, especially the Northern Territory and Queensland. The tree itself will grow to about 20 metres (65 feet) high.
- Grow in full sun or part-shade
- Suitable for pots
- Hates frost
- Biodiversity habitat

Gumbi gumbi | Native apricot | *Pittosporum angustifolium*

This native apricot, known as gumbi gumbi (particularly in inland Australia), was one of the very first plants we learnt about when foraging with Damien's uncle Nola. The leaves make a very special cup of tea, which is not just aromatic and delicious, but also fights coughs and colds. We don't bother with the fruit — they're so bitter as to be inedible — but they're beautiful. Be very careful to get the correct plant as there are several species referred to as gumbi gumbi. In other parts of Australia, it's also called cumbi cumbi, meemeei, kurti (Adnyamathanha), weeping pittosporum, bitterbush, kurti, mondroo and mutja (Kaurna).

USE: Just for tea and only the leaves. Must be boiled, cooked or processed
BUY: As fresh or dried leaves. Or pick leaves to use straight from the tree.
PICK/FORAGE: Only pick the leaves and be sure to boil them before drinking.
STORE: If dried, store in an airtight container.
GROW: Gumbi Gumbi is one of the toughest plants out there. It will grow in a wide array of conditions but prefers it hot and dry with well-drained soil.
- Grow in full sun and part-shade
- Suitable for pots
- Biodiversity habitat
- Tolerates sandy soil and drought
- Provides great shade

Eeepaeep | Atherton raspberry | *Rubus probus*

There's more than one variety of native raspberry, but this one, known as eeepaeep in Wurundjeri (Yarra River, VIC) is the most commonly available. It's a lighter red than the raspberry we see at the shops, and tends to be softer and more tart. The shelf life is short for these (as is the season), so the best thing to do is eat them quickly, or freeze them. Grows wild throughout tropical, subtropical and warm, temperate Queensland, although we have two in pots at home in South Australia.

USE: As you would strawberries or raspberries, raw or cooked.
BUY: Online either fresh, frozen or as a freeze-dried powder. Occasionally at farmers' markets and shops in the right regions.
PICK/FORAGE: In the wild in tropical climates.
STORE: Use fresh or freeze.

GROW: Thrives in warm climates and pots.
- Grow in full sun or part-shade.
- Suitable for pots
- Really hates frost, so not suitable for cold climates unless sheltered
- Will grow up to 2 metres (6 feet) high and wide, likes trellising
- OK in sandy soil, needs quite a bit of water
- Great biodiversity habitat
- Loves a good prune

War-rak | Banksia | *Banksia spp.*

These beautiful shrubs with orange and yellow flowers grow all over Australia, and while the flowers are lovely to decorate your house with, they also can be soaked in water to make a sweet nectar. This is a traditional practice for war-rack, as it's known in Wurundjeri (Yarra River, VIC), as is sucking on the stamens for a little sugar hit. If you're picking banksias, do it when they're full of nectar — and make sure you leave plenty behind. Silver and swamp banksias make great alternatives, too.

USE: As edible flowers (picked) or in drinks. Best freshly picked and used immediately. They can also be fermented for drinks. Dried petals make great decoration, too.
BUY: Fresh or dried as petals, or whole flowers in bunches. Or pick your own.
PICK/FORAGE: In abundance all over but there are many species, so always ID three times to make sure it is an edible species.
STORE: In the fridge, picked and kept like herbs or in vases.

GROW: Common ornamental garden plant, likes good drainage. Choose the right species for your soil and climate.
- Grow in full sun
- Suitable for pots if kept small and trimmed as they can grow as tall as 20 metres (65 feet)
- Needs well-drained soil
- Biodiversity habitat
- Adds stunning pops of colour and fragrance
- Save seeds to plant out

Birira | Barilla or bower spinach | *Tetragonia implexicoma*

A coastal shrub, known as birira in Kaurna (Adelaide, SA), that's much like warrigal greens in terms of texture and nutrients. The plant, which grows in clumps, has small yellow flowers and bright red berries.

USE: Like spinach. Fresh, wilted or blanched is best.
BUY: Fresh.
PICK/FORAGE: This grows in abundance by the coast, so if foraging, do it there, which also means it won't be overly polluted.
STORE: In the fridge, sealed in a paper bag.

GROW: A groundcover that can be kept as small as you like. High salt tolerance, and so easy to grow.
- Propagate from seed or seedling
- Grow in full sun or part-shade
- Suitable for pots and garden beds
- Biodiversity habitat
- Tolerates sandy soil and drought
- Good in gaps and makes a great groundcover
- Save seeds to plant out

Native basil | *Plectranthus graveolens*

A mint relative with soft, fluffy leaves that's more basil than basil. It's also very easy to grow at home, either in pots or planted straight into beds — we've had luck with both. Like wild basil, it has a beautiful purple flower.

USE: Wherever you'd use basil. Use much less, though, as it's very strong.
BUY: Fresh or dried.
PICK/FORAGE: Young leaves to use fresh, older leaves to dry. The purple flowers are edible, too.
STORE: In the fridge or a vase. If dried, in an airtight container.

GROW: In part-shade for best results. This basil has large fuzzy leaves and lovely purple flowers. The plant makes a great mozzie repellent too.
- Propagate from seeds or plant seedlings
- Grow in full sun or part-shade
- Suitable for pots
- Good in gaps and makes a great groundcover
- Remove yellow leaves
- Biodiversity habitat
- Tolerates sandy soil and drought
- Save seeds to plant out

Wild basil | *Ocimum tenuiflorum*

A relative of Asia's holy basil with beautiful violet flowers, this wild variety really lends an intense fragrance to dishes. It's believed to have made its way to Australia through Indonesia, then adapted to our climate over time.

USE: Like basil.
BUY: Fresh or dried. Or pick leaves straight from the plant.
PICK/FORAGE: Always ID three times to make sure you're picking an edible species. You can also eat the flowers.
STORE: In the fridge or a vase. If dried, in an airtight container.

GROW: This is very easy to grow either in the ground or in pots. Like most soft herbs, it does not love frost and needs some water.
- Propagate from seed or seedling
- Grow in full sun or part-shade
- Suitable for pots and garden beds
- Biodiversity habitat
- Tolerates sandy soil
- Save seeds to plant out

Meen | Bloodroot | *Haemodorum spicatum*

Known as meen in Noongar (south-western WA), and elsewhere as bohn, mardja or menang, this native bulb vegetable is revered as both a food source and a medicine to help with dysentery, mouth sores and toothache. Known as bloodroot in English, it oozes a reddish sap when cut — hence the name — and its flavour lingers, so use sparingly. Perfect for a curry paste or to make flavoured oil, like chilli oil.

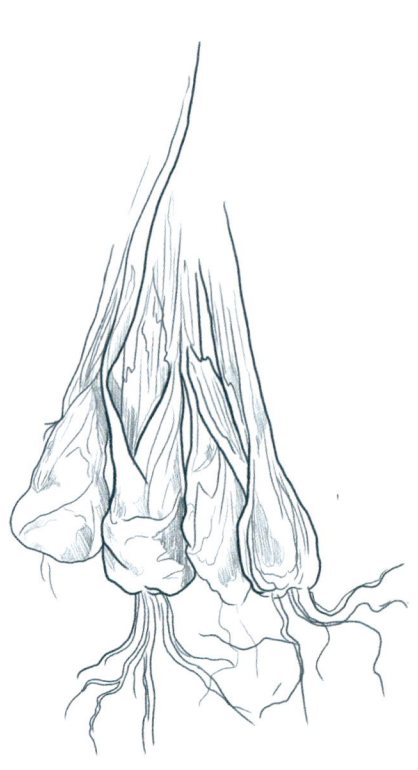

USE: Like chilli (really hot chilli) or radish. The roots are great eaten fresh, but very hot, so it's good to roast or otherwise cook it before use.
BUY: Hard to find. Best to try to grow it yourself.
PICK/FORAGE: Not advisable; safer to grow your own.
STORE: In the fridge.

GROW: Native to WA, bloodroot is a very slow-growing bulb that can handle really poor soils. Best planted in groups.
- Grow in full sun and part-shade
- Suitable for pots
- Biodiversity habitat
- Good groundcover
- Tolerates sandy soil
- Likes water when young to help it establish itself

Larrkardiy | Boab | *Adansonia gregorii*

A large, bulbous tree found in the Kimberley and parts of the Northern Territory and Western Australia. Sometimes known as larrkardiy, these long-lived trees produce large fruits with a tough husk; when cracked open, they reveal chalky nuts that taste a little like sherbet. Ground up, they turn into a powder that adds creamy, zesty flavour to sweet or savoury dishes. Fresh is best, but freeze-dried is more common and still tastes amazing. Also, studies have shown the fruit to be high in vitamin C. Boab roots are a little like kohlrabi in texture and have a subtly sweet carrot-like flavour and crunch.

USE: Anywhere you want something zesty or minerally. Boab powder is great sprinkled on yoghurts, cereals, fruit salads, veggies and more. It can also be cooked into dishes.
BUY: Online as a freeze-dried powder. Occasionally as a whole nut when in season.
PICK/FORAGE: Boab trees are of immense importance to the peoples of the Kimberley as they can be places for camping or landmarks, and some even have maps and stories etched into them like living libraries. They are also protected, so it is illegal to gather any parts of the tree from the wild.
STORE: In an airtight container away from direct sunlight. Or in the freezer.
GROW: Out of respect, this is best left to Indigenous people.

Birdak | Bottlebrush | *Callistemon spp.*

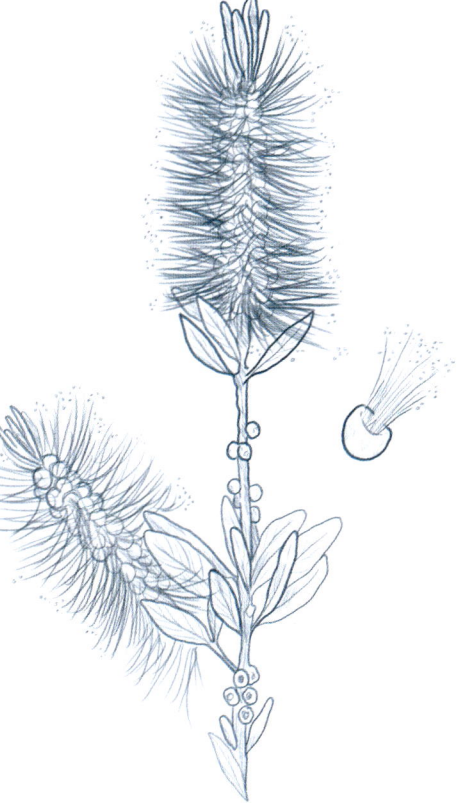

These bright red flowers, known as birdak in Noongar (south-western WA), can be (and were) used in much the same way as banksia flowers, either soaked in water to make a sweet nectar, or sucked on fresh for a sugar hit. Again, be sparing when you pick them, making sure to leave plenty on the plant for regeneration — and for the wildlife, of course.

USE: As edible flower or in drinks. Best freshly picked, but dried petals are good for decoration, too. Great fermented.
BUY: Fresh or dried petals, or in bunches. Or pick your own.
PICK/FORAGE: In abundance all over, but there are many species so be careful to do your research to ensure you pick only edible varieties.
STORE: Picked and kept like herbs in the fridge, or in vases.
GROW: In well-drained soil.
- Grow in full sun.
- Not suitable for pots, as plants can grow to 25 metres (80 feet)
- Great biodiversity habitat
- Adds stunning pops of colour and fragrance
- Great for providing shade

Bunya | Bunya pine | *Araucaria bidwilli*

These enormous, ancient trees — known as bunya in Kabi Kabi (south-eastern QLD) — date back to the time of the dinosaurs, which were known to have eaten the cones. Aboriginal people did the same, often climbing the trunks to harvest the enormous cones, then cracking them open to reveal their seeds, with the fruiting season attracting large gatherings. (It's also a dangerous time to walk under a bunya pine, since the cones can weigh up to 10 kilograms.) The large seeds inside the cones, which must be cracked open to expose the nuts, taste a little like pine nuts, and can be used in much the same way. (They're also high in protein, carbohydrates and good fats.) In season, you can source them fresh, but more often the peeled, halved nuts will be available frozen.

USE: Raw or cooked, wherever you'd use pine nuts.
BUY: Online when in season; often comes peeled and frozen.
PICK/FORAGE: Can you climb a 30-metre (100 foot) tree and carry down a cone the weight of a bowling ball? That said, you might chance upon one on the ground.

STORE: In the freezer. Or if still in the shells, just in an airtight container is fine.
GROW: This one is best left to the professionals.

Ballee | Native cherry | Cherry ballart | *Exocarpos cupressiformis*

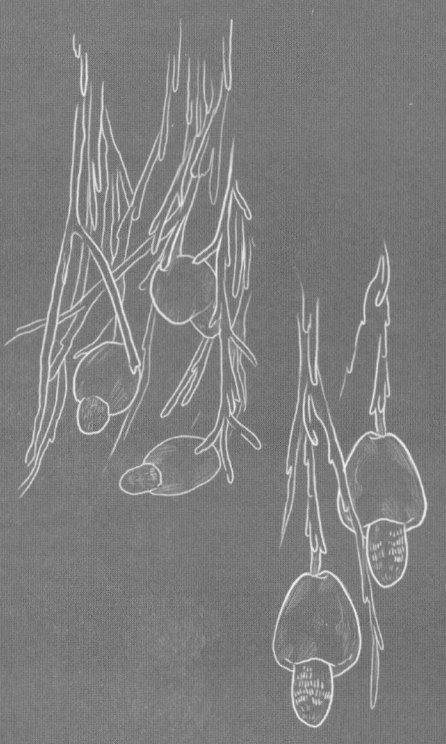

These native cherries or cherry ballart — known as ballee in Wurundjeri (Yarra River, VIC) or elsewhere as palatt, ballot and pul-loitch — grow in the Atherton Tablelands in Queensland, in southern Victoria, in southern Tasmania, and across in the Eyre Peninsula in South Australia. Environmentally they are quite extraordinary, as they control their immediate environment. Research shows that they create moderate micro-climates with their foliage, reduce soil temperatures, increase water retention in the soil, concentrate nutrients in the ground beneath their canopies, and alter the understory vegetation. The tiny red fruits are astringent and tart, popping with flavour in the mouth. They aren't as plump or sweet as cherries, so use them more as you would cranberries, rather than putting them out for dessert on the Christmas table.

USE: Like cherries or cranberries. Use fresh, cooked or dried.
BUY: Online, either fresh, frozen or (sometimes) as a freeze-dried powder. Occasionally at farmers' markets and shops in the right regions.
PICK/FORAGE: These are only really found in tropical climates. Pick when plump and red.

STORE: In the fridge or freezer, or the pantry if dried.
GROW: Best left to nature and for professionals because it is a semi-parasitic which can make it challenging to grow.

Cinnamon myrtle | *Backhousia myrtifolia*

A lovely native rainforest tree with pretty cream-coloured flowers and cinnamon-scented leaves. Use it in place of traditional cinnamon, but be sparing because the flavour is stronger. The leaves usually come dried; we tend to grind them to a powder with a spice grinder then keep it in a jar. Also known as carrol, grey myrtle, ironwood, neverbreak and Australian lancewood.

USE: Instead of cinnamon. Can be dried and ground, then sprinkled or cooked into dishes.
BUY: Online, fresh or dried.
PICK/FORAGE: Pick young, fresh leaves any time of year. More mature leaves are best for drying and infusions.
STORE: In the fridge or freezer. If dried, in the pantry in an airtight container.

GROW: Cinnamon myrtle prefers well-drained, nutrient-rich soil in a sunny position, but may also be grown in part-shade. Established trees are relatively hardy and will tolerate dry weather.
- Grow in part-shade or morning sun
- Suitable for pots
- Tolerates sandy soil and drought, but keep well watered when flowering
- Good in gaps and for hedges and screens
- Provides shade

Ahakeye | Native currant | *Canthium latifolium*

They may be tiny, but these stunning red berries that grow around sand hills and ranges in the Central Desert are mighty in flavour, with a sharp tartness. Known as ahakeye in Eastern Arrernte languages (Alice Springs, NT), they're best eaten fresh but can be frozen. Try them in salads and desserts, as a cocktail garnish or in jams and chutneys. You can also dry them out for longer storage.

USE: As you would raisins, sultanas or cranberries. Best freshly picked, but can also be frozen or dried.
BUY: Frozen, or as a plant. Always rinse before eating.
PICK/FORAGE: They are not in abundance, so we wouldn't suggest you go searching.
STORE: In the fridge or freezer.

GROW: Quick-growing tree/shrub. Actually pretty easy to grow, especially in pots.
- Grow in full sun or part-shade
- Suitable for pots
- OK in sandy or salty soil and tolerates drought
- Makes a great screen, hedge and biodiversity habitat

Morr | Wild currant | *Antidesma erostre*

Known as morr in Wurundjeri (Yarra River, VIC), this wild currant could be mistaken for a grape vine as the berries grow in bunches like grapes. The berries themselves, which are extremely tart, get sweeter as they mature and have a similar flavour to cranberries — they really make amazing sauces. Also known as currant tree and currant wood.

USE: Wherever you'd use raisins, sultanas or cranberries. Best fresh, but can be frozen or dried.
BUY: Frozen, or as a plant.
PICK/FORAGE: The berries are ripe when purple and the plant will produce more fruit as they are picked. We recommend harvesting and freezing to build up quantity and encourage growth.
STORE: In the fridge or freezer.

GROW: Quick-growing tree/shrub.
- Grow in full sun or part-shade
- Suitable for pots
- OK in sandy or salty soil and tolerates drought
- Makes a great screen, hedge and biodiversity habitat

Cut-leaf mint or native oregano | *Prostanthera rotundifolia*

A fast-growing bush shrub with a herbal aroma and a hint of menthol. Not only does this leaf make a great palate cleanser, it also promotes digestion, and the freshly cut leaves can help relieve nausea and headaches. We grow ours in small pots.

USE: Like mint, when you want a menthol tinge. The purple flowers are also edible.
PICK/FORAGE: Always ID three times to make sure you pick the right plant. Always ask permission if on someone else's property and avoid roadsides because of pollution.
BUY: Fresh or dried and ground. Or pick leaves to use straight from the plant.
STORE: In the fridge or a vase. If dried, in an airtight container.

GROW: This plant is a perennial and will put up with a little bit of cold and frost. It prefers to be watered in summer. Cut frequently to ensure continuous growth.
- Grow in part-shade, especially in pots and raised beds
- Biodiversity habitat
- Best in well-drained soils
- Likes water but can tolerate dry spells

Ooray | Davidson's plum | *Davidsonia pruriens*

The fruit of a rainforest plant known as ooray, most often found in Queensland and northern New South Wales, Davidson's plums are bright purple, with vibrant, almost magenta flesh. The trees grow to be quite tall and skinny, and the mature fruits are covered with irritant hairs. The fruit is more tart than it is sweet, and makes beautiful jams and sauces or, in powdered form, adds sharpness. They're also known colloquially as 'Davos'.

USE: Instead of plums. We prefer them cooked, but they can be eaten fresh rather like the Japanese sour plum.
BUY: Find them online either fresh, frozen or as a freeze-dried powder. Occasionally sold at farmers' markets and shops in the right regions.
PICK/FORAGE: Fruits are green when under-ripe, purple when ripe, and the plant will produce more fruit as they are picked. We recommend harvesting and freezing to encourage growth.

STORE: In the fridge or freezer.
GROW: Best in the tropics but some people have success in other regions; we have two growing in a sheltered area at home with other tropical plants. Can also be grown indoors.
- Grow in full sun or part-shade
- Suitable for pots
- OK in sandy soil, but likes water
- Shade provider — can grow to 8 metres (25 feet) high
- Biodiversity habitat
- Makes amazing fruit forests

Desert lime | *Citrus glauca*

These delicious fruits taste like a sherbet bomb. We keep them in the freezer and use them at just about every opportunity — try putting them in cakes, stir-fries, salads, desserts, even cocktails. They grow from Queensland to South Australia and are a true citrus. The trees are slow to mature, sometimes growing for a decade before they produce. Also known as bush lime, native lime and native cumquat.

USE: Wherever you'd use citrus. Great fresh, but can be cooked or processed into jams and sauces. Eat the whole thing.
BUY: Fresh, frozen or freeze-dried and powdered. Sometimes available at farmers' markets.
PICK/FORAGE: Always ID three times to make sure you pick the right fruit.
STORE: In the fridge or freezer. If dried, in an airtight container.

GROW: Desert limes thrive in dappled light, as well as in full sun. They actually like clay soil, which is great as not much else does! The stems have thorns to protect the fruit, making a wonderful shelter for birds and critters.
- Grow in full sun or part-shade
- Suitable for pots
- Tolerates light frost
- Biodiversity habitat
- Good in gaps and for hedges and screens

Gulalung | Finger lime | *Citrus australasica*

Known as gulalung in Bundjalung (south-eastern QLD and north-eastern NSW), finger limes can be found in a variety of colours, ranging from deep red through to bright green. A true citrus, the fruit has the flavour of lime, but instead of juicy flesh, inside is a pocket of tiny pearls that pop with acid — 'lime caviar'. No wonder they're so sought after by chefs all over the world. They're also a great source of folate, potassium and vitamin E, not to mention vitamin C. Finger limes are incredibly versatile. Try them with raw fish, on oysters, in salads or even in a G&T.

USE: Wherever you'd use citrus, but especially lime. The pearls can be squeezed fresh into sweet or savoury dishes and drinks, and the whole limes can be cooked, or used in jams.

BUY: Fresh, frozen or as a freeze-dried powder. Sometimes available in grocers and farmers' markets. Keep your eyes peeled for neighbours with trees and offer to swap fruit for some lime curd.

PICK/FORAGE: A hugely commercialised crop — it's much easier to buy them than try to forage for them.

STORE: If fresh, with your other citrus. If packaged, keep frozen or in an airtight container as recommended. Thaw out on paper towel if frozen. Can be re-frozen.

GROW: We have planted in the ground in our temperate climate and in pots; we are finding that the ones in pots are doing better. Whichever you decide, plant in free-draining soil and protect from frost and drying winds.

- Grow in full sun or part-shade
- Suitable for pots
- Biodiversity habitat
- Tolerates sandy soil and drought
- Good in gaps and for hedges and screens
- Very spiky spines — be careful
- Fruits from November to March, depending on where you live; the fruit will break off the branch easily with a twist when ready

Geraldton wax | *Chamelaucium uncinatum*

A real favourite, native to Western Australia. This tree has an incredible scent, and a flavour much like pine infused with lemon. The leaves, which look and taste a little like pine needles, work with a lot of dishes, but they're especially good with seafood. The flowers can also be used as an edible garnish in small quantities.

USE: Like juniper berries or lemon zest. Very versatile.
BUY: Online, fresh or dried and ground. If you have a plant, pick leaves to use straight away.
PICK/FORAGE: Always ID three times to make sure you pick the right fruit. These trees thrive when picked.
STORE: In the fridge or a vase. If dried, in an airtight container.
GROW: Likes dry climates, sandy soils, and sun. Very comfortable in heat and drought. When you first plant them they will need water for the first few months until established. We have a dozen or so plants in the ground that are doing well and two we have had in pots for five years that we use for cooking. They respond well to pruning.
- Grow in full sun or part-shade
- Suitable for pots
- Biodiversity habitat
- Tolerates sandy soil
- Likes water when young

Native ginger | *Alpinia caerulea*

The roots and fruit of this native ginger can be substituted wherever you'd use the more common variety; the berries have a slight citrusy, ginger flavour — just don't eat the seeds. Also known as 'red back' ginger, shell ginger and pink porcelain lily, its large leaves were traditionally cut and used to build thatch shelters and to wrap foods during cooking. Wrapping ingredients like fish or chicken is a great way to impart a fragrant zing to them, while a leaf or two will add fragrance to broths and soup.

USE: In place of ginger. Use fresh or cooked.
BUY: Hard to find except in nurseries, so best to grow your own.
PICK/FORAGE: Pick young roots.
STORE: In the fridge.
GROW: Like common ginger, it loves shade and thrives in high-rainfall areas.
- Suitable in full sun and part-shade and pots
- Hates frost
- Biodiversity habitat
- Tolerates salt and sandy soil
- Needs water

Bolwarra | Native guava | *Eupomatia laurina*

Known as bolwarra in Wonnarua (Hunter Valley, NSW) and sometimes as scented laurel or copper laurel, the perfume from this tree's cream flowers is intoxicating. Endemic to the Hunter region, the pulp of the sweet fruit inside is edible, and although there are lots of seeds to navigate, it's worth the trouble.

USE: In place of tropical fruit. Great fresh, cooked or processed into jams and sauces.
BUY: Hard to find, so best to grow your own.
PICK/FORAGE: Always ID three times to make sure you're picking the right fruit.
STORE: In the fridge or freezer.

GROW: As a rainforest native this needs to be protected from super hot, dry winds. It can also be grown as an indoor plant and kept small.
- Grow in full sun or part-shade, but ideally in morning sun
- Suitable for pots
- Hates frost
- Biodiversity habitat
- Tolerates salt and sandy soil
- Needs plenty of water

Goongum | Illawarra plum | *Podocarpus elatus*

A beautiful deep purple in colour, these plums are almost olive-like, with a large seed inside and about the size of a grape. Known as goongum in Eastern NSW and QLD, they are loved for their piney flavour. Also known as gidneywallum, pine plums and bush plums.

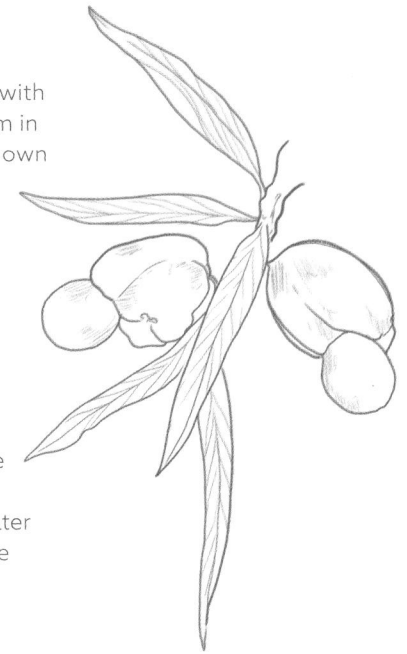

USE: Like plums or other sour fruits and when you want a citrusy/pine flavour.
BUY: Fresh, frozen or dried.
PICK/FORAGE: They are ripe when purple and more fruit will be produced as they're picked. We recommend harvesting and freezing to build up yields and maintain growth.
STORE: In the fridge or freezer.

GROW: Best in the tropics but some people have success in other regions; we have two growing in a sheltered area at home in a food-forest arrangement with other tropical plants.
- Grow in full sun or part-shade
- Suitable for pots
- OK in sandy soil, and likes water
- Great shade provider because they grow to 8 metres (26 feet) high
- Biodiversity habitat

Boonwurung | Island sea celery | *Apium insulare*

Known as boonwurung in Palawa kani (TAS), this plant, which grows around Flinders Island and Lord Howe Island, looks and tastes just like celery. Sub it in wherever you'd use celery, or use the dried powder in place of celery seeds.

USE: As you would celery. The leaves are better than the stalks.
BUY: Fresh or dried and ground into a powder. If you have a bush, pick leaves and small stems straight from it.
PICK/FORAGE: This grows in abundance by the coast, so if foraging, do it there, which also means it won't be overly polluted.
STORE: In the fridge or in a vase. If dried, store in an airtight container.

GROW: This drought-tolerant, frost-tolerant plant loves sun, but can still thrive in dappled shade. Choose a soil or potting mix that drains easily, and water well.
- Propagate from seed or seedling
- Grow in full sun or part-shade
- Suitable for pots and garden beds
- Biodiversity habitat
- Tolerates sandy soil and drought
- Good in gaps and makes a great groundcover
- Save seeds to plant out

Boobialla | Native juniper or Common boobialla | *Myoporum insulare*

It is said that boobialla is the Palawa kani (TAS) name for this plant but was more likely pronounced 'bubialla'. Close in flavour to juniper, this berry has been made popular by gin companies Australia wide. The berry starts out green and is ready to pick when it starts to turn pink. Best dried and used as a spice.

USE: Instead of juniper berries or allspice.
BUY: Fresh or frozen, dried whole berries or dried and ground.
PICK/FORAGE: Pick only ripe berries.
STORE: In the freezer or an airtight container.

GROW: Grow in full sun where possible and keep well pruned to promote new growth and replenishment of berries. We have them in the ground in several spots and in pots too.
- Grow in full sun and part-shade
- Suitable for pots
- Biodiversity habitat
- Tolerates sandy soil
- Great screen or hedge

Gubinge | Kakadu plum | *Terminalia ferdinandiana*

Known as gubinge in Bardi (Kimberley, WA), the kakadu plum is a flowering plant in the *Combretaceae* family. 'Magic plant' is also how many refer to it — particularly those who, like us, take it in powdered form whenever they're travelling or feeling run down. It's known for being the world's highest natural source of vitamin C and, interestingly, we haven't had any colds or flus since we started taking it. The pale green fruit, which can be eaten raw, is about the size of an olive and has a large seed. It's also known as madoorr in Bardi, garbiny in Yawuru, kabinyn in Nyul Nyul and colloquially as billy goat plum.

USE: Fresh, use like olives. As a powder, it's fresh and zesty — sprinkle it on yoghurt, muesli, fruit salads or veggies, or add it to smoothies and juices. We also brine them like olives.
BUY: Available fresh, frozen or dried and ground into a powder.
PICK/FORAGE: This fruit is of incredible importance to First Nations people and so we would discourage any picking or foraging.
STORE: In an airtight container or in the freezer.
GROW: Given its cultural significance, this is best left to Indigenous people. The commercialisation of this fruit is sensitive, but has been making progress through groups such as NAAKPA (Northern Australia Aboriginal Kakadu Plum Alliance) and there are many great Indigenous growers to buy from.

Mookitch or Mayakitch | Kangaroo apple | *Solanum aviculare*

Known as mookitch or mayakitch in Gunditjamara (south-western VIC), this is a member of the nightshade family that's rather like a tomato with one big seed. A beautiful fruit indeed, it's slightly sweet and turns orange when ripe. Try it in both sweet and savoury dishes.

USE: Like cherry tomatoes or tomatoes, but in small amounts.
BUY: Hard to find. Best to grow it yourself.
PICK/FORAGE: Very important — the fruits of many species of Solanum can be poisonous until they are soft-ripe. Only pick when ripe and make extra-sure they are the correct species (see page 137 for more).
STORE: In the fridge.
GROW: A dwarf, evergreen tree. Prefers no frost and likes a combination of sun and shade. Its leaves look like kangaroo paws and its flowers and fruits are pretty.
- Grow in full sun or part-shade
- Suitable for pots
- Biodiversity habitat
- Grows as a dwarf tree
- Likes good drainage
- Needs water when young

Pike | Native leek | *Bulbine bulbosa*

Known as pike in Wurundjeri (Yarra River, VIC), and also called native lily, the above-ground parts of this native leek aren't edible — except the seeds — once the flower has finished, but the corms (the underground bulb-like parts) are edible and have a leek- or onion-like flavour.

USE: Like leek or spring onion. Can be eaten fresh, cooked, roasted or baked. Only eat the corms and seeds.
BUY: Hard to buy. Better to grow your own.
PICK/FORAGE: Always ID three times to make sure you pick the right fruit.
STORE: In the fridge.

GROW: This is a small plant, and we've successfully grown many of them in our onion and garlic bed at home. Its flowers are bright yellow and make a lovely addition to your garden. Prefers moist soil.
– Grow in full sun or part-shade
– Suitable for pots and raised beds
– Biodiversity habitat
– Easy to grow in cool climates
– Likes water
– Keep pruned
– Save seeds to plant out

Aherre-aherre | Native lemongrass | *Cymbopogon ambiguus*

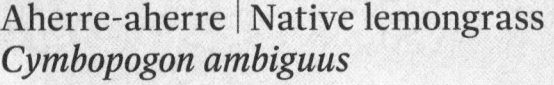

This is nature's paracetamol, known as aherre-aherre in Arrernte (south-eastern NT). An amazing medicinal plant that doubles up as a wonderful addition to cooking too. We prepare it as a tea if we feel like a cold is coming, or just for a refreshing and uplifting drink.

USE: Like lemongrass, for flavouring. Not pleasant raw, so cook it or use it dried.
BUY: Dried, or pick fresh from your garden.
PICK/FORAGE: Grows wild in arid areas such as the Flinders Ranges. Snip tops of long stems to allow for regrowth.
STORE: In an airtight container.
GROW: Really drought-hardy and easy to grow in a home garden. Happy in dry weather but will produce more with water. You can grow it in pots or in clumps of three seedlings in the ground. They grow up to 1 metre (3 feet) high and love to be trimmed regularly, so we just cut and use as we go.
– Grow in full sun or part-shade
– Suitable for pots
– Dislikes frost
– Biodiversity habitat
– Great for hedging and screens
– Loves a prune
– Save seeds to plant out

Ingredients guide: Kakadu plum, kangaroo apple, leek, lemongrass

Lemon-scented gum | *Corymbia citriodora*

A gum with leaves that pack a lemony punch. It's both invigorating and energising, but is quite strong, so use it sparingly. We hang a bunch of them upside-down in our house to keep insects away and add a beautiful lemon freshness to the air, tearing off the occasional leaf for teas or to add to dishes. Also known as blue-spotted gum, lemon-scented eucalyptus, lemon-scented ironwood and citron-scented gum.

USE: In place of lemon or bay leaves. Mature leaves are best for drying and young leaves are best used fresh.
PICK/FORAGE: Always ID three times to make sure you pick the right leaves. Ask permission if on someone else's property and avoid roadsides because of pollution. Pick leaves from your own plant as needed. The more you pick, the more growth you will encourage.
STORE: Keep fresh leaves in the fridge or freezer. If dried, store in an airtight container.

GROW: Makes fabulous shade and is easy to grow at home. Once established, they're low-maintenance. In spring, they produce small white flowers.
- Grow in full sun or part-shade
- Especially good for pots
- Tolerates sandy soil and drought, keep moist when flowering
- Grows tall and thin, up to 20 metres (65 feet)
- Shelter from wind if in pots
- Good in gaps and for hedges and screens
- Biodiversity habitat

Lemon aspen | *Acronychia acidula*

This fruit is a bit like a lemon crossed with an apple, with a bit of grapefruit tartness. When you cut it open it has pretty little seeds like an apple too. It's a really special fruit and can be used whole or with the core removed. Also known as pigeon berry and lemonwood.

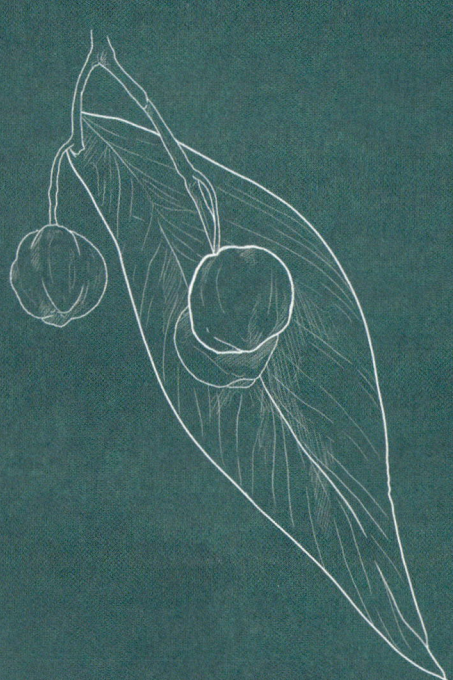

USE: Where you might reach for lemon, Granny Smith apple or want a burst of sharpness.
BUY: Fresh or dried and ground. If you have a bush, use it straight from the plant.
PICK/FORAGE: In autumn and winter, they begin falling when ripe and will also fall if you shake the branch.
STORE: If buying fresh, you can store in the freezer. If dried, in an airtight container.

GROW: Grows quite tall, loves sun and hates wind. Needs well-drained soil and lots of organic matter. Once established, it is low-maintenance.
- Grow in full sun or part-shade, or indoors in a well-lit spot
- Suitable for pots
- Biodiversity habitat
- Provides great shade
- Prune like citrus, and prune well in the first year

Girri girri | Lemon myrtle | *Backhousia citriodora*

Known in some Countries as girri girri, lemon myrtle is one of the better-known bush foods. It is a native rainforest plant loved for its fragrant, citrusy leaves that go with just about everything; it also happens to be the purest natural source of citral, a component of many essential oils. Use it wherever you'd use lemon or citrus to brighten sweet or savoury dishes. Also known as lemon ironwood, lemon-scented myrtle and sweet verbena tree.

USE: As a substitute for citrus flavour or even bay leaves. Fresh or dried leaves can be cooked, and the ground leaves can be used cooked or as is. Great in tea.

BUY: As dried leaves, or ground. If you have a plant, you can use them fresh, too. Pro tip: mature leaves are best for drying and young leaves are best used fresh.

PICK/FORAGE: Reasonably widespread. The more you pick, the more growth you will encourage.

STORE: Keep fresh leaves in the fridge or freezer. If dried, store in an airtight container.

GROW: Provides fabulous shade or hedging, and they're easy to grow at home. Once established, they're easy to maintain, and in season they produce small white flowers. Best in part-sun, likes morning sun.
- Especially good for pots
- Tolerates sandy soil and drought, but keep moist when flowering
- Keep sheltered from wind if in pots
- Good in gaps and for hedges and screens
- Biodiversity habitat

Wanduin | Lilly pilly | *Syzygium paniculatum*

Lilly pillies, of which Australia has more than 40 species, come in a variety of colours, from bright magenta and to blue, through to cherry red. This magenta-coloured one, known as wanduin by some Aboriginal groups, is one of the more readily available varieties. The small, tart fruits taste a bit like Granny Smith apples spiked with clove (imagine an apple pie filling before you add the sugar), and can be used fresh, cooked, pickled or preserved. They're prolific in season, but it's a short season, so we like to pickle them, then we can use them throughout the year (you can freeze them too, but they lose their colour when thawed). Fresh, they're wonderful in salads and desserts. Also known as small-leaved lilly pilly, clove lilly pilly.

USE: Instead of blueberries or raspberries. Great fresh, cooked or processed into jams and sauces. They have a great crisp crunch, and are awesome in salads.

BUY: Available fresh, frozen or as a freeze-dried powder. Sometimes available in farmers' markets, and almost always available somewhere in your neighbourhood. Keep your eyes peeled and offer to swap with your neighbours for some jam in return.

PICK/FORAGE: In abundance all across Australia.

STORE: In the fridge or freezer. If dried, in an airtight container.

GROW: Once you have seen lilly pillies growing, you will notice them everywhere. They make an amazing tree and/or hedge. Filled with stunning scarlet berries in different sizes (depending on the species) when in season. Best to learn how to climb a tree or get a ladder, though, as they can grow to 10 metres (33 feet) high.
- Grow in full sun or part-shade
- Suitable for pots
- Happy in sandy or clay soil and will tolerate drought
- Good in gaps and for hedges, screens and shade
- Biodiversity habitat

Dirramaay or Bo-an | Chocolate lily | *Arthropodium strictum* and Vanilla lily | *Arthropodium milleflorum*

These plants, known as dirramaay in Wurundjeri (Yarra River, VIC) and bo-an in Bunganditj (south-eastern SA), have such pretty little purple and white flowers. They mainly grow in South Australia, New South Wales and Victoria, and we're lucky enough to have them on our farm, where in the springtime, the blossoms fill the air with a strong caramel and chocolate scent. We use their flowers decoratively, but the tubers are edible, too.

USE: As edible flowers, particularly in place of borage flowers. Best freshly picked. Make a gorgeous fragrant posy.
BUY: We haven't seen this for sale except as seed.
PICK/FORAGE: Once you've seen these flowers you'll be notice how common they can be in arid climates. Only take what you need and always leave plenty behind.
STORE: In the fridge, picked and kept like herbs.

GROW: Lily tubers generally grow to a few centimetres in length, but one plant can produce multiple tubers in a season. Grow for its edible flowers, as an ornamental plant, or for the birds and bees.
- Can be propagated from seed or seedling
- Grow in full sun or part-shade
- Suitable for pots.
- Tolerates drought and sandy soil
- Adds colour and fragrance
- Save seeds to plant out

Kindal kindal | Macadamia | *Macadamia integrifolia*

Known as kindal kindal by First Nations people in New South Wales, these are one of the most well-known and widely available native ingredients. Macadamia nuts are great in sweet or savoury dishes, and make an incredible nut milk. If you've ever tried to crack their shells, you'll realise why they're so expensive (they're bloody hard!), but they really are worth it. Also known as boomberra and jindall.

USE: Everywhere and anywhere you use nuts — milk, butter or roasted.
BUY: Raw or roasted.
PICK/FORAGE: You might be able to pick them, but you will be hard-pressed to crack them open without a hardcore nut cracker.
STORE: In an airtight container

GROW: They prefer a warmer climate but will grow in cooler areas too. Just wait for the last frost before planting in well-drained soil.
- Grow in full sun or part-shade
- Biodiversity habitat
- Tolerates sandy soil, likes well-drained soil
- Hates frost and loves water
- Offers great shade
- Will grow indoors in good light

Midyim | Midyim berry | *Austromyrtus dulcis*

Known as midyim or midgin in eastern Australia, this plant produces white berries similar to blueberries with a spicy, almost nutmeg-like flavour — especially when baked into muffins! Also known as midgen berry or silky myrtle (or sometimes even bush marshmallows), not only are the fruits delicious, but the plant also makes a wonderful shrub or hedge and the birds and bees love it.

USE: As you would blueberries. Fresh, cooked or processed into jams and sauces.
BUY: Fresh or frozen, although it's quite rare. Better to grow your own and pick berries to use straight from the bush.
PICK/FORAGE: When the berries are white with small grey marks, which makes them look lilac.
STORE: In the fridge or freezer, although they have a short shelf-life.

GROW: As a dwarf tree or climber. Keep well pruned to encourage new growth. We have them in the ground in several spots, and in pots too.
- Grow in part-shade; likes morning sun
- Suitable for pots
- Biodiversity habitat
- Grows Likes good drainage
- Likes water when young
- Good on trellises

Native mulberry | *Pipturus argenteus*

This one you will have to fight the birds for. The pearl-coloured berries are just amazing. More like a strawberry than a mulberry, with tiny seeds on the outside. They're very soft, so have a short shelf-life.

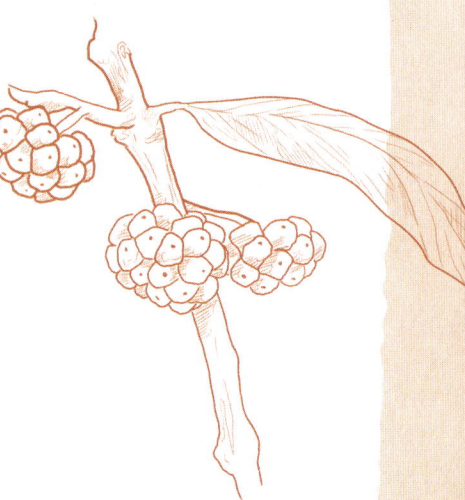

USE: Like other berries, especially strawberries, raspberries and, of course, mulberries. Great fresh or cooked.
BUY: Hard to buy. Better to grow your own.
PICK/FORAGE: Flowers in summer, fruits from early winter, when it's easy to spot.
STORE: In the fridge or freezer.

GROW: Better in warm climates as they love full sun and well-drained soils. Prune well and use netting in fruiting season (winter).
- Grow in full sun
- Suitable for pots
- Hates frost
- Tolerates sandy soils
- Biodiversity habitat
- Great screen or hedge
- Loves a good prune

Munter | Muntries | *Kunzea pomifera*

Native to Australia's south coast and known as munter or muntharri in Ngarrindjeri (Murray River, SA) and as ngurp in Bunganditj (south-eastern SA), muntries are small berries that are crunchy and juicy, with a taste like spiced apple. Kids tend to love them, and the green and red tinge makes them extra pretty. Also known as emu apple and native cranberry, they were traditionally used by the Ngarrindjeri people, who either dried them or pounded them to a paste, which was then dried to make a sort of fruit leather. These are great ways to use them, but we also love them in salads or eaten like grapes.

USE: Fresh, use like apples. Use dried muntries in place of cloves.
BUY: Fresh (rare), frozen, dried or as a freeze-dried powder.
PICK/FORAGE: The berries are tiny, about the size of a pea. Pick when a pinky tone appears on them, usually February to April.
STORE: In the fridge or freezer. If dried, in an airtight container. They have a long shelf-life.

GROW: We have tried this beautiful groundcover in our temperate climate in the ground and also in pots, both of which work, but for a first-time grower we would highly recommend trying them in pots.
- Grow in full sun or part-shade
- Suitable for pots
- Biodiversity habitat
- Tolerates sandy soil and drought
- Good in gaps and for hedges; makes a great groundcover

Tyulern or Irreye | Old Man Saltbush | *Atriplex nummularia*

Tell any farmer over the age of 60 that saltbush is now considered a delicacy and they'll probably find it hard to believe — but just like the cuts of meat that used to be reserved for dogs are now fetching top-dollar at the butcher, saltbush (which used to be used for grazing) has had its own surge. Known as tyulern in Wemba Wemba (Murray River, VIC) and Irreye in Arrernte (south-eastern NT), you'll still find it running wild across properties, but it really is wonderful and should be eaten by all of us. The two best-known varieties are old man saltbush and ruby saltbush (see page 45 for more; it's quite different). After spring and autumn the plants produce an enormous amount of seeds that taste like salty popcorn kernels. Traditionally, these were ground and mixed into a dough to cook in the coals, but the fleshy leaves are deliciously salty as they are. They're great cooked, but just as the sheep do, we like to graze on them fresh as we walk around the farm.

USE: Like you would Swiss chard, or use the powder as an alternative to salt. Fresh leaves are best used soon after they're picked. Highly recommend drying them out and using as spice on anything that calls for salt. The seeds can be toasted for use on everything.
BUY: Available fresh or dried and ground into a powder.
PICK/FORAGE: In abundance all over, but there are more than 60 saltbush species in Australia alone and not all are edible. Always ID three times before picking to make sure you pick an edible species.
STORE: In the fridge, picked and kept like herbs. Or fresh from the garden. Stems of fresh saltbush can also be kept in a vase and make stunning flower arrangements.

GROW: An easy, fast-growing shrub that grows all over Australia. It is easily adaptable and will grow in most conditions.
- Can be propagated from seed or seedling
- Will grow in full sun or part-shade.
- Very adaptable and tolerates salinity, drought, frost and sandy soil.
- Makes a great hedge or screen and acts as a natural fire-retardant — it's perfect planted around your house, especially if you live in fire-danger areas.
- Makes great fodder for livestock

Yarrinyari | Bush onion or Wild onion | *Cyperus bulbosus*

Known as yarrinyari in Yawuru (Broome region, WA), these small edible bulbs are little pops of nutty, crunchy goodness. More like a nut than an onion, they are also known as merne yalke in Arrernte (south-eastern NT), erreyakwerra in Kaytetye (central NT) and jurnta in Walmajarri (Great Sandy Desert, WA). When they're ready to harvest, the thin blades of vibrant green grass turn yellow and dry out.

USE: Fresh.
BUY: Hard to find, but some native growers have them.
STORE: In the fridge.
PICK/FORAGE: They have skin like onions, but are small, so best to slough off the skin as you would with garlic. Pick in April and May.

GROW: Hard to find seeds, but try Melbourne Bushfood (see page 234).
– Grow in full sun or part-shade
– Likes water, but needs free-draining soil
– Harvest tubers after a few years

Rlaarluk or Wakiri | Pandanus | *Pandanus spp.*

A glorious plant with proud, spiky leaves, this plant is known as rlaarluk in Dhuwal (Arnhem Land, NT) and wakiri in Walmajarri (Great Sandy Desert, WA). The Australian pandanus, or screwpine, has large pineapple-like fruits comprising edible segments, but it's better known for the nuts inside. The leaves, which are soft and white when young, can also be eaten. This is an important plant to Indigenous people, and the leaves are often woven into baskets. The nut is considered to be a real luxury. Try it in all sorts of ways: raw, roasted or fermented. There are a few varieties in Australia, but in general they're different to the familiar pandanus that is used for its leaves throughout Asia.

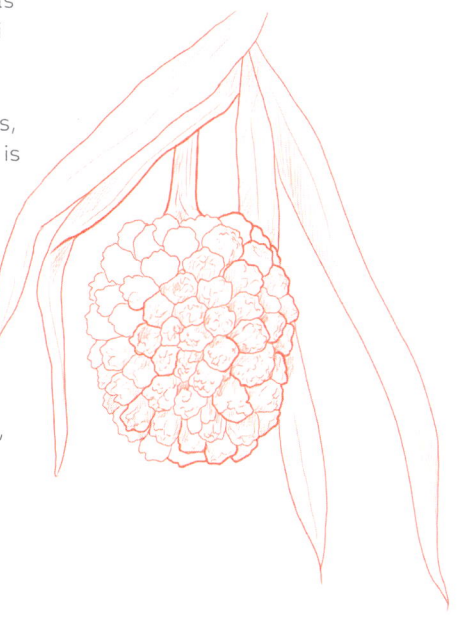

USE: As you would other nuts, although they're best cooked. The fruit is soaked before eating and then the kernel is pounded and the nut extracted.
BUY: Fresh or frozen, but they might take some tracking down.
STORE: In the fridge or freezer.
PICK/FORAGE: Leave this one to the Indigenous peoples whose land it grows on.

STORE: In the freezer. Or if the nuts are still in the shell, an airtight container is fine.
GROW: Prefers a tropical or sub-tropical climate. Needs three trees for pollination: two females and a male.
– Grow in full sun and part-shade
– Hates frost
– OK in sandy soil; likes water
– Biodiversity habitat
– Provides shade

Kurrajong or Dundil | Peanut tree | *Sterculia quadrifida*

This is such a beautiful tree, called kurrajong or dundil by Indigenous people in Queensland and the Northern Territory. Related to hibiscus and cacao, it produces large red pods containing vibrant black nuts with a papery shell like peanuts that are total stunners. Also known as the orange-fruited sterculia, kuman, orange-fruited kurrajong, native peanut and koralba.

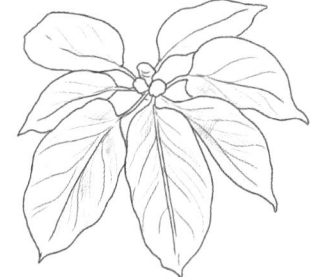

USE: Instead of peanuts. Fresh, cooked, roasted or in baking.
BUY: Online, fresh.
PICK/FORAGE: Always ID three times to make sure you pick the right plant. Always ask permission if on someone else's property and avoid roadsides because of pollution.
STORE: In an airtight container

GROW: Likes well-drained soils and full sun, but can tolerate poor soil. With lots of pruning it can be kept in pots.
- Grow in part-shade
- Suitable for pots and raised beds
- Biodiversity habitat
- Easy to grow in cool climates
- Provides great shade

Pepperberry | *Tasmannia lanceolata*

Pepperberry, also known as mountain pepper and Dorrigo pepper, is used for both its fragrant leaves and its potent berries. The plant, which is endemic to Palawa Country (TAS), among other places, was traditionally used to treat sore gums and teeth, and is renowned for its antiseptic qualities as much as its flavour. Whenever pepper is mentioned in the book or anytime we season a dish, we're using dried pepperberries (unless the leaves are specifically stated). We encourage you to do as we've done, and replace the peppercorns in your grinder too.

USE: Anywhere you'd use pepper or chilli. Can be used fresh or cooked, or dried and ground like pepper. Use one tenth of the amount of pepperberry as you would normal pepper, and use the leaves fresh or dried also — they have a gorgeous sweetness.
BUY: Fresh or dried whole berries or milled. They come frozen too.
PICK/FORAGE: Accessible in high areas of Tasmania and Dorrigo. Pick leaves and berries.

STORE: Fresh, in the fridge or freezer. If dried, in an airtight container (or your pepper grinder).
GROW: You will need both male and female plants for pollination; only the females produce fruit.
- Grow in part-shade, likes morning sun
- Suitable for pots
- Biodiversity habitat
- Tolerates sandy soil and drought, but keep moist when flowering
- Good in gaps and for hedges and screens
- Provides shade when mature

Nganangi or Keeng-a or Katwort | Pig face | *Disphyma crassifolium*

Known as nganangi in Ngarrindjeri (Murray River, SA), keeng-a in Bunganditj (south-eastern SA), and katwort in the Gippsland region of Victoria, this coastal plant grows prolifically in sandy soil. The leaves are incredibly juicy and succulent, with an addictive salty crunch. It has bright pink or purple flowers that are also edible, along with its fruit, which is like a juicy, salty fig. Once you know how to spot them, you'll always be on the lookout when you're at the beach. Karkalla (Mallee pigface/*Carpobrotus rossii*) is a similar variety you can also find along the coast.

USE: Instead of Swiss chard or lettuce, for a salty burst. Great fresh, cooked or pickled.
BUY: Fresh, online or from select grocers.
PICK/FORAGE: This grows in abundance by the coast so if foraging, do it there, which also means it won't be overly polluted. Pick a little; be respectful.
STORE: In the fridge or a vase. Or dried in a paper bag.

GROW: Grow as groundcover that can be kept as small as you like. Propagate from seed or seedling.
- Grow in full sun or part-shade
- Suitable for pots
- Biodiversity habitat
- Tolerates salinity, sandy soil and drought
- Good in gaps and makes a great groundcover
- Grows quickly

Urti or Bidjigal | Quandong | *Santalum acuminatum*

Often referred to as native or desert peach, quandongs are one of the more common fruits in our pantry, and are relatively easy to source. Known as urti in parts of South Australia and bidjigal in parts of Victoria, we always look forward to their season, and to seeing what colours they come in — from bright pink to dark pink and ruby red. We've also heard stories of 'ghost quandong', which are pure white. Quandongs are popular for their tart flesh, and for the kernel inside, which is sometimes used decoratively. They also hold an important place in Damien's culture, being the jewel of the Flinders Ranges where his Country is, and in many of his Yarta Mudra (history and creation stories). The kernel is delicious — it tastes like an almond — and is highly medicinal. Quandong is also known as wolgol in Noongar (south-western WA) and as kurti in Nukunu (Yorke Peninsula, SA).

USE: As you might peaches or rhubarb — fresh, cooked or preserved.
BUY: Fresh, frozen or dried in halves or pieces. Occasionally found at farmers' markets and shops in the right regions.
PICK/FORAGE: Pick when the fruit has turned pink or red. Depending on where you live, this will be between October and March.
STORE: In the fridge or freezer, or in an airtight container if dried. They'll last a long time dried and will quickly plump up again when soaked.

GROW: Quandongs are amazing because they will grow in poor soil. They do, however, need host plants as they are semi-parasitic. Acacias make great hosts for quandong and then you get a double harvest too.
- Grow in full sun or part-shade
- Can be grown from seed or seedlings; always plant in groups of five or more
- Not suitable for pots as they definitely need space and a host or companion tree
- Will grow up to 6 metres (20 feet) high and 5 metres (16 feet) wide
- Likes free-draining soil and plenty of water when first planted
- Frost-tolerant

Blue quandong | *Elaeocarpus grandis*

Sometimes called blue fig, this is mostly grown as an ornamental tree, although traditionally the fruit was pounded to make a paste. Blue quandong is popular for its tartness, but it's also prized for its large seed, which can also be made into a paste and dried, then eaten or used in bread. The fruit ban be used to make a dye for fabric as well.

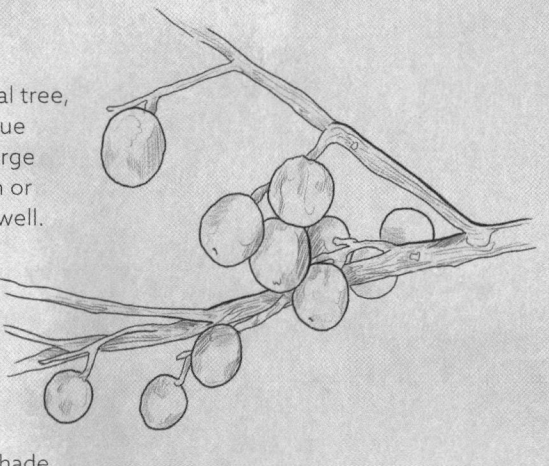

USE: Can be eaten fresh, cooked or preserved, like peaches or plums. Just note they are very tart and so are best cooked.
BUY: Fresh, frozen or dried in halves or pieces. Occasionally found at farmers' markets and shops in the right regions.
PICK/FORAGE: In spring, when fruit is purple or blue.
STORE: In the fridge or freezer, or in an airtight container if dried. They'll last a long time dried and quickly plump up when soaked.

GROW: This really will only grow in tropical climates. Given it is such a large tree, we wouldn't try unless you have a lot of space.
- Grow in full sun or part-shade
- Suitable for large pots in which you can manage the height
- Will grow up to 50 metres (165 feet) high, so bear that in mind
- Likes nutrient-rich, well-drained soil

Manjart | Raspberry jam wattle | *Acacia acuminata*

This wattle, known as manjart in Noongar (south-eastern WA), has great significance in Noongar culture. It's known for its resin, and its seeds are a food source. We love to use the flowers in drinks — they really do smell like raspberry jam.

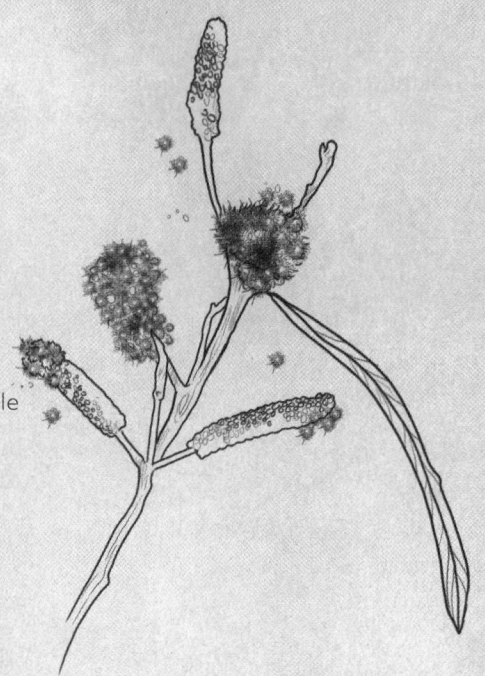

USE: Use the seeds, flowers and resin to flavour drinks and desserts.
BUY: Better to find a plant and pick it straight from the tree. Or grow your own.
PICK/FORAGE: Be careful to shake out any little critters before use.
STORE: Use it fresh.

GROW: Grow in full sun if possible and in free-draining soil. It can handle drought, salt and frost and is a beekeeper's best mate. Like other acacias, it is a super nitrogen-fixer and makes an excellent companion plant for quandong.
- Grow in full sun or part-shade
- Not suitable for pots
- Biodiversity habitat
- Tolerates salt, sandy soil, frost and drought
- Provides great shade

Ngwan | Riberry | *Syzygium luehmannii*

A sweet, sour and nicely spiced bright pink berry, known as ngwan in Bunjalung (south-eastern QLD and north-eastern NSW). Riberries might be tiny, but they pack a punch in the health stakes: they are nutrient-dense, and packed with antioxidants and vitamins, including A, C and E. It is said that traditionally the fruit was mashed into a paste and used to treat earache. Also known as clove lilly pilly and cherry alder.

USE: Instead of raspberries or blueberries. If dried, treat more like cloves.
BUY: Available fresh, frozen or as a freeze-dried powder. Sometimes available in farmers' markets. Almost always available somewhere in your neighbourhood. Keep your eyes peeled and offer to swap with your neighbours in return for some jam.
PICK/FORAGE: In early summer. Freeze straight from the bush.
STORE: In the fridge or freezer. If dried, in an airtight container.

HOW TO GROW: Makes fabulous shade or hedging, and is easy to grow. Once established, it's low-maintenance and will yield lots of fruit.
- Grow in full sun or part-shade
- Suitable for pots
- Biodiversity habitat
- Tolerates sandy soil and drought
- Good in gaps, hedges and screens
- Provides great shade
- Note that dropped fruit can stain

Panaryle or Poang-gurk | River mint | *Mentha australis*

Native river mint is the badass mint of the mint family, known as panaryle in Wurundjeri (Yarra River, VIC) and poang-gurk in Djab Wurrung (central VIC). Bursting at the seams with flavour, this will take any mint dish to another level. It is not just wonderful in cooking, it is also a great digestive if prepared as a tea.

USE: Anywhere you'd use mint or basil.
BUY: Fresh or dried and ground.
PICK/FORAGE: If foraging, the best place to look is by rivers, creeks and bodies of fresh water — hence the name river mint.
STORE: In the fridge or a vase. If dried, in an airtight container.

GROW: In the wild you will find this growing along rivers and creeks, as it is a plant that likes moisture. Having said that, we have had success even through dry spells by planting in part-shade and in pots.
- Propagate from seed or seedlings
- Grow in part-shade
- Suitable for pots
- Biodiversity habitat
- Tolerates sandy soil and drought
- Good in gaps and makes a great groundcover
- Keep well pruned

Wyrrung | Rosella | *Hibiscus sabdariffa*

While this plant is not technically endemic to Australia, it has been here for long enough to be treated as native. Known as wyrrung by Aboriginal people in New South Wales, the rosella (sometimes called native hibiscus) is known for enlivening pots of tea or glasses of Champagne. This vibrant red flower is very versatile and is good in both sweet and savoury dishes.

USE: As you would sorrel, lemon sorrel or rhubarb. Can be eaten fresh, cooked or preserved in syrups or similar. The leaves are also delicious.
BUY: Fresh, frozen or as a freeze-dried powder. Sometimes available from farmers' markets.
PICK/FORAGE: Always ID three times to make sure you picking the right plant. Always ask permission if on someone else's property and avoid roadsides because of pollution.
STORE: In the fridge or freezer. If dried, in an airtight container.
GROW: Rosella prefers warmer climates, so we wouldn't attempt growing them anywhere you get heavy frosts. They love to be pruned.
- Grow in full sun
- Suitable for pots
- Hates frost
- Biodiversity habitat
- Good in gaps, hedges and screens
- Rabbits love them; keep Peter well away!

Kurrkuty or Paranghuni | Ruby saltbush | *Enchylaena tomentosa*

Known as kurrkuty in Wemba Wemba (Murray River, VIC) and paranghuni in Ngarrindjeri (Murray River, SA), this is a plant with amazing salty leaves and fabulous sweet fruit in an array of colours from yellow and red to bright pink. So, so delicious.

USE: Anywhere you'd use spinach, mustard leaf or watercress. Good fresh or cooked. Use the fruit in salads or sweets.
BUY: Fresh.
PICK/FORAGE: Pick to use direct from the bush. The fruit is ripe when it turns red/pink.
STORE: In the fridge, freezer or in a vase.
GROW: So easy to grow in pots or the ground. It prefers lots of sun, but also grows well in dappled shade and can even cope with a little frost.
- Grow in full sun or part-shade
- Suitable for pots and raised beds
- Biodiversity habitat
- Easy to grow in cool climates
- Likes water
- Makes a great hedge or groundcover

Milyu | Samphire | *Tecticornia ssp.*

Across the continent, there are several varieties of samphire that are endemic or unique to our shores. Known in some Aboriginal languages as milyu, it grows in coastal areas and in salt marshes, in large clumps close to the ground, and the leaves have a distinctive, refreshing saltiness to them. They sometimes have beautiful patches of red on them too. Blanch as you would asparagus, then serve with roast lamb, fish, in salads or tossed in a wok with stir-fried vegetables. Also known as sea asparagus, swamp grass, glasswort, pickleweed and sea beans.

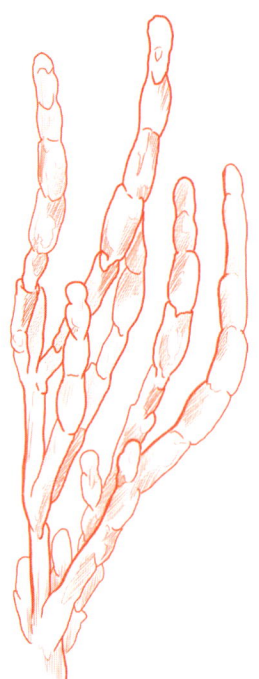

USE: Like green beans or asparagus. Great with lamb.
BUY: Fresh.
PICK/FORAGE: Almost always available along the coast, so keep your eyes peeled. Only pick a little; be respectful. Check the rules where you live on foraging samphire, as they differ depending on the region.
STORE: In a paper bag in the fridge.

GROW: As a groundcover that can be kept as small as you like. Very easy to grow.
- Propagate from seed or seedlings
- Grow in full sun or part-shade
- Suitable for pots
- Biodiversity habitat
- Tolerates salinity, sandy soil and drought
- Good in gaps and makes a great groundcover

Uilarac or Wolgol or Waang | Australian sandalwood | *Santalum spicatum*

Sandalwood, called uilarac, wolgol, waang and other names in Noongar (south-western WA), is famous for its price tag as much as its precious oil and perfume. But the plant has another gift that remains largely unused: the sandalwood nut. It is comparable to a flavourless macadamia for its texture, and reminds us a little of puffed rice. Sandalwood nuts are great for simply roasting with spices or honey, as well as for bulking out nut milks and for baking. Sandalwood is also known as dutjahn in Martu (Western Desert, WA).

USE: Like puffed rice, macadamias and cashews. Great fresh, roasted or baked into sweets.
BUY: Fresh or dried.
PICK/FORAGE: Best to grow your own.
STORE: In an airtight container.

GROW: This is semi-parasitic, so will steal from other plants. For this reason, we recommend growing it in pots.
- Grow in full sun and part-shade
- Suitable for pots
- Biodiversity habitat
- Tolerates salinity, sandy soil and drought
- Provides great shade

Sea parsley | *Apium prostratum*

Unlike your average parsley, this one adds a seriously peppery kick to meals. Smells like celery and can be used in much the same way as celery leaves or parsley.

USE: Instead of flat-leaf parsley.
BUY: Fresh or dried and ground into a powder.
PICK/FORAGE: This grows in abundance by the coast so if foraging do it there, which also means it won't be overly polluted.
STORE: In the fridge, or a vase. If dried, in an airtight container.

GROW: This is very easy to grow, either in the ground or in pots. Like most soft herbs, it dislikes frost and needs some water.
- Propagate from seed or seedlings
- Grow in full sun or part-shade
- Suitable for pots
- Biodiversity habitat
- Tolerates sandy soil and drought
- Good in gaps and makes a great groundcover
- Save seeds to plant out

Winggi Kuranthantha | Sea rosemary | *Olearia axillaris*

A silver-leaved coastal plant that resembles common rosemary known as winggi kuranthantha in Ngarrindjeri (Murray River, SA), and sometimes known as coastal daisybush or wild or native rosemary. Unsurprisingly, it was one of the first native plants to be used by Europeans. This plant loves sandy soils and sea air. We use it anywhere we'd use rosemary — it's way tastier and has such a beautiful fragrance.

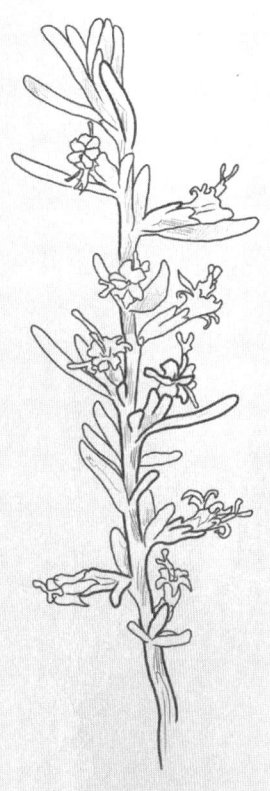

USE: Instead of rosemary. Use it fresh, cook it, or dry it in bunches upside down.
BUY: Fresh or dried.
PICK/FORAGE: This grows in abundance by the coast so if foraging do it there, which also means it won't be overly polluted. Only pick a little; be respectful.
STORE: If dried, in an airtight container. If fresh, in the fridge; picked and kept like herbs, or in a vase.

GROW: Grow as a hedge or shrub that can be kept as small as you like.
- Grow in full sun or part-shade
- Suitable for pots
- Biodiversity habitat
- Tolerates salinity, sandy soil and drought

Seablite | *Suaeda australis*

Seablite grows in salty conditions, especially around the coast and salt marshes of South Australia. Use it in small quantities to add a pleasant, salty kick to dishes, especially salads, or add it to vegetables to give them an extra edge.

USE: Wherever you'd use Swiss chard or lettuce.
BUY: Fresh.
PICK/FORAGE: This grows in abundance by the coast so if foraging do it there, which also means it won't be overly polluted.
STORE: In a paper bag in the fridge.

GROW:
- Propagate from seed or seedling
- Grow in full sun or part-shade
- Suitable for pots
- Biodiversity habitat
- Tolerates sandy soil and drought
- Good in gaps and makes a great groundcover
- Save seeds to plant out

Native sorrel | *Hibiscus heterophyllus*

This stunning plant is not to be confused with the more common rosella that's used a lot in Australia (see page 45), instead the flowers are big, like the Hawaiian variety of hibiscus, and come in an array of colours. You might also see it called native rose, green kurrajong or common wood sorrel. The flowers are edible — just like nasturtiums.

USE: Anywhere you'd use mixed green leaves. Especially salads.
BUY: Fresh.
PICK/FORAGE: Look for flowers in multiple shades of purple.
STORE: In the fridge.

GROW: Grows well in all soil types, but prefers well-drained soil and lots of water.
- Grow in part-shade
- Suitable for pots and raised beds
- Biodiversity habitat
- Likes water

Strawberry gum | *Eucalyptus olida*

Growing largely in the Northern Tablelands of New South Wales, strawberry gum is renowned for its leaves, which have a strawberry-bubblegum or Allen's Strawberries & Cream scent. Also known as the forest berry herb, it suits a range of cooking styles, but we love it for flavouring tea, or in desserts. Apart from the great taste, this tree is also rich in antioxidants, and has anti-fungal and antibacterial properties. Also look out for its sweet, minty cousin, the narrow-leaved peppermint gum (*Eucalyptus radiata*).

USE: To impart a berry flavour, or add it to anything with berries to enhance the flavour. Can be baked, cooked or made into tea.
BUY: Online, fresh or dried.
PICK/FORAGE: Always ID three times to make sure you pick the right plant. Always ask permission if on someone else's property and avoid roadsides because of pollution.
STORE: In an airtight container.

GROW: Grows to 30 metres (100 feet) tall, so best grown in a pot and kept small if you want to give it a go. Not available to grow in all states because of restrictions, so check first. Grows best in areas with higher rainfall.
- Grow in full sun and part-shade
- Suitable for pots
- Loves water and warm weather
- Biodiversity habitat
- Provides great shade

Kunduwi | Sweet apple berry | *Billardiera cymosa*

Such a pretty plant with stunning flowers, this is known as kunduwi in Bunganditj (south-eastern SA). The fruit is sweet with an aniseed flavour.

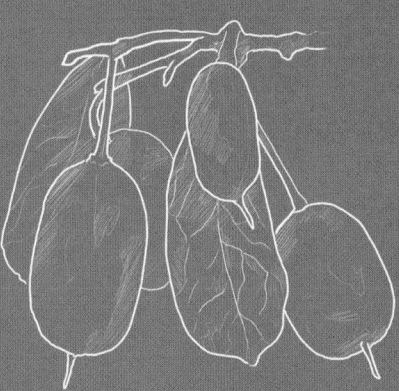

USE: Like berries, either fresh or cooked.
BUY: Best to grow your own.
PICK/FORAGE: Pick them when they change from green to maroon.
STORE: In an airtight container in the fridge or freezer. Best fresh.

GROW: This is a great climber and really easy to grow directly in the ground; they're really resilient plants.
- Grow in full sun and part-shade
- Biodiversity habitat
- Tolerates sandy soil
- Loves well-drained soil
- Great climber with pretty flowers

Boonjie | Small-leaved tamarind | *Diploglottis campbellii*

A stunning bright red fruit that can be eaten raw (it's super-fresh and refreshing) or used in a few different ways. Tamarind typically makes great pastes, chutneys and sauces. Unfortunately, there are very few of these trees left growing wild, which is why we think it's good to create a demand for them — we source ours from Rainforest Bounty (Atherton Tablelands, QLD; see page 235).

USE: Anywhere you'd use tamarind or something else that's sweet and sour, like unripe pineapple. We prefer it cooked.
BUY: Fresh or frozen. Found Occasionally at farmers' markets and shops in the right regions.
PICK/FORAGE: Very difficult to find, so we'd discourage foraging for these.
STORE: In the fridge or freezer, or preserve as a paste.

GROW: This rainforest beauty prefers part-shade for optimal growth. It also likes a lot of water, so it's best to grow it in non-drought areas.
– Grow in part-shade
– Suitable for pots
– OK in sandy soil; likes water
– Biodiversity habitat
– Provides shade

Native thyme | *Prostanthera incisa*

One of our favourite native herbs. Growing wild in Australia's south-east, this is sometimes called cut-leaf mint for its strong menthol scent, which also explains why it was traditionally used for its medicinal properties. We use it to make a flavoured oil, but we like to add it, fresh or dried, to almost anything. The pretty purple flowers are also edible.

USE: Instead of thyme or oregano.
BUY: Fresh or dried and ground.
PICK/FORAGE: If picking, take from the top. It will grow back better if picked regularly.
STORE: In the fridge or in a vase. If dried, in an airtight container.

GROW: This native thyme is a fragrant, fast-growing, beautiful hardy herb with bright purple flowers and tiny little micro leaves. The more you pick the more it will grow.
– Grow in part-shade
– Especially good for pots and raised beds
– Biodiversity habitat
– Beautiful purple flowers
– Best in well-drained soils
– Likes water, but can tolerate dry spells

Kutjera | Bush tomato or Desert raisin | *Solanum centrale*

These are wonderful eaten fresh, but the intensity and flavour really steps up when they're dried. The flavour has a hint of caramel or carob, but crossed with that savoury aspect you get in a sun-dried tomato. Called kutjeri by Aboriginal groups in central Australia, it almost tastes like caramelised Vegemite. You can leave the fruits on it to dry in the sun, then gather them up all at once. Ground, fresh or dried (we like ground best) they're great in just about anything. Total umami.

USE: Like sun-dried or sun-blushed tomatoes, subbed for raisins or as an alternative to Vegemite. Eat raw, cooked, dried or semi-dried. Powdered, it's a great spice.
BUY: Fresh, frozen or dried and ground into a powder.
STORE: In the fridge or freezer, or in an airtight container if dried.
PICK/FORAGE: There are over 100 species but only six are edible. **Be absolutely sure to only pick the non-toxic ones.** Even if you know it is the right species, **never** eat green or unripe berries.
GROW: We have had success in the ground and pots at home, largely because we don't get frost.
– Grow in full sun or part-shade
– Suitable for pots
– Really dislikes frost (like, really)
– Biodiversity habitat
– Save seeds to plant out

Warrigal | Warrigal greens | *Tetragonia tetragonioides*

Sadly, there is not a lot of information available how First Nations people ate these greens — known as warrigal ('wild') in Dharug (Western Sydney, NSW). But we do know that the European settlers used it as a substitute for spinach and to help prevent scurvy. Today, we do the same. Well, the spinach substitute bit at least, not the scurvy bit. The plant is also known as warrigal cabbage, New Zealand spinach and Botany Bay greens.

USE: Like spinach, chard, silverbeet or bok choy. Really versatile. Must be cooked.
BUY: Fresh.
PICK/FORAGE: Young leaves are less bitter.
STORE: In the fridge, in a paper bag.
GROW: This seems to pop up everywhere in our garden. It's easy to grow, so if you don't have much space, use a pot because there's no stopping it.
– Propagate from seed or seedlings
– Grow in full sun or part-shade
– Suitable for pots
– Tolerates salinity, sandy soil and drought
– Good in gaps, makes a great groundcover
– Save seeds to plant out

Warreah | Native watercress | *Barbarea australis*

A relative of the Brassica family — alongside kale, broccoli, cauliflower, cabbage, Brussels sprouts, mustard plants and other cress — this native watercress produces giant leaves of peppery green goodness. Also known as native wintercress or Tasmanian watercress.

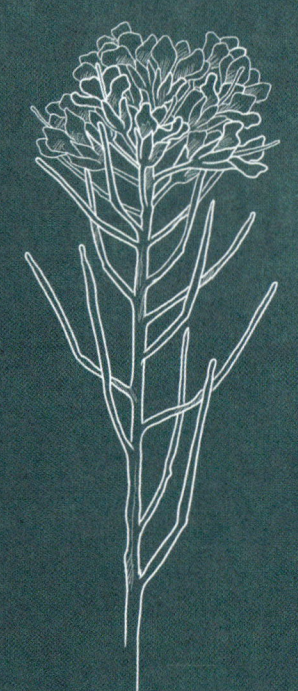

USE: Like spinach, mustard leaf or watercress. Good raw or cooked.
BUY: Fresh.
STORE: In the fridge or freezer, or in a vase.
PICK/FORAGE: This is a critically endangered plant, so although it grows wild, you shouldn't pick it. Best to grow it yourself or buy it fresh, if you can find it.

GROW: Grows well in all soil types, but prefers well-drained soil and lots of water.
- Grow in part-shade
- Suitable for pots and raised beds
- Biodiversity habitat
- Easy to grow in cool climates
- Likes water

Ariepe | Wattleseed | *Acacia victoriae*

Known as ariepe in Arrernte (south-eastern NT), these tiny seeds from several species of acacia (*A. victoriae* being the most used commercially) have an aroma of roasted coffee, sweet spice, raisins and chocolate. These seeds were an important food for First Nations people, who would eat the fresh seeds cooked, or dry them to grind and bake into a kind of bread. Not only are they delicious, they're also high in nutrients, especially proteins and — depending on the variety — good fats. While there are many kinds of acacia, only a handful of species are harvested or grown for commercial use. Among many other names, they are also known as minga in Adnyamathanha (Flinders Ranges, SA).

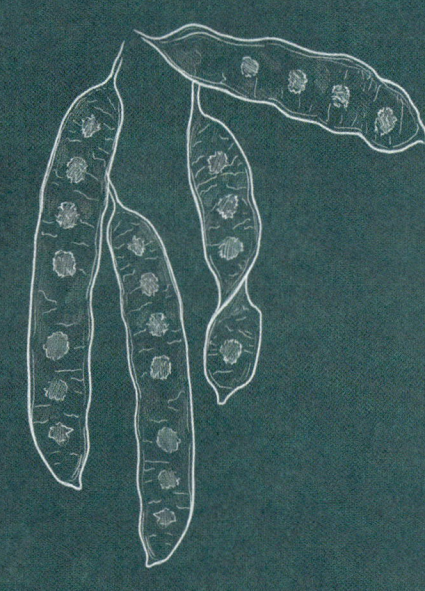

USE: In dishes where you'd reach for coffee, nuts or chocolate. Cook or boil whole seeds, or roast and grind them.
BUY: As whole seeds, roasted and ground, or as an extract.
PICK/FORAGE: Always ID three times to make sure you pick the right plant. Ask permission if on someone else's property and avoid roadsides because of pollution. However, collecting wattleseed is a super time-consuming process, so we would recommend leaving it to the professionals.
STORE: Seeds will keep dried for 20+ years. If already roasted and ground, store in an airtight container and use within a year.
GROW: An all-round legend, this is nitrogen-fixing, makes good fodder for livestock and has edible seeds. Prefers well-drained soils. The climate-resilient dream tree.
- Grow in full sun or part-shade
- Tolerates frost
- Drought-hardy
- Will grow up to 10 metres (33 feet) tall but can be kept small
- Biodiversity habitat

White kunzea | *Kunzea ambigua*

Part of the myrtle family, this is a fragrant shrub with beautiful white flowers that blossom in vast quantities come spring. You can use both the dried flowers and the leaves, which have a subtle eucalyptus and honey flavour, making them perfect in sweets, savouries and medicines. This plant is found mainly in eastern Australia.

USE: In anything herbal, both sweet and savoury. Use sparingly, as it packs a medicinal punch.
BUY: Dried or in essential oil form. With any essential oil, always make sure it is edible before using it in cooking or medicine.
PICK: The leaves and flowers, then dry them before use; just leave them in the sun until there's no moisture left.
STORE: In an airtight container.
GROW: This beautifully aromatic shrub has delightful white flowers. It is really low-maintenance and makes great borders or hedges.
- Grows best in the ground
- Tolerates poor soil and frost
- Likes sunny positions
- Biodiversity habitat

And these beauties ...

These aren't available commercially, but might be growing in your neighbour's backyard, or even yours! Keep your eyes open or try to grow your own.

BARBED WIRE GRASS
Cymbopogon refractus
Edible seeds

BEACH FLAX LILY
Dianella congesta

BLUE FLAX LILY
Dianella atraxis

BLUE TRUMPET / BLUE YAM
Brunoniella australis

BROAD-LEAVED PAPERBARK
Melaleuca quinquenervia
Bark used to wrap food before steaming or grilling

CAPE BARREN TEA
Correa alba
Used for tea

COASTAL WATTLE
Acacia longifolia var. sophorae

CORAL PEA
Kennedia rubicunda
Vine with spectacular flowers and sweet pink berries

COTTONWOOD
Hibiscus tiliaceus
Edible yellow flowers

RED COTTONWOOD
Hibiscus rubra
Edible flowers and leaves

DEERINGIA
Deeringia amaranthoides
Edible fruit

DESERT FIG / ROCK FIG
Ficus brachypoda

DEVIL'S MARBLES
Eremophila debilis
Edible fruit

FALSE SARSAPARILLA
Hardenbergia violacea
Makes a refreshing drink

NATIVE FUCHSIA
Correa reflexa
Flowers and leaves used for tea

FUCHSIA HEATH
Epacris longiflora
Edible fruit; red and pink flowers

NATIVE GRAPE
Cayratia clematidea
Vine with edible black berries

NATIVE GUAVA
Eupomatia laurina
Perfumed flowers and edible fruit

GYMEA LILY
Doryanthes excelsa

ILLAWARRA FLAME TREE
Brachychiton acerifolius
Edible seed, potential coffee or nut-flour substitute

KANGAROO GRASS
Themeda australis
Seeds can be ground into flour; see Black Duck Foods for more

KANGAROO VINE BERRY
Cissus antarctica
Edible berry

KURRAJONG
Brachychiton bidwilli
Edible fruit, potential coffee or nut-flour substitute

YELLOW MANGOSTEEN
Astractocarpus fitzlanii
Edible fruit and scented flowers

MEADOW RICE GRASS
Microlaena stipoides

MURNONG
Microseris lanceolata
Also known as yam daisy; edible tubers

PALM LILY
Cordyline rubra

PARRAMATTA WATTLE
Acacia parramattensis

PINK-FRUITED LIME BERRY
Glycosmis trifoliata
Edible pink berries; related to citrus, with stunning white flowers

PRICKLY MOSES
Acacia ulicifolia

QUEENSLAND BOTTLE TREE
Brachychiton rupestris
Edible seed

WILD QUINCE
Guioa semiglauca

SANDPAPER FIG
Ficus coronata

SCRAMBLING LILY
Geitonoplesium cymosum
Shoots that taste like asparagus

SILVER-LEAVED MOUNTAIN GUM
Eucalyptus pulverulenta

SUNSHINE WATTLE
Acacia terminalis

SWEET-SCENTED WATTLE
Acacia suaveolens

TEN CORNERS FRUIT
Astroloma pinifolium
Edible leaves and fruit

WHITE FEATHER HONEYMYRTLE
Melaleuca decora

Green ants (page 74)

Stock your pantry, freezer and garden

It's safe to say that First Nations peoples' pantries were very, very expansive, filled with thousands of nutritious and functional seasonal goodies. The seasons themselves vary from Nation to Nation (with some having two seasons, while others have twelve). Alongside the fresh ingredients, there would also be a bounty of preserved goods from previous seasons that had been foraged, harvested or cultivated, much like today. With First Nations ingredients becoming more accessible than ever before, there's never been a better time to change up our pantries and freezers to include these amazing local foods.

Opposite is a list of ingredients we use in our everyday cooking. Over time we've learned how to substitute native spices, fruits and greens for more common ingredients, and we've also come to enjoy them in their own right. There's no need to overhaul your pantry, freezer or garden, but by beginning to buy, grow and store some of these items, you'll soon be adding them to recipes and increasing your confidence and knowledge. The most important part is to have fun with the incredible flavours, and enjoy the process of learning about First Nations foods.

Where to buy all of the things

There are a plethora of online retailers today where you can buy fresh, frozen or dried First Nations ingredients, as well as seedlings. The best place to start is by researching your area and checking out local farmers' markets and farm gates; if there's nothing nearby, then try buying frozen or dried. Even better, use the handy tips in the ingredients guide and try growing some yourself. We've provided a wide-ranging list of stockists, including major supermarkets, specialists and wholesalers, on pages 234–35.

Frozen, fresh, dried or grown

Given the very short seasons of many of these plants and their accessibility, for the most part you will be buying them preserved in some way. That's not a problem, because dried ingredients or spices are actually wonderful with learning how to cook, so think of it as experimentation, and have a play! Where you can get fresh, always give it a go. Don't forget, like all ingredients that are rare or new, the more we ask for them, the more widely available they will become. The more you buy, the more the growers can grow …

Our most-used pantry staples

Ground herbs and spices (dried and ground)
- Anise myrtle
- Cinnamon myrtle
- Davidson's plum
- Finger lime
- Lemon myrtle
- Native lemongrass
- Native thyme
- Native basil
- Sea parsley
- Sea rosemary
- Pepperberries
- Peppermint gum
- River mint
- Saltbush
- Strawberry gum
- Wattleseed

Whole fruit or leaves (dried or fresh)
- Anise myrtle
- Bush tomatoes
- Cinnamon myrtle
- Finger lime
- Geraldton wax
- Lemon myrtle
- Pepperberries
- Pepperberry leaves
- Quandongs

Other pantry staples
- Bush honey
- Davidson's plum
- Desert lime
- Finger lime
- Kangaroo grass
- Lemon aspen
- Macadamia nuts
- Macadamia oil
- Muntrie powder
- Sandalwood nuts
- Warndu thyme oil and wattleseed balsamic (from warndu.com)
- Wattleseeds
- White kunzea

Freezer staples
- Bunya nuts
- Desert limes
- Finger limes
- Green ants
- Native cherries
- Native currants
- Plums (Davidson's and Illawarra)
- Quandongs
- Riberries
- Rosella
- Small-leaved tamarind

Our favourite garden staples
- Anise myrtle
- Cinnamon myrtle
- Finger lime
- Geraldton wax
- Island sea celery
- Kangaroo apple
- Lemon myrtle
- Lilly pilly
- Midgin berry
- Muntries
- Native basil
- Native lemongrass
- Native thyme
- Old man saltbush
- Pepperberry
- River mint
- Ruby saltbush
- Seablite
- Sea parsley
- Sea rosemary

Karkalla (Mallee pigface, page 41)

First Nations flavour wheel

This visual guide is an essential part of this book. Flavour wheels are so useful and my favourite one is in Niki Segnit's book The Flavour Thesaurus. *The flavour wheel opposite is a handy place to begin learning about the vibrant flavours First Nations foods offer, so you can appreciate why these ingredients are so special, and experiment with your own recipes and adaptations.*

*Gumbi Gumbi
(Native Apricot, page 17)*

Spice:
Bloodroot
Cinnamon myrtle
Pepperberry
Pepperberry leaf
Watercress

Floral:
Banksia
Bottlebrush
Grevillea
Native lilies
Rosella

Earthy:
Black ants
Davidson's plum
Kangaroo

Forest / Bramble:
Atherton raspberry
Ilawarra plum
Native fig
Native juniper
Sea rosemary

Nutty:
Boab
Bunya nut
Macadamia
Pindan nut
Sandalwood
Wattleseed

Vegetal:
Bush onion
Bush tomato
Dusty yam
Native lilies
Youlk

Citrusy:
Desert lime
Finger lime
Geraldton wax
Green ants
Lemon myrtle
Lemon-scented gum
Lemon tea tree
Rosella leaf
Tamarind

Marine:
Barramundi
Crocodile
Iceplant
Karkalla
Oysters
Samphire
Yabbies

Fruity:
Bush apple
Kangaroo apple
Midyim berry
Muntries
Native grape
Quandong
Riberry
Tanami apple

Herbal:
Anise myrtle
Eucalypt
Island sea celery
Native basil
Native thyme
Peppermint gum
River mint
Sea parsley
Strawberry gum
Warrigal greens

Flavour Wheel

First Nations flavour wheel

spice

Whether it's the tang of pepperberries, the zing of native ginger, the earthiness of bush tomatoes or the citrus-tang of green ants, the native pantry is brimming with an array of ingredients ready to fill your spice cupboard. Where you can source fresh, great — but in most cases the recipes that follow call for dried, which brings even more potency and flavour to a wide variety of dishes, from tea cake and spiced apple cider, to a fresh take on that old favourite: cheese on toast. Just want to dip your toe into using native ingredients? This is where to start.

Bush Tomato Cheese on Toast

Use the Native Worcestershire Sauce (see page 73) to top this beauty and you've got footy or netty snack sorted — OK, it's every snack sorted. The quantities here are for one slice of bread. Scale it up as needed.

Serves 1

2 slices of bread (pick your favourite)
Olive oil, for drizzling
2 tablespoons Kangaroo Apple and Bush Tomato Chutney (page 210)
4 dried bush tomatoes
2 slices Gruyère or cheddar
Native Worcestershire Sauce (page 73), to serve

Substitution options:

Bush tomatoes
→ Vegemite or sun-dried tomatoes

Toast bread lightly, just so it starts to go crisp (you don't want it too brown as it will get toasted more under the grill later). Preheat oven grill to high.

Drizzle toast with olive oil, spread on chutney, then grate bush tomato on top with a microplane. Lay on cheese, then grill until melted and golden.

Drizzle with Native Worcestershire Sauce and sprinkle with salt and ground pepperberry to serve.

Pickled Quandongs

Apart from quandongs, this base recipe (see page 71 for the finished product) can also be used to pickle Tanami or other bush apples, as well as firm vegetables such as cauliflower, carrots, fennel or cabbage. Use this as you would any other pickle, with cheese, cold meats or in salads.

Makes 2 large (500ml/17 fl oz) jars

1.2 kg (2 lb 10 oz) quandongs, halved, seeds removed
2 cups (500 ml) apple cider vinegar
1 cup (250 ml) white vinegar
1 cup (220 g) white sugar
4 anise myrtle leaves
2 teaspoons yellow mustard seeds
1 teaspoon black mustard seeds
1 teaspoon ground turmeric
½ teaspoon fennel seeds
½ teaspoon pepperberries

Place quandongs in a large heatproof bowl. Combine remaining ingredients in a large saucepan, bring to the boil and simmer for 20 minutes or until sugar dissolves and flavours are infused.

Pour liquid over quandongs, stand for 5 minutes, then transfer apples and liquid back to saucepan and simmer for a further 3 minutes. Ladle into sterilised jars (see page 232), seal and cool.

Label and store in a cool, dark place for up to 2 years. For best results, let the pickle mature for at least 3 months before eating.

Substitution options:

Quandongs
→ Tanami apples, cauliflower, carrots, fennel or cabbage
Anise myrtle
→ ground fennel seeds
Pepperberries
→ black peppercorns

Herb Powders

A great go-to method for all your potted herbs from the garden, these powders make great additions to soups or stews, roast veggies and salads or used on meat as rubs. We like to use saltbush, sea rosemary, island sea celery, sea parsley, myrtles, curry bush, the list goes on. For every 5 g (⅛ oz) dried leaves, you'll end up with about 1 tablespoon of powder. You'll need a spice grinder.

Makes ¼ cup (15 g)

15 g (½ oz) dried herbs (pick fresh and leave to dry), stems removed

Once leaves are completely dry, add to a spice grinder and blitz to a powder. Store in a jar and use to sprinkle over and into dishes as needed.

Lilly Pilly Cordial

Lilly pilly is one of those fruits that, when you know what it looks like, you start to see everywhere (there always seems to be at least one tree somewhere on the street). It works in both sweet and savoury dishes, but try to save some to make this delicious cordial.

Makes 1 litre (4 cups)

2 cups (500 g) lilly pillies, plus extra to serve
1 teaspoon tartaric acid
2 cups (220 g) caster sugar
Juice of 2 lemons
Myrtle leaves (optional), to serve

Combine lilly pillies, tartaric acid, sugar and lemon juice in a saucepan, add 1 litre (4 cups) water and bring to the boil. Boil for 5 minutes or until the fruit is just starting to soften. Remove from heat, mash fruit, then strain through a fine sieve. Pour into a sterilised bottle.

Use like any cordial — put a splash in a glass and add water and ice to taste, garnishing with extra lilly pillies and perhaps a lemon myrtle leaf — or use it in the jelly on page 184.

'Lime'ade

A fab cordial alternative for kids and grown-ups alike. The base recipe works with any citrus at all, so mix and match whatever you have with whatever is growing on your or your friends' trees. And of course, you can add a shot of vodka for the perfect garden-party cocktail. This also makes an amazing bubble when topped up with soda.

Makes 1 litre (4 cups)

4 finger limes, coarsely chopped
4 sunrise limes (similar to finger limes, and from similar stockists), coarsely chopped
12 desert limes, coarsely chopped
2 cups (500 ml) boiling water
½ cup (110 g) caster sugar
Water or sparkling water, to serve

Place all limes in a large heatproof bowl and squeeze with your hands to draw out juice and oils. Pour boiling water over the top, then leave for 10 minutes to steep. Strain into a large bowl or jug (reserve some limes to serve), then whisk in sugar until dissolved.

Pour into a jug or bottle, topping it up with cold tap water or sparkling water to make about 1 litre (4 cups). Pour over ice and serve with reserved limes.

Substitution options:

Finger limes, sunrise limes and desert limes
→ limes or other citrus

From left to right: Lilly Pilly Cordial; 'Lime'ade; Spiced Bush Apple Cider (page 72)

Aussie Olives

It isn't commonly known, but all olives that are sold as ready to eat have gone through a brining process, so this is a recipe to treat fresh olives straight from the tree. We also love this recipe with Kakadu plums — frozen Kakadu plums can sometimes go soggy, so try to get hold of fresh if you're doing this. Otherwise, any edible olive works. The brine recipe here is based on 1 kilogram of olives; once they're brined, you can keep them in the brine and marinade in smaller batches.

Makes 1 kg (2 lb 4 oz)

1 kg (2 lb 4 oz) fresh olives
2 tablespoons salt
2 cups (500 ml) warm filtered water
100 ml (3½ fl oz) apple cider vinegar or white vinegar

MARINADE
For every 1 cup (150 g) brined olives

1 cup (250 ml) good-quality olive oil, plus extra for topping up
¼ cup (60 ml) lemon juice
1 garlic clove, crushed
1 strip finger lime or lemon zest
½ teaspoon dried cut-leaf mint or thyme leaves
¼ teaspoon pepperberries
2 anise myrtle leaves
4 lemon myrtle leaves

Substitution options:

Cut-leaf mint
→ oregano
Native thyme
→ thyme or lemon thyme
Pepperberry
→ any pepper
Anise myrtle
→ fennel seeds
Lemon myrtle
→ Lemon zest

With a sharp knife, make a single straight cut into each olive or poke each one with a fork (this will allow them to release some of their bitterness and soak up flavour faster). Place olives in a large saucepan or bucket, cover with water and place a heavy plate on top to keep olives fully submerged. Leave at room temperature for 2 weeks, changing the water every day.

Add olives to sterilised jars (see page 232), packing them in as tightly as possible.

To brine olives, add salt to a large bowl, add 3–4 tablespoons warm filtered water and stir to dissolve, then add vinegar and remaining water and stir to combine. Pour brine into jars right to the top and until it begins to overflow; it's important that no air remains in the jar (make up more brine if necessary). Screw on lids, label jars, then leave them in a cool, dark place for 2 months.

Now olives are ready to marinate. Drain and rinse the desired quantity of olives to remove excess brine. Combine marinade ingredients in a bowl, add olives and stir to coat well. Transfer olives, with their marinade, to jars, adding more oil if needed to coat them. Refrigerate for 1–2 days to marinate before serving. Marinated olives will keep, refrigerated, for 2–3 weeks.

*From left to right:
Saltbush and Pepper
Vinegar (page 72);
Aussie Olives; Pickled
Quandongs (page 66)*

Spiced Bush Apple Cider

Bec hasn't been drinking for nearly two years now, so we're always trying to find fun things to drink that aren't alcoholic. This non-alcoholic cider is not only refreshing, it's also easy to make quite low in sugar — play around and experiment with the quantities to see what you like. You'll need some muslin and sterilised bottles (see page 232).

Makes around 3 cups (750 ml)

1 kg (2 lb 4 oz) native apples (muntries, Tanami, bush or a mix), halved, any seeds removed
¼ cup (55 g) caster sugar
4 cinnamon myrtle leaves
2 lemon myrtle leaves
2 anise myrtle leaves
1 whole nutmeg

Place apples in a large saucepan with 1 cup (250 ml) water, adding extra if necessary to cover. Stir in sugar, leaves and nutmeg. Bring to the boil, then reduce heat to low. Cover and simmer for 3 hours or until apples are very tender. Strain through muslin, change cloth, then strain again. Pour into sterilised bottles and refrigerate. Drink within 3–5 days.

Substitution options:

Native apples
→ apples
Cinnamon myrtle
→ cinnamon quill
Anise myrtle
→ ground fennel seed
Lemon myrtle
→ lemon zest

Saltbush and Pepper Vinegar

The best thing about infusing your own vinegars is the experimentation. For every vessel, we aim to fill it approximately a third full with foraged, harvested or picked goodies, then top it up with a choice of vinegar (we like apple cider). Use this as a guide and go wild, or stick to the script for salt and pepperberry perfection (see page 71 for the end product). You'll need a 1 cup (250 ml) sterilised jar.

Makes 1 cup (250 ml)

2 sprigs saltbush (or 1 teaspoon dried)
6 pepperberries, bruised
1 cup (250 ml) apple cider vinegar
Caster sugar or maple syrup, to taste

Add saltbush and pepperberries to your jar, top up with vinegar and seal, then leave in a cool, dark place to infuse for 1 month.

Strain and sweeten with sugar or maple syrup to taste. Vinegar will keep in a cool, dark place for up to a year.

Substitution options:

Saltbush
→ salt
Pepperberries
→ black or pink peppercorns

Native Worcestershire Sauce

As a kid, I used to eat cheese on toast sprinkled with Worcestershire sauce. Me and my childhood bestie Amanda loved it. Not the Lea & Perrins fancy stuff, the good old Spring Gully sweetened one. This recipe is a take on that childhood favourite, but much more grown up. That said, it's still fantastic with cheese on toast (see page 64).

Makes 350 ml (12 fl oz)

½ cup (125 ml) malt vinegar
½ cup (125 ml) apple cider vinegar
150 g (5½ oz) molasses, maple syrup or brown sugar
2 tablespoons small-leaved tamarind paste (make by blitzing tamarind in a food processor with a splash of water)
1 tablespoon soy sauce
8 anchovies, mashed with a fork (for a vegan version, substitute 8 crushed bush tomatoes or sun-dried tomatoes)
4 garlic cloves, finely chopped
2 teaspoons native ginger, finely chopped
1 teaspoon pepperberries, ground
1 teaspoon ground pepperberry leaves
1 teaspoon ground cinnamon myrtle (or 4 whole leaves)
4 cloves

Combine all ingredients in a sterilised jar (see page 232). Stir well (or put the lid on tightly and shake). Store in a cool, dark place for 2 weeks.

Try a little, then adjust to taste with vinegar, molasses or soy, paying attention to the balance of acid, sweetness and saltiness. Strain through muslin into a clean bottle. If you used anchovies, the sauce will keep for up to 3 months, or up to a year if it's the vegan version.

Substitution options:

Small-leaved tamarind paste
→ tamarind paste
Pepperberries
→ black peppercorns
Native ginger
→ fresh ginger
Pepperberry leaves
→ bay leaves
Cinnamon myrtle
→ ground cinnamon

Green Ant Curry Paste

Yes, you read that right. Green ants have the most incredible flavour, like citrus crossed with coriander seeds, which make them a perfect addition to curry pastes. You can buy green ants at selected specialty shops, such as Something Wild (see page 235), and online.

Makes 100 ml (3½ fl oz)

4 green chillies, seeds removed, chopped
2 red eschalots, chopped
5 garlic cloves
4 cm (1½ in) piece native ginger, thickly sliced
2 tablespoons chopped native lemongrass (or 4 lemongrass stalks, finely chopped)
2 teaspoons green ants
1 teaspoon ground cumin
1 small handful native basil, coarsely chopped
1 small handful coriander, coarsely chopped
2 tablespoons soy sauce
1 tablespoon fish sauce
Finely grated zest and pearls of 1 finger lime
⅓ cup (80 ml) coconut cream

Place all ingredients except coconut cream in a small food processor and blitz until coarsely chopped. With the motor running, add coconut cream a tablespoon at a time until everything comes together into a smooth paste.

Store in an airtight container in the fridge until ready to use. Use in recipes in place of shop-bought curry paste. Curry paste will keep refrigerated for 2 weeks or frozen for 3 months.

Substitution options:

Native ginger
→ ginger
Native basil
→ basil
Green ants
→ coriander seeds
Finger lime
→ lime

Salt 'n' Pepper Popcorn

Movie night sorted!

Serves 1 (or 2 if you share)

50 g (1¾ oz) salted butter
1 small pinch ground saltbush
1 small pinch ground bush tomato
1 large pinch ground pepperberry
⅓ cup (80 g) popcorn kernels

Substitution options:

Saltbush
→ extra salt
Bush tomato
→ chopped sun-dried tomato
Pepperberry
→ ground pepper

Melt butter in a large shallow saucepan (with a lid) over medium-high heat with saltbush, bush tomato, pepperberry and a large pinch of flake salt, stirring to combine. Once foaming, add popcorn kernels and shake to coat evenly.

Cover with a lid and cook, shaking pan occasionally, for 6–8 minutes. You'll hear kernels popping, and you'll know it's done when the popping has mostly stopped. Remove lid and stir popcorn to make sure it's nicely coated. Serve warm or at room temperature.

Cinnamon Myrtle and Maple Popcorn

A variant on the saltbush popcorn, this gives you a sweet and slightly spicy version. Add the cinnamon a little at a time, tasting as you go.

Serves 1 (or 2 if you share)

50 g (1¾ oz) salted butter
2 tablespoons maple syrup
1 tiny pinch ground pepperberry (optional)
⅓ cup (80 g) popcorn kernels
1 teaspoon ground cinnamon myrtle, or 4 leaves

Substitution options:

Pepperberry
→ ground pepper
Cinnamon myrtle
→ ground cinnamon

Melt butter in a large shallow saucepan (with a lid) over medium-high heat with maple syrup, pepperberry and a large pinch of flake salt, stirring to combine. Once foaming, add popcorn kernels and shake to coat evenly.

Cover with a lid and cook, shaking pan occasionally, for 6–8 minutes. You'll hear kernels popping, and you'll know it's done when the popping has mostly stopped. Once it's finished popping, add cinnamon myrtle to taste, tossing to coat. Serve warm or at room temperature.

Pepperberry Cookies with Lemon Aspen

Like the German spice cookie, but Aussie. And moreish. Very moreish. The flour is easily substituted with others, as are the spices, making this a fun recipe to play around with as you stock your pantry with amazing First Nations ingredients like pepperberry and different kinds of myrtle.

Makes 20 large or 40 small cookies

2 cups (300 g) wholemeal flour
1 cup (130 g) buckwheat flour
1 cup (50 g) macadamia nut meal
1 teaspoon baking powder
1 teaspoon ground pepperberries (or 2 teaspoons if you like spice)
Pinch each ground nutmeg, ground cloves, ground allspice and ground cardamom
2 teaspoons ground cinnamon myrtle
1 teaspoon ground anise myrtle
1 teaspoon ground lemon myrtle
1 teaspoon finger lime powder
2 free-range eggs
1 cup (185 g) lightly packed brown sugar
Finely grated zest of 1 lemon
1 tablespoon spirits (we love Økar amaro or Applewood gin), for brushing

WATTLESEED EXTRACT
1 tablespoon ground wattleseed
¼ cup (60 ml) boiling water

ICING
1 egg white, beaten
1 tablespoon pure icing sugar, plus extra for sprinkling
1 tablespoon lemon aspen powder, for sprinkling
Karkalla petals or strips of lemon zest, for garnish

For wattleseed extract, add wattleseed to a small coffee plunger and pour in boiling water. Leave for 2 minutes to steep, then plunge as normal. (Alternatively, brew it in a tea infuser.) Reserve 2 tablespoons extract for the cookies.

Whisk flours, macadamia meal, baking powder, spices, ground leaves and finger lime powder in a bowl to combine. Put eggs, brown sugar, lemon zest and reserved wattleseed extract in the bowl of a stand mixer fitted with the whisk attachment and beat until thick and pale. Add dry ingredients and a large pinch of salt and beat to form a firm dough. Divide dough into four, then roll each piece into a 20 cm (8 in) log. Wrap each one in plastic wrap and chill for 2 hours.

Cut each log into 1 cm-thick (½ in) cookies and place onto a baking tray lined with baking paper, flattening the cookies slightly. Leave out of the fridge, but in a cool place, overnight.

The next day, heat oven to 160°C (315°F). Turn each biscuit over, then brush lightly with spirits (not too much). Transfer to oven immediately and bake for 20 minutes until golden brown. Transfer to a wire rack to cool completely.

For icing, mix egg white and icing sugar in a small bowl until smooth. Brush each cookie with icing, adding a little water if it becomes too thick. Dust with lemon aspen powder.

Leave on a wire rack until icing is almost set, then dust with more icing sugar and garnish with strips of lemon zest. Store in an airtight container. Try to wait at least 3 days before eating (they get better with time).

Substitution options:

Macadamia nut meal
→ almond meal
Cinnamon myrtle
→ ground cinnamon
Anise myrtle
→ ground fennel seeds
Lemon myrtle
→ lemon zest
Finger lime powder
→ lime zest
Wattleseed
→ ground coffee
Lemon aspen powder
→ any freeze-dried fruit powder

Myrtle Tea Cake

If anything reminds me of being a kid it's tea cake. My Auntie Sally made the most moist, buttery cake ever, always with white icing and sprinkles. This is a little more grown up but just as much fun.

Makes 1 cake

160 g (5¾ oz) butter, grated and softened, plus extra for greasing
1 cup (220 g) caster sugar
1½ cups (225 g) self-raising flour
¼ cup (35 g) custard powder
2 free-range eggs
¾ cup (175 ml) milk
1 teaspoon ground cinnamon myrtle
1 teaspoon ground anise myrtle
1 teaspoon ground lemon myrtle
Finely grated zest of 2 finger limes

DESERT LIME ICING

140 g (5 oz) butter, melted
200 g (7 oz) pure icing sugar, sifted
2 egg yolks
1 teaspoon desert lime powder or finely grated zest of 1 lemon

---

Substitution options:

Cinnamon myrtle
→ ground cinnamon
Anise myrtle
→ fennel flowers
Lemon myrtle
→ lemon zest
Finger lime zest
→ lemon zest

Preheat oven to 160°C (315°F). Grease and line a 20 cm (8 in) square cake tin.

Combine all ingredients, except those for the icing, in a stand mixer fitted with the whisk attachment. Start on low, then slowly increase speed to high. Beat on high for 4–5 minutes, scraping down bowl occasionally if needed, until batter is pale and fluffy.

Pour batter into tin and bake for 40–45 minutes or until light golden and a skewer inserted into the centre comes out clean. Cool in tin for 5 minutes, then turn out onto a wire rack to cool completely. Cut in half lengthwise.

For icing, mix butter and icing sugar in a small bowl until well combined. Stir in egg yolks and desert lime powder. Spread top and sides of one cake generously with icing, top with the other cake and spread with remaining icing.

Barb and Lil's Christmas Pudding

This recipe is a combination of two generations of recipes: one from Bec's great-grandmother and another from Damo's nan. We've made it our own, with native fruits and spices to boot. A delicious and deeply flavoured family affair.

Serves 8–10

250 g (9 oz) butter, melted and cooled, plus extra for greasing
200 g (70 oz) raisins, finely chopped
100 g (35 oz) dried muscatels, finely chopped
100 g (35 oz) dried quandongs, finely chopped
⅔ cup (100 g) candied orange rind, finely chopped
100 g (3½ oz) candied ginger, finely chopped
1 Granny Smith apple (skin on), finely chopped
200 g (7 oz) riberries (dried or fresh)
1 cup (155 g) muntries
1 cup (150 g) macadamia nuts, finely chopped
1 cup (250 ml) orange juice
Juice of 1 lemon
4 finger limes, pearls squeezed
1 cup (150 g) plain flour
1 cup (150 g) self-raising flour
1 teaspoon bicarbonate of soda
1 teaspoon ground pepperberry leaf
1 teaspoon ground cinnamon myrtle
½ teaspoon ground anise myrtle
2 teaspoons ground lemon myrtle
1 tablespoon ground wattleseed
1 teaspoon ground nutmeg
250 g (9 oz) brown sugar
3 large free-range eggs, lightly beaten
100 ml (3½ fl oz) Økar amaro, or orange liqueur such as Grand Marnier or Cointreau
Cream and custard, to serve

Grease a 2-litre (8 cup) pudding bowl with butter.

Combine dried and candied fruit, apple, riberries, muntries, macadamia nuts, orange and lemon juice and finger lime pearls in a large saucepan. Place over medium heat and cook, stirring occasionally, for 10 minutes or until fruit softens.

Sift flours and bicarbonate of soda into a large bowl, add spices and stir to combine. Add fruit mixture, melted butter, brown sugar, eggs and liqueur and stir until well combined.

Gently spoon pudding mixture into bowl, smooth the top, then cover the top tightly with buttered baking paper then foil, sealing it tightly with string. Place pudding in a large saucepan filled with enough simmering water to come halfway up the sides of the bowl. Steam, covered with a lid for 4–5 hours, topping up with extra boiling water as necessary. Remove pudding from pan (it's hot, so use mitts), allow to dry and cool completely, then store in the fridge for up to 3 months.

To reheat, place pudding bowl in a large saucepan filled with enough simmering water to come halfway up the sides and simmer for 45 minutes. Allow to cool for 5–10 minutes before unwrapping and serving with lashings of cream and custard.

Substitution options:

Quandongs
→ dried apricots
Finger limes
→ lime juice
Muntries
→ Granny Smith apples

Cinnamon myrtle
→ ground cinnamon
Anise myrtle
→ fennel seeds
Lemon myrtle
→ lemon zest
Wattleseed
→ ground coffee

herbal

Just like the mint and basil you might grow at home but a hundred
times more intense, native herbs are packed with flavour, and they're
really nutritious too. These recipes show them off in savoury dishes,
as well as in fragrant desserts and rubs with countless uses.
We've said it before, but many of these ingredients are so easy
to grow in pots — 'thyme' to get planting.

Warrigal Greens and Saltbush Cob

A cob is a very Australian kind of dish, but what better way to make it extra Aussie than by using First Nations ingredients? We add saltbush, then rather than spinach we use warrigal greens, but you can also use bower spinach — both are a stunning bright green, nutritious and easy to grow.

Serves 4-6

1 cob loaf
1 tablespoon olive oil
4 spring onions, thinly sliced
250 g (9 oz) bacon, diced
2 sprigs saltbush leaves, finely chopped
10 warrigal greens leaves, finely chopped
2 tablespoons thinly sliced chives
250 g (1 cup) cream cheese
⅔ cup (160 ml) pure cream
⅔ cup (160 g) sour cream
2 cups (200 g) grated cheddar
½ baguette, sliced
Sea parsley, native thyme, saltbush and seablite, to serve

Substitution options:

Saltbush
→ karkalla, seablite, samphire, capers or caper leaves
Warrigal greens
→ bower spinach or spinach

Preheat oven to 160°C (315°F). Cut the top off the loaf (reserve), then pull out the bread from the centre, leaving a 2 cm (¾ in) shell. Tear or chop bread into coarse pieces.

Heat oil in a large frying pan over medium heat. Add spring onion and bacon and cook, stirring, for 5 minutes or until bacon is browned and onion has softened. Add greens and toss quickly until wilted. Remove from the heat.

Add chives to frying pan, stir in cream cheese, then add cream, sour cream and cheddar and stir to combine. Season with salt and ground pepperberry.

Spoon dip mixture into cob shell. Arrange lid, bread pieces and sliced baguette in a single layer on a baking tray around loaf. Bake for 20 minutes or until lightly toasted. Top dip with herbs, replace lid and serve warm.

Dolmades with River Mint Yoghurt

How good are dolmades? They have their own rich heritage, but we decided to put a local spin on them by using First Nations ingredients in the stuffing. We've sometimes made these in miniature with saltbush leaves replacing the vine leaves entirely rather than being rolled inside them. You could also try this with fig or rosella leaves.

Makes 10 dolmades

1½ tablespoons olive oil, plus ¼ cup (60 ml) extra for drizzling
1 brown onion, finely diced
4 spring onions, thinly sliced
3 carrots, finely diced
200 g (7 oz) button mushrooms, finely diced
1 kg (2 lb 4 oz) minced kangaroo
1 cup (200 g) white rice
3 cups (750 ml) chicken stock
6 tomatoes, diced
1 bunch of dill, chopped
1 bunch of sea parsley (about 4 tablespoons), chopped
10 island sea celery leaves, chopped
2 spring garlic sprigs, thinly sliced or 3 garlic cloves, finely diced
10 fresh vine leaves
10 saltbush leaves

YOGHURT DRESSING
1½ cups (390 g) Greek yoghurt
1 tablespoon river mint, chopped, plus extra to serve
Juice of 1 lemon
2 teaspoons olive oil

For yoghurt dressing, whisk all ingredients together and season with salt and ground pepperberry to taste. Refrigerate until needed.

Heat 1 tablespoon oil in a large, deep frying pan over medium-high heat. Add onion, spring onion, carrot and mushroom and sauté, stirring occasionally, for 5 minutes until softened.

Meanwhile, heat 1 teaspoon oil in another large frying pan over high heat, add mince and fry, stirring occasionally, for 8–10 minutes until browned all over (do this in batches if necessary to avoid crowding the pan).

Add mince to vegetables, stir to combine, then add rice and stir over medium-high heat until transparent. Pour in stock, add tomatoes and season to taste with salt and ground pepperberry. Reduce heat to low-medium, cover with a lid and simmer, adding a splash of water if necessary, for 30 minutes or until the rice is tender and has absorbed all the liquid. Stir in herbs and garlic. Cool.

Preheat oven to 200°C (400°F). Blanch vine leaves in a large saucepan of boiling water for 1 minute, refreshing them immediately in iced water. Dry on a clean tea towel.

Lay out a vine leaf and top with a saltbush leaf, then place 1 tablespoon rice filling in the centre and roll up, sealing the filling inside. Place in the base of a casserole. Repeat with remaining leaves and filling, packing them into casserole tightly. Drizzle with ¼ cup (60 ml) olive oil, then bake, uncovered, for 45 minutes or until tender. Serve with yoghurt dressing.

> **Substitution options:**
>
> River mint
> → any mint
> Minced kangaroo
> → minced beef, lamb or pork
> Sea parsley
> → parsley
> Island sea celery leaves
> → celery
> Saltbush
> → caper leaves or capers

Green Baked Eggs

Easy. Tasty. Healthy. This makes a great, light mid-week supper or Sunday brunch.

Serves 1

2 teaspoons olive oil
2 handfuls native sorrel
1 handful warrigal greens
1 handful native watercress
Lemon juice, to taste
1 large free-range egg
¼ cup (25 g) finely
 grated parmesan

Preheat oven grill to high. Heat oil in a small frying pan over low heat, add sorrel, warrigal greens and watercress and stir until just wilted. Squeeze in a little lemon juice (if you're not using sorrel) and season with salt and ground pepperberry to taste.

Place greens in the base of a ramekin, crack egg on top, then cover with cheese and grill until egg is cooked to your liking.

Substitution options:

Native sorrel
→ lemon sorrel or spinach
Warrigal greens
→ spinach
Native watercress
→ watercress

Fragrant Coconut Rice

Coconut rice is a staple in our house because the leftovers can be used to make rice pudding or as a versatile side dish. You can use any myrtle leaf here; try anise or cinnamon myrtle.

Serves 2–3

1 cup (200 g) jasmine rice
8 lemon myrtle leaves
 (fresh or dried)
½ cup (125 ml) coconut cream

Put rice 2 cups (500 ml) water and lemon myrtle leaves in a saucepan and bring to the boil. Cover with a lid, reduce heat to low and simmer for 5–10 minutes or until liquid is nearly absorbed. Add coconut cream, remove from heat, stir, cover and leave for at least 5 minutes. Remove lemon myrtle leaves and fluff rice before serving.

Substitution options:

Lemon myrtle leaves
→ lemon zest

Green Garden Soup

This is the goods. Jam-packed with nutrients and flavour, this soup can be totally mixed and matched, depending on what's in season and/or in the garden at the time. Eat soup, all of the soup.

Serves 2

2 cups (90 g) dandelion, nettle or any other edible wild weeds or leaves (we tend to forage these or pick them from the garden), chopped
1 cup (45 g) warrigal greens
½ cup (25 g) purslane or bower spinach
20 g (¾ oz) butter
1 brown onion, diced
2 island sea celery sprigs, chopped
2 garlic cloves, finely chopped
2 cups (500 ml) vegetable stock
1 sea rosemary sprig, leaves chopped
5 saltbush leaves, chopped
Finely grated zest of 1 lemon
1 parmesan rind (optional)
1 cup (250 ml) pure cream
Edible flowers and leaves, to serve

Blanch wild leaves, warrigal greens and purslane in a large saucepan of boiling water for 1 minute, then plunge into iced water. Drain.

Melt butter in a large saucepan over medium heat, add onion, celery and garlic and stir occasionally for 5 minutes until softened. Season to taste with salt and ground pepperberry, then add stock, rosemary, saltbush, lemon zest, parmesan rind (if using) and blanched leaves and bring to a simmer. Cover with a lid, reduce heat to medium-low and simmer, stirring occasionally, for 4–5 minutes or until everything has collapsed.

Remove parmesan rind and discard. Cool soup slightly, then pour into a blender and blend until smooth. Return to saucepan, stir in the cream, season to taste and reheat gently (without boiling) until hot. Ladle into soup bowls and serve topped with flowers and leaves.

Substitution options:

Warrigal greens
→ spinach
Purslane or bower spinach
→ spinach
Island sea celery
→ celery
Sea rosemary
→ rosemary
Saltbush
→ extra salt

Native Watercress and Lentil Soup

Green and packed full of protein, this hearty soup is full of flavour and easily tweaked to suit your taste: the stock can be meat- or vegetable-based, and if you prefer a creamy soup, you can add some sour cream, cream or crème fraîche at the end. I try not to cook this for too long at the end so that it stays fresh and bright and the peas don't turn to mush.

Serves 4-6

2 litres (8 cups) chicken stock
20 g (¾ oz) butter
1 small brown onion, diced
2 island sea celery sprigs
1 garlic clove, finely grated
200 g (7 oz) ham, chopped (optional)
1 cup (80 g) cooked Puy or green lentils
1 cup (140 g) frozen peas
1 cup (30 g) native watercress (this is very peppery, so adjust to taste)
Sea parsley and wild basil, to serve

Bring stock to a simmer in a saucepan.

Meanwhile, melt butter in a small frying pan over medium heat, add onion, celery, garlic and a small pinch of salt. Stir for 3-5 minutes until almost soft.

Add ham to stock, if using, increase heat and bring to the boil, then reduce heat to low and add onion and celery mixture, stirring to combine. Add lentils, peas and watercress and season to taste with salt and ground pepperberry. Stir gently for 1-2 minutes until heated through, then serve topped with parsley and basil.

Substitution options:

Island sea celery
→ celery leaves
Native watercress
→ watercress
Sea parsley
→ parsley
Wild basil
→ holy basil

Barramundi Poached in Geraldton Wax, Kunzea Flower and Lemon-scented Gum

These three leaves, in our opinion, are the queens of citrus, eucalypt and honey flavours and their perfumes, infused in the broth, will draw you into the bowl. The base is flexible and can be experimented with in many ways, with different herbs or spices. You can also swap the nut milk for whole milk, coconut milk or even stock or broth and use chicken in place of fish. This is fantastic with coconut rice infused with more lemon-scented gum (see page 90).

Serves 2

2 tablespoons olive oil
2 eschalots, finely diced
10 g (¼ oz) Geraldton wax leaves
2 teaspoons dried ground lemon-scented gum (or 4 whole leaves)
1 teaspoon dried ground white kunzea flower
2 anise myrtle leaves (fresh or dried)
700 ml (24 fl oz) macadamia milk
½ small fennel bulb, chopped
2 garlic cloves, bruised
2 skinless barramundi fillets

TO SERVE

Sliced finger limes, blood limes and desert limes
Geraldton wax flowers, to serve
Lemon myrtle and Geraldton wax leaves
Fragrant coconut rice (page 90)

Heat oil in a large saucepan over low heat. Add eschalot, Geraldton wax, lemon-scented gum, kunzea and anise myrtle and stir occasionally for 3–4 minutes until softened. This will help to release their oils.

Stir in macadamia milk, fennel and garlic and season to taste with salt and ground pepperberry. Increase heat to medium and bring to a simmer. As broth comes to a simmer, season barramundi on both sides with salt and ground pepperberry.

Reduce heat to low and add barramundi. Cover with a lid and simmer gently for 8–10 minutes, or until barramundi is opaque and flakes easily. Gently remove from broth with a fish slice and place in serving bowls. Strain broth, discarding solids, then pour it over fish. Top fish and broth with limes, flowers and leaves and serve with rice.

Substitution options:

Geraldton wax
→ lemongrass
Lemon-scented gum
→ lime leaves
White kunzea
→ juniper berries
Anise myrtle
→ fennel seeds
Barramundi
→ any flaky white fish
Native limes
→ limes

Peppermint Gum Slice

Old school, with a new twist. Peppermint gum tastes more like peppermint than peppermint itself; use it sparingly to avoid everything tasting like chewing gum.

Serves 8–10

⅔ cup (100 g) self-raising flour
⅔ cup (110 g) macadamia nuts, finely chopped
¼ cup (55 g) caster sugar
¼ cup (30 g) raw cacao powder
1 teaspoon ground wattleseed
140 g (5 oz) butter, melted
1 free-range egg, beaten

FILLING
4 cups (500 g) pure icing sugar
2½ tablespoons boiling water
1 teaspoon ground peppermint gum

TOPPING
200 g (7 oz) dark chocolate, chopped
1 tablespoon macadamia oil
2 peppermint crisp bars (optional), crushed

Substitution options:

Macadamia nuts
→ sandalwood nuts or cashews
Wattleseed
→ ground coffee
Peppermint gum
→ chopped fresh mint

Preheat oven to 180°C (350°F). Grease a 20 cm x 30 cm (8 in x 12 in) baking tin and line it with baking paper. Mix flour, macadamia nuts, sugar, cacao powder, wattleseed, butter and egg in a bowl until it comes together to form a dough.

Press dough into base of tin. Bake for 12 minutes or until soft and lightly golden brown. Leave to cool.

When base is completely cooled, make the filling. Stir icing sugar, boiling water and peppermint gum in a bowl to combine, then immediately spread filling onto base, tapping tin on bench to make sure it's flat and level. Chill for 1 hour to set.

For topping, melt chocolate and macadamia oil in a heatproof bowl set over a saucepan of simmering water, stirring until smooth. Pour onto slice and tap tin on bench until smooth. Sprinkle with crushed peppermint crisp bars and refrigerate for 1 hour until set.

Lift out and slice into squares to serve. Slice will keep refrigerated in an airtight container for 5 days.

River Mint Granita

A flavourful dessert or palate cleanser. Also known to be great at curing hangovers.

Serves 4–6

2 cups (40 g) fresh river mint
2 cups (500 ml) boiling water
2¼ cups (500 g) caster sugar
1 teaspoon finger lime pearls
Fresh violets or other edible flowers, to serve

Substitution options:

River mint
→ mint or basil
Finger lime pearls
→ lemon or lime juice

Place mint in a heatproof bowl, then pour in boiling water. Cover with a clean tea towel and leave overnight at room temperature to infuse.

The next day, strain liquid through a sieve into a saucepan, pressing on the mint as you go. Discard leaves. Stir in sugar and heat slowly, stirring, until very gently simmering. Don't let it boil, just heat until sugar dissolves. Add finger lime and stir to combine.

Pour into a deep baking tray or shallow freezer-proof dish and place in freezer. After 1 hour, use a fork to scrape the iced mixture, bringing the crystals from around the edges into the centre and mashing well. Return to freezer and repeat this process 3 more times, waiting an hour between each time, until completely frozen, light and fluffy (it should be the texture of snow).

To serve, run a fork through the granita a few times to break it up, then transfer to glasses or bowls and top with edible flowers.

Herby Ice Pops

These ice pops recipes, one made with soda, one with yoghurt, recall super-hot summer days running under the garden hose in the backyard, ice pops dripping down onto the hot concrete, only to be quickly eaten by ants. The only difference here is that we've made ants a part of the ice pops! These are less sweet than those you may remember from your youth, and much more about the flavourings. We encourage you to play around with different additions to suit your tastes. You'll need popsicle moulds and 4-6 sticks — we like to use thoroughly cleaned (and safe) sticks from the garden.

Makes 4-6

SODA WATER POPS
100 g (3½ oz) raw honey
1 tablespoon green ants (optional, see page 74)
Finely grated zest and pearls of 6 finger limes
2 cups (500 ml) soda water

YOGHURT POPS
1¾ cups (460 g) natural yoghurt
2 tablespoons raw honey
1 teaspoon green ants
1 small handful chopped native basil leaves (optional)
Honey, to serve

Substitution options:

Green ants
→ citrus zest
Finger lime
→ lime zest and juice
Native basil
→ basil

For soda water pops, pour 100 ml (3½ fl oz) fresh water into a small saucepan and bring to the boil. Remove from heat, add honey and stir to dissolve. Add half the green ants (or whatever flavouring you're using; with these we also like desert limes, lilly pillies, quandongs, midyim berries, Tanami apples or muntries), return to the heat and simmer for 5 minutes, then remove from heat and leave to infuse for 30 minutes. (This can be done the day before and left in the fridge overnight to infuse.)

Pour through a sieve into a jug, squashing ants with the back of a spoon to squeeze out all the liquid. Add finger lime zest and pearls and stir well. Add enough soda water to bring the total volume up to 600 ml (21 fl oz).

Add your choice of ingredients to moulds, then pour in the liquid. Freeze for 1-2 hours, insert popsicle sticks, then allow to freeze overnight. Unmould and enjoy.

Note, for two different colours like in our soda pops in the photo, freeze half first, then pour in the second half once the first is set — this will take about 2 hours. We used only a little soda for the orange part, and mostly soda for the white part.

For yoghurt pops, add yoghurt and honey to a food processor and whiz to combine. Stir in green ants and basil (or whatever flavouring you're using; with these we also like rosella leaves, river mint or petals of native flowers).

Pour into popsicle moulds, pushing some ants and herbs to the edges of the moulds so you can see them when they're unmoulded. Place a popsicle stick into each mould, then freeze overnight. Unmould and enjoy with some honey.

Preserving native herbs

Drying picked herbs
- Pick the leaves from your herbs. Lay some sheets of paper towel on trays and spread out the individual leaves, keeping them apart so the air can circulate. The paper helps to draw any moisture away from the leaves.
- Find a place out of draughts to dry the leaves, preferably inside. They like dry heat, no humidity. Near a window will give them sufficient sunlight for drying — direct sunlight dries them more quickly, but they'll fade a little.
- Leave them for 1–2 days. Check frequently as they may dry faster than this, depending on your home. They like dry heat, no humidity.
- You will know they're dry when they feel like tissue paper and have wrinkled up a little.

Once your herbs have dried, play around with mixtures to make the perfect mix to add to your meals. I love using native rosemary, thyme and oregano (cut-leaf mint) together in equal parts. Grind them up or leave them whole and store in jars or airtight containers — they'll last for ages, and the flavour is stronger than using fresh herbs.

Drying in bunches
Hanging up woody herbs in bunches to dry lets you do them in bulk, and they also look pretty tied to a shelf or hanging overhead. Simply gather bunches of herbs, tie a bunch together and hang upside-down out of direct sunlight. If you want to speed up the process you can dry them outside in warm, not humid, air and bring them inside when dried. If you live in a humid climate, dry them inside. Leave the bunch hanging and snip off leaves as needed.

Freezing in oil
Pick off individual leaves and place into ice cube trays. Cover with oil of your choice (use 3 parts oil to 1 part herbs), freeze, then pop out a couple of cubes when cooking. You can use them straight from frozen.

Herbal oil infusions
Herb-infused oils are not only great for cooking, they can also be used as massage oil or as bath additives, which means they make lovely gifts. You can use any oil you like for this, but it's best to use one you like to cook with.

Sterilise and thoroughly dry a large jar or bottle (see page 232). Fill it with herbs, then add some chillies, garlic or edible flowers, of course depending on what you want to use the oil for.

Slowly pour oil over the herbs. Use a skewer to move the herbs around in the oil to ensure no air pockets remain. Add enough oil to completely cover all the herbs, filling your vessel right up to the brim.

Tightly seal the jar or bottle, give it a few shakes, and put it in a cool, dark place. Shake every few days and let it sit for at least 4–6 weeks so the herbs can infuse. After that time, strain the oil through a muslin-lined sieve into sterilised storage bottles (see page 232). Give the herbs a squish to get all the oil out before discarding. Seal and label your bottles. Store in a cool, dark place for up to 2 years.

Herby Salt Rub

Turn plain old meat and vegetables into a restaurant-quality meal simply by adding some herbs and spices. Make a jar of this, keep it in your pantry and use it on everything. It's also worth making one or two extra, since a jar of herby salt rub really makes a lovely gift.

Makes 1½ cups (200 g)

10 g (¼ oz) sea rosemary leaves
⅓ cup (50 g) paprika
⅓ cup (15 g) fresh native thyme leaves
1½ tablespoons chilli flakes
1½ tablespoons garlic powder
1½ tablespoons yellow mustard seeds
2 dried lemon myrtle leaves, ground
1 cup (130 g) flaked sea salt

Place everything in a jar, shake well and store. Sprinkle on veggies and meats before roasting.

Substitution options:

Sea rosemary
→ rosemary
Native thyme
→ thyme
Lemon myrtle leaves
→ dried lemon zest

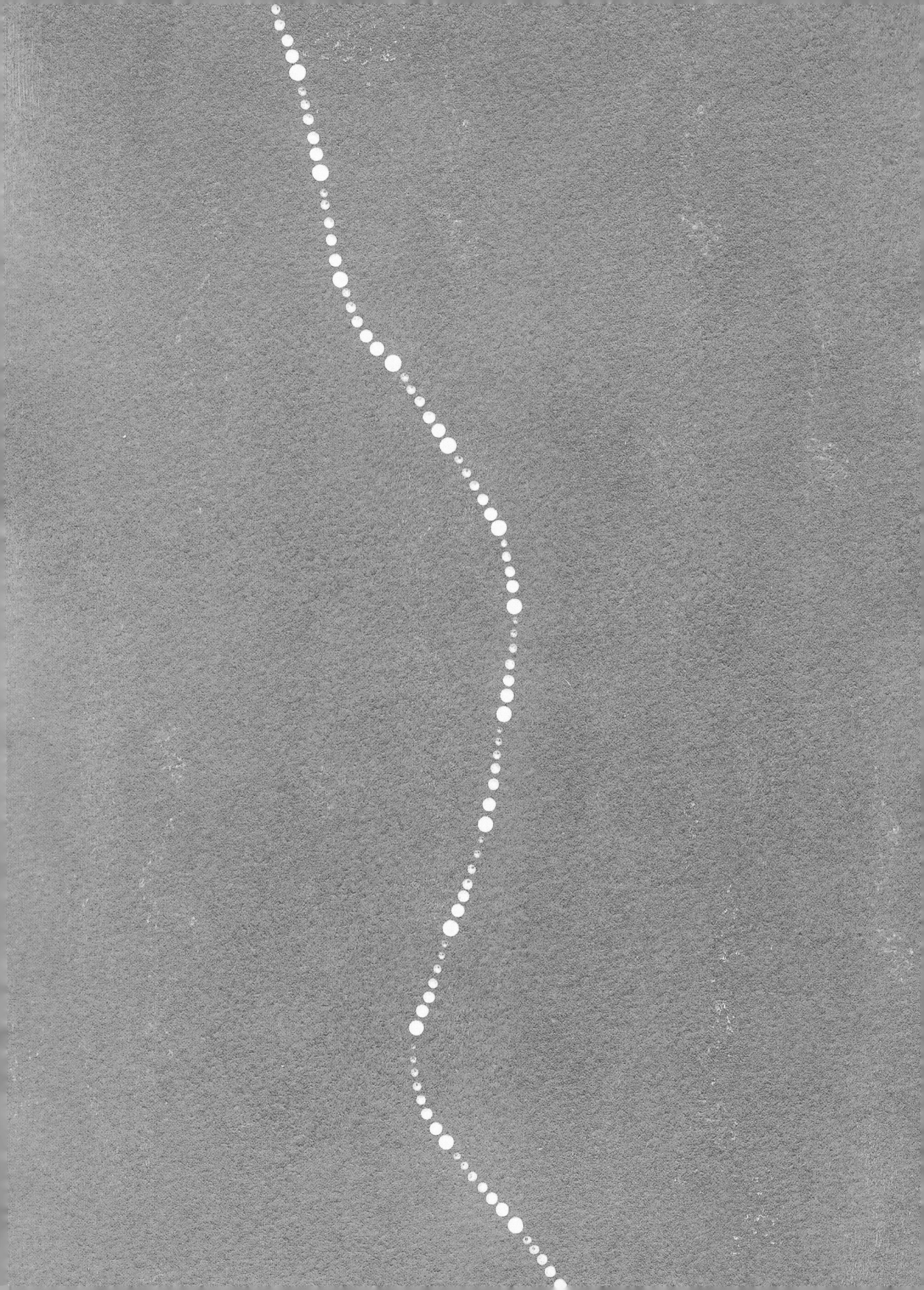

nutty

Not just macadamias, the native nut scene is a party! Sandalwood and bunya nuts are often neglected; it's time to introduce them to your everyday regime. As well as nuts, think about the nutty flavours of wattleseed and the like, too. These recipes show these ingredients off in an array of cooking styles.

Wattella

Like Nutella, but not. This Aussie version has less bad stuff and more good stuff, and although it's a little thicker than the real deal, we prefer it. Just like the original, this requires liberal spreading, right to the edges, so don't skimp.

Makes 1 cup (250 ml)

1¼ cups (200 g) macadamia nuts, roasted
10 dates, pitted
⅓ cup (40 g) raw cacao powder
2 teaspoons wattleseed extract (page 78),
1 teaspoon ground wattleseed
2 tablespoons macadamia oil
1 tablespoon maple syrup
1 teaspoon ground cinnamon myrtle

Substitution options:

Wattleseed extract
→ vanilla extract
Wattleseed
→ ground coffee
Cinnamon myrtle
→ ground cinnamon
Macadamia oil
→ another nut oil

Blitz macadamia nuts in a food processor until they begin to form a paste. Add remaining ingredients and continue to blitz, adding 1 teaspoon water at a time until you reach a thick, spreadable consistency. Add a pinch of salt and stir through.

Serve on toast, crumpets or whatever else takes your fancy. Wattella will keep refrigerated in an airtight container for up to 3 weeks.

Macadamia Butter

I'm not sure why this hasn't replaced every Aussie's peanut butter yet, but it should — especially if you make your own. You can roast the nuts first if you want a deeper flavour.

Makes 350 g (12 oz)

3 cups (400 g) macadamia nuts (roasted or unroasted)
Pinch of salt
Pinch of ground wattleseed or lemon, anise or cinnamon myrtle (optional)
1 teaspoon raw honey (optional)
Macadamia oil (optional), to cover

> **Substitution options:**
>
> Wattleseed
> → ground coffee
> Cinnamon myrtle
> → ground cinnamon

Place macadamia nuts, salt, wattleseed and honey (if using) in a food processor and blitz on medium speed, stopping to scrape down sides occasionally, until you get a consistency you're happy with. The time it takes will depend on the power of your processor; the longer you blitz, the smoother it'll be.

Transfer to an airtight container. If you prefer a less dry butter, cover it with 1 cm (½ in) layer of macadamia oil; stir before use. Macadamia butter will keep refrigerated for 3 months.

Macadamia Butter Cups

If you love Reese's Peanut Butter Cups, make these. If you've never heard of Reese's, make them anyway — they're so good that you'll soon be addicted.

Makes 12 biscuits

10 Nice biscuits (or Milk Arrowroot biscuits)
½ cup (60 g) pure icing sugar
1½ cups (400 g) macadamia butter (see above)
½ cup (75 g) macadamia nuts, coarsely chopped
2½ cups (425 g) chocolate chips or pieces, melted

Line a 12-hole muffin tin with paper cases. Crush the biscuits to a fine crumb in a food processor, or smash them up in a bag as small as you can — both fine and coarse consistencies work great for this recipe.

Add the crushed biscuits, sugar, macadamia butter and nuts to a heatproof bowl set over a saucepan of simmering water (don't let base of bowl touch water) and stir until melted and combined.

Place 1 tablespoon melted chocolate in each paper case, spreading it evenly over the base, then top with 1 tablespoon nut-butter mixture. Top with another spoon of chocolate, then tap trays on the bench to help it settle. Refrigerate until set. Pop out of moulds to serve. Macadamia butter cups will keep in an airtight container for up to a week.

Macadamia Blondies

For your sweet-toothed mates — make a tin as a gift and you will be loved.

Makes 8

⅔ cup (180 g) macadamia butter (page 108)
150 ml (5½ fl oz) macadamia oil
100 g (3½ oz) maple syrup or honey
1 free-range egg, beaten
¼ cup (40 g) macadamia nuts, roasted and coarsely chopped
1 tablespoon grated native ginger or 1 teaspoon ground roasted wattleseed
100 g (3½ oz) dark, milk or white chocolate, coarsely chopped

Preheat oven to 180°C (350°F). Grease and line a 20 cm (8 in) square baking tin. Mix all ingredients except chocolate in a large bowl until well combined.

Transfer to tin, push flat and scatter chocolate over the top. Bake for 15–20 minutes until fudgy. Cool, then cut into squares.

Blondies will keep in an airtight container at room temperature for 5 days.

Substitution options:

Macadamia oil
→ coconut oil
Macadamia nuts
→ sandalwood nuts or cashews
Native ginger
→ ginger
Wattleseed
→ ground coffee

Breakkie muffins

Our breakfast or break muffins, jam-packed with protein and good fats from wattleseed and nuts. These make a great portable snack, are brilliant for the kids and also freeze well.

Makes 12 mini muffins

Macadamia oil, for greasing
½ cup (50 g) rolled oats or quinoa flakes
30 g (1 oz) macadamia nuts
25 g (1 oz) sandalwood nuts
25 g (1 oz) almonds
25 g (1 oz) bunya nuts
20 g (¾ oz) wattleseeds, plus 1 teaspoon ground roasted wattleseed
2 free-range eggs
2 cups (100 g) chopped kale leaves
1 zucchini, chopped
1½ tablespoons pepitas or sunflower seeds

Preheat oven to 180°C (350°F). Grease a 12-hole muffin tray with oil. Put all ingredients except pepitas in a food processor and blitz until just combined. Transfer to muffin tray, filling holes two-thirds full. Sprinkle tops with pepitas.

Bake for 20 minutes or until centre springs back to the touch. Muffins will keep in an airtight container at room temperature for 4 days, or for several months frozen.

Substitution options:

Wattleseed
→ ground coffee
Bunya nuts
→ pine nuts
Sandalwood nuts
→ use more macadamia nuts

Spiced Honey Nuts

A brilliant gift and a brilliant snack — plus it's so simple to make. We like to make a batch of these nuts whenever we're blind-baking pastry, using the nuts in place of baking beads or beans.

Makes 200 g (7 oz)

¼ cup (90 g) honey
100 g (3½ oz) macadamia nuts
⅔ cup (100 g) sandalwood nuts
Pinch of crushed pepperberries
Pinch of ground lemon myrtle
Pinch of ground wattleseed
Pinch of sea rosemary, chopped

Preheat oven to 180°C (350°F). Line a baking tray with baking paper. Place honey in a small saucepan over medium heat and swirl until warmed. Place nuts in a heatproof bowl, pour in honey, add spices and a pinch of salt and mix until coated.

Pour onto tray and spread out. Roast for 15–20 minutes or until golden; keep your eye on them, they can burn within minutes. Cool before serving. Spiced honey nuts will keep in an airtight container for 4 weeks.

Substitution options:

Pepperberries
→ pepper or dried chilli flakes
Lemon myrtle
→ lemon zest
Sea rosemary
→ rosemary
Wattleseed
→ ground coffee

Sandalwood nuts, in and out of their shells

Macadamia, Finger Lime, Native Lemongrass and Cauliflower Soup

This is one of those simple mid-week soups that can be altered to suit whatever you have in the fridge or pantry. Swap the cauliflower for potatoes, for example, or the macadamia milk for coconut milk. Whatever you have is whatever you use.

Serves 4

1 small cauliflower, cut into florets, stalk coarsely chopped
1 tablespoon olive oil
1 small brown onion, finely diced
4 garlic cloves, chopped
5 cm (2 in) piece ginger, chopped
2 teaspoons ground native lemongrass
1 long red chilli, finely chopped
4 dried lemon myrtle leaves
1 teaspoon ground turmeric
800 ml (28 fl oz) macadamia milk or coconut milk
2 tablespoons soy sauce
2 tablespoons coconut sugar
4 finger limes, pearls squeezed

Preheat oven to 180°C (350°F). Spread cauliflower on a lined baking tray, drizzle with 2 teaspoons oil, season with salt and ground pepperberry and toss to coat. Roast for 10–15 minutes or until starting to turn golden.

Meanwhile, heat 2 teaspoons oil in a saucepan over medium heat, add onion and a pinch of salt and cook, stirring, for 2–3 minutes until beginning to soften. Add garlic, ginger, lemongrass, chilli, lemon myrtle and turmeric and cook, stirring, for another 3 minutes until fragrant.

Add roasted cauliflower to saucepan along with macadamia milk, soy sauce and sugar and simmer, stirring occasionally, for 15 minutes or until cauliflower is soft and flavours have melded.

Add finger lime, cool briefly, then blitz the soup in a blender in two batches (or use a stick blender) until smooth. Season to taste with salt and ground pepperberry and gently reheat before serving.

Substitution options:

Native lemongrass
→ lemongrass
Lemon myrtle leaves
→ lime leaves
Finger lime
→ lime juice

Macadamia Lentil Curry

One to batch-cook on the weekend then eat during the week. Try replacing the pumpkin with sweet potato, and the macadamia milk with whatever milk you prefer.

Serves 4-6

1 butternut pumpkin, peeled and diced
2 carrots, coarsely chopped
2 brown onions, finely chopped
4 garlic cloves, finely chopped
10 cm (4 in) piece ginger, grated
4 cups (1 litre) vegetable stock
2 cups (500 ml) macadamia milk
250 g (9 oz) Puy lentils
5 cm (2 in) piece turmeric, grated
1 long red chilli, finely chopped
½ tsp cayenne pepper
2 cups (500 ml) boiling water
Juice of 1 lemon
Small bunch of native herbs (such as island sea celery or sea rosemary), chopped
Roasted macadamia nuts, to serve

Substitution options:

Native herbs
→ coriander
Macadamia milk
→ almond milk

Put pumpkin, carrot, onion, garlic, ginger, stock and macadamia milk in a large saucepan over medium heat. Cover with a lid and bring to a simmer.

Simmer for 15 minutes, season with salt and ground pepperberry, then add lentils, turmeric, chilli, cayenne pepper and boiling water. Simmer for 20 minutes, then turn off heat. Squeeze in lemon juice, season to taste with salt and ground pepperberry and stir in herbs.

Bunya Nut Risotto with Bush Green Pesto

We like to use bunya nuts as a straight substitute for pine nuts. The best thing about them is they're also about a hundred times bigger (slight exaggeration), so you only need a few to pack a punch.

Serves 4

4 cups (1 litre) vegetable or chicken stock
2 tablespoons macadamia oil
2 eschalots, finely diced
1 garlic clove, crushed
2 Geraldton wax sprigs, needles finely chopped (or 1 teaspoon powder)
150 g (5½ oz) arborio rice
2 cups (500 ml) white wine
½ cup (50 g) finely grated parmesan
Native herbs, crisp-fried, to serve

BUNYA NUT BUTTER

225 g (8 oz) bunya nuts, chopped
2½ tablespoons macadamia oil

BUSH GREEN PESTO

5 cups (250 g) warrigal greens
2½ cups (50 g) sea parsley
1 cup (50 g) native basil
3 finger limes, pearls squeezed
1 cup (250 ml) macadamia oil
20 desert limes
¾ cup (100 g) macadamia nuts, roasted and chopped
¾ cup (100 g) bunya nuts, toasted and chopped
3 garlic cloves
Juice of 2 lemons
⅔ cup (70 g) parmesan, finely grated

For bunya nut butter, heat oven to 180°C (350°F). Roast bunya nuts for 3–4 minutes until hot but not browned. Reserve about 6 nuts to serve, then place the rest in a food processor or blender, add oil, 150 ml (5 fl oz) water and blitz on high speed until very smooth, scraping down sides occasionally if needed. If it's a little dry, add a splash more water; you're aiming for a nut butter consistency. Season to taste with salt and ground pepperberry. Nut butter will keep refrigerated for a month.

For bush green pesto, blanch warrigal greens in boiling water for 1 minute then refresh in iced water. Drain well, roughly chop, then add to a food processor with herbs, finger lime and a drizzle of oil. Blitz to a coarse puree, then add desert limes, macadamia nuts, bunya nuts and garlic and continue to blitz, drizzling the remaining oil in slowly. Stir in lemon juice, then parmesan and season to taste with salt and freshly ground pepperberry. Pesto will keep refrigerated for 1–2 weeks.

Bring stock to a simmer in a saucepan over high heat, then turn off and cover with a lid to keep warm. Heat oil in another large saucepan over medium heat, add eschalot, garlic and Geraldton wax and sweat, stirring occasionally, for 3–5 minutes until just soft but not coloured. Add rice and stir for 1–2 minutes (it will crackle and pop) until edges of rice just start to turn transparent. Add wine, let it sizzle to burn off alcohol, then add stock ladle by ladle, stirring constantly and allowing each ladleful to be absorbed before adding the next. Continue this process until rice is just cooked, and the texture is like that of thick cream, about 15–20 minutes.

Stir in ¼ cup (40 g) bunya nut butter until thick and creamy, then stir in parmesan. Cover with a lid and leave for 1–2 minutes to melt through. Season to taste with salt and ground pepperberry, stirring one more time. Serve with bush green pesto and crisp-fried herbs on top.

Substitution options:

Macadamia oil
→ olive oil
Geraldton wax
→ ground juniper berries
Bunya nuts
→ pine nuts
Sea parsley
→ parsley

Warrigal greens
→ spinach
Native basil
→ basil
Finger limes
→ lime juice
Desert limes
→ lemon juice

Bunya Nut Rice Paper Rolls with Macadamia Dipping Sauce

These beauties can be made with or without the meat, and using any of your favourite veggies.

Serves 4–6

- 75 g (¾ cup) dried rice vermicelli noodles
- 1½ cups (225 g) cooked minced kangaroo or pork, or sliced chicken
- 1 carrot, julienned or grated
- ⅓ cup (10 g) chopped river mint leaves, plus extra leaves to serve
- 6 large native basil leaves, sliced, plus extra leaves to serve
- 2 tablespoons coriander leaves, chopped
- ¼ cup (30 g) roasted bunya nuts, chopped
- 20 x 22 cm (8 in) rice paper wrappers
- Edible flowers, to serve

FINGER LIME SAUCE
- 8 finger limes, pearls squeezed
- 1 teaspoon brown sugar
- 1 garlic clove, crushed
- 2 cm (¾ in) piece ginger, finely grated

MACADAMIA AND BUNYA NUT DIPPING SAUCE
- ½ cup (60 g) macadamia nuts, roasted
- ½ cup (60 g) bunya nuts, roasted
- 1 garlic clove, finely grated
- ½ cup (125 ml) macadamia oil
- ½ cup (125 ml) coconut cream
- 4 finger limes, pearls squeezed

Place noodles in a heatproof bowl. Cover with boiling water and leave for 5 minutes to soften. Once softened, rinse under cold water and drain. Cut noodles into short lengths with a pair of scissors.

For finger lime sauce, combine finger lime, sugar, garlic and ginger in a bowl, whisk with a fork until mixed. (You can double this recipe if you want your rolls extra-tangy.)

For dipping sauce, combine everything except lime in a food processor and blend until smooth. Transfer to a bowl and top with finger lime.

Combine noodles, mince, carrot, herbs and bunya nuts in a bowl. Add finger lime sauce and toss to coat.

Now get rolling. Lay a damp tea towel on a baking tray. Fill a shallow bowl with warm water. One by one, dip rice paper wrappers in water to soften, then transfer to a dry tea towel to absorb excess water. Place a couple of tablespoons noodle mixture in centre and top with edible flowers, then roll up, folding in edges, to enclose filling. Place on tray, cover with another damp tea towel and repeat until all filling is used.

Serve the rice paper rolls with macadamia and bunya nut dipping sauce.

Substitution options:

River mint
→ mint
Native basil
→ basil
Minced kangaroo
→ minced pork, lamb, beef or veal
Bunya nuts
→ cashews
Finger lime
→ lime juice

Strawberry gum (page 49)

Sandalwood and Custard Cake with Tanami Apples and Bush Pears

Custard and cake, brought together with two of the most exciting fruits in the bush-food forest. If you can't get the bush pears (also known as makaya) or Tanami apples, use extra muntries and bush apples, or use pears and apples instead. If you prefer, you can use very thick or set bought custard in place of homemade.

Serves 6-8

75 g (2¾ oz) butter, softened
½ cup (100 g) lightly packed brown sugar
2 free-range eggs
60 g (2¼ oz) plain flour
1½ teaspoons baking powder
½ teaspoon ground cinnamon myrtle
Cream or crème fraîche, to serve

WATTLESEED CUSTARD

¾ cup (180 ml) milk
1 free-range egg
50 g (1¾ oz) light brown sugar
2 tablespoons cornflour
1 teaspoon wattleseed extract (page 78)

APPLE TOPPING

10 Tanami apples, seeds removed, sliced
6 bush pears, peeled and halved (or 1 small pear, cored and sliced)
1 cup (155 g) muntries
½ cup (80 g) sandalwood nuts, coarsely chopped
50 g (1¾ oz) light brown sugar
75 ml (2½ fl oz) Kangaroo Island Spirits honey and walnut liqueur (from select bottleshops), or mead or brandy

To make custard, whisk all ingredients together in a saucepan over medium heat. Bring to the boil, whisking constantly, until very thick. Transfer to a small bowl and refrigerate until set — it should be thick enough that you can slice it.

For apple topping, combine Tanami apples, bush pears, muntries, nuts, sugar, liqueur and 1¼ tablespoons water in a large frying pan. Cook over high heat, stirring occasionally, until liquid evaporates and fruit is soft. Allow to cool.

Preheat oven to 180°C (350°F). Grease and line a 20 cm (8 in) cake tin. Beat butter and sugar in a stand mixer fitted with the whisk attachment until pale and fluffy. Add eggs one at a time, making sure each egg is fully incorporated before adding the next, then stir in flour, baking powder and cinnamon myrtle. Chop the custard coarsely (or pour it in if it's thin enough) and fold it through.

Pour batter into cake tin, spoon three-quarters apple topping on top, reserving the rest to serve, then bake for 40–50 minutes or until a skewer inserted in the centre comes out clean.

Top with remaining apple topping and serve with cream or crème fraîche. This cake is best eaten on the day of baking.

Substitution options:

Cinnamon myrtle
→ ground cinnamon
Wattleseed extract
→ vanilla extract
Tanami apple
→ apples
Muntries
→ apples
Sandalwood nuts
→ cashews

Campfire S'mores with Davidson's Plum

Camping is the best. OK, not the sleeping on the floor bit, but the campfire bit. We've since discovered the joys of cooking on fire and toasting marshmallows, but really this recipe came about as we were determined to beat our American mates in a from-scratch s'mores contest. You'll need a sugar thermometer if you're making the marshmallows, but you can cheat that bit by melting shop-bought ones in the microwave for a few seconds, then shaping and sprinkling with Davidson's plum powder.

Makes 6–8 large s'mores

Your favourite chocolate, to serve

MACADAMIA BISCUITS
250 g (9 oz) butter, softened
½ cup (110 g) white sugar
½ cup (100 g) lightly packed brown sugar
2 large free-range eggs
1 teaspoon wattleseed extract (page 78) or ground wattleseed
2½ cups (375 g) plain flour
1 teaspoon bicarbonate of soda
1½ cups (230 g) macadamia nuts, coarsely chopped

DAVIDSON'S PLUM MARSHMALLOWS
Olive oil spray, for greasing
1¼ tablespoons powdered gelatine
¾ cup (165 g) caster sugar
½ cup (125 ml) light glucose syrup
2 teaspoons Davidson's plum powder, plus extra for dusting

Substitution options:

Wattleseed extract
→ vanilla extract
Wattleseed
→ ground coffee
Davidson's plum powder
→ goji berry powder

For the marshmallows, lightly coat a large, deep-sided baking tray with olive oil spray. Whisk gelatine in a microwave-safe bowl with ¼ cup (60 ml) water, then leave to sit for 5 minutes.

Combine sugar, ¼ cup (60 ml) glucose syrup, a pinch of salt and ½ cup (125 ml) water in a saucepan and bring to the boil, stirring occasionally to dissolve. Continue to boil rapidly, stirring occasionally, until the temperature reaches 115°C (230°F) on a sugar thermometer.

Meanwhile, add remaining glucose syrup to the bowl of a stand mixer fitted with the whisk attachment. Microwave gelatine mixture on high for 30 seconds until melted, stirring once or twice. Pour into the mixer bowl, then turn mixer on low and keep it running. Once syrup in the saucepan reaches 115°C (230°F), remove from heat and slowly pour into the mixer bowl, whisking continuously. Increase speed to medium, whisk for 5 minutes, then increase speed to medium-high and whisk for a further 5 minutes. Add Davidson's plum powder, then increase speed to high and whisk until fluffy. Transfer marshmallow into greased baking tin, banging the base on the bench to spread evenly, then smooth with a palette knife. Dust with a little extra plum powder, then leave in a cool, dry place for 6 hours to set.

For macadamia biscuits, preheat oven to 170°C (325°F). Grease and line a baking tray with baking paper. Cream butter and sugars in stand mixer fitted with the whisk attachment until light and fluffy. Add eggs and wattleseed extract and continue to beat on medium for another 2 minutes. Add flour, bicarbonate of soda and a pinch of salt, beat for 1 minute, then turn off and stir in macadamia nuts with a large spoon.

Place tablespoonfuls of dough on tray 2 cm (¾ in) apart, then bake for 12 minutes or until golden brown; we like these biscuits chewy as opposed to crunchy. Cool briefly, then transfer to a wire rack to cool.

Turn set marshmallow slab out onto a chopping board lined with baking paper and cut into small squares with a knife (a pizza cutter also works great for this). Marshmallows will keep in an airtight container (with baking paper between each layer) in a cool, dry place for up to 2 weeks.

To assemble s'mores, take two biscuits, sandwich them around a square of chocolate and a piece of marshmallow, then wrap in foil. Put them in the coals of a campfire for 1–2 minutes until chocolate and marshmallow are melted. Squish down a little and devour.

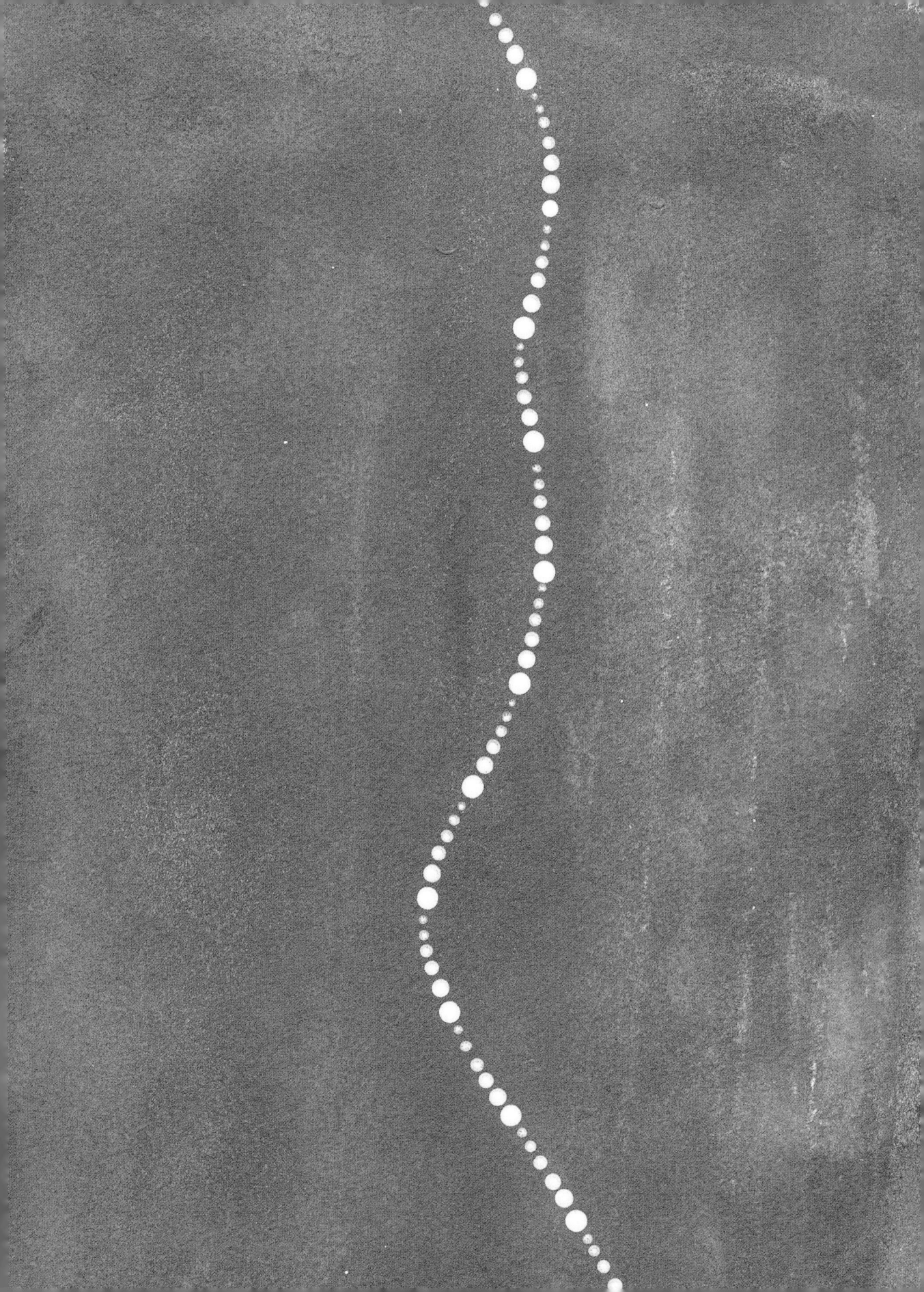

fruity

For anyone who hasn't tried native fruits, they're truly new and exciting for your palate. Don't expect bursts of sweetness, but more tart, sour and sometimes spicy flavours (with a load of antioxidants and vitamins as a bonus). There are a few sweeter berries, but even then the taste tends to be more like honey than sugar. These recipes explore the range of sweet and savoury offerings.

Davidson's Plum and Sandalwood Nut Brownies

Chocolate and Davidson's plum is such an amazing pairing. This sweet-and-sour combination was the first chocolate tablet we released for our Haigh's collaboration. If it's good enough for Haigh's ... As well as Davidson's plum, this recipe works well with quandongs, desert limes, lilly pillies and muntries.

Serves 10

65 g (2½ oz) butter
250 g (9 oz) caster sugar
2 egg whites
¼ cup (30 g) raw cacao powder
125 g (4½ oz) self-raising flour
1 tablespoon Davidson's plum powder
¼ cup (60 ml) macadamia oil
½ cup (75 g) chopped Davidson's plum (fresh or frozen and thawed)
⅔ cup (100 g) sandalwood nuts (optional), roasted and chopped
Toasted wattleseeds, to serve

DAVIDSON'S PLUM ICING

1½ cups (185 g) pure icing sugar
2 tablespoons butter, at room temperature
1 tablespoon milk (or water), plus extra if needed
1 teaspoon Davidson's plum powder

Preheat oven to 180°C (350°F). Grease and line a Lamington tin or similar with baking paper, leaving some overhanging. Cream butter and sugar in a stand mixer fitted with the whisk attachment on low speed until pale and creamy. With the motor running, add egg whites, beating to combine, then add cacao powder and flour, a little at a time, mixing until fully incorporated. Add Davidson's plum powder, macadamia oil and a pinch of salt, increase speed to medium, beat well, then add Davidson's plum and nuts and beat until just combined.

Transfer batter to tin and bake for 25 minutes until fudgy and set. (This will give you a soft, chewy brownie; bake it a few minutes longer if you like it firmer.) Remove from oven and cool in tin.

For icing, combine ingredients in a bowl and stir together until smooth, adding extra drops of milk (or water) to loosen if needed. Ice brownie and top with toasted wattleseed.

Cut into squares to serve. Brownies will keep in an airtight container for 5 days.

Substitution options:

Davidson's plum powder
→ goji berry powder
Macadamia oil
→ any nut oil
Sandalwood nuts
→ macadamia nuts

White Chocolate Quandong Truffles

You can totally change the flavourings here to any you like, as well as swapping the type of chocolate. Some of our favourites are dark chocolate truffles with Davidson's plum and strawberry gum, milk chocolate with finger lime and lemon myrtle, and milk chocolate with pepperberry and pepper leaf.

Makes about 15 truffles

2 cups (280 g) chopped white chocolate (use the best quality you can find; couverture is great)
20 g (¾ oz) salted butter
¼ cup (60 ml) thickened cream
Pinch ground cinnamon myrtle
½ cup (70 g) fresh quandongs, seeds removed, chopped (or ¼ cup dried, coarsely chopped)
Finger lime powder, for rolling
Toasted wattleseeds, for rolling

Substitution options:

Cinnamon myrtle
→ ground cinnamon
Quandong
→ Dried apricots, pears or apples

Combine chocolate, butter, cream and cinnamon myrtle in a heatproof bowl set over a saucepan of simmering water (don't let base of bowl touch water). Stir constantly until melted, then stir in the quandongs. Cool to room temperature, then chill for 1–2 hours to set.

Roll into walnut-sized balls with your hands, then roll in finger lime powder or wattleseeds to coat. Transfer to an airtight container lined with baking paper and keep refrigerated for up to 1 week.

Strawberry Gum Rice Pudding

Dessert, breakfast, a snack. Whatever the occasion, this is just so good. You can swap the strawberry gum for any native flavouring you like, and the fruit combination can be altered to your taste, too.

Serves 6

3½ cups (875 ml) milk
⅔ cup (160 ml) pure cream
¼ cup (60 ml) sugar, honey or golden syrup
6 dried strawberry gum leaves (or 2 tablespoons ground)
4 dried cinnamon myrtle leaves (or 1 teaspoon ground)
1 teaspoon vanilla paste
¾ cup (150 g) jasmine rice
Edible flowers and chopped sandalwood nuts, to serve

QUANDONG COMPOTE

2 cups (300 g) quandongs (fresh or frozen and thawed), halved
2 tablespoons caster sugar, plus extra to taste
1 cup (250 ml) orange juice
3 dried lemon myrtle leaves

Combine milk, cream, sugar, leaves, vanilla and a pinch of salt in a large saucepan over medium-high heat and bring to a simmer. Stir in rice and reduce heat to medium-low. Simmer, stirring often, for 20 minutes or until rice is tender and mixture is thick and luscious.

Meanwhile, for quandong compote, combine quandongs, sugar, orange juice and lemon myrtle in a saucepan and bring to the boil. Reduce heat to medium-low, then simmer gently for 5–10 minutes until quandongs are tender and juices have thickened slightly. Adjust sugar to taste. Remove from heat.

Divide most of compote evenly among bowls, reserving a little to serve. Top with rice pudding, then remaining compote, spooning the juices over. Serve with edible flowers and chopped nuts.

Substitution options:

Strawberry gum
→ blueberry or strawberry powder
Cinnamon myrtle
→ ground cinnamon
Quandong
→ peach (unripe, if possible)
Lemon myrtle leaves
→ lemon zest
Sandalwood nuts
→ macadamia nuts

Not-quite-blueberry Muffin with Illawarra Plum and Midyim Berry

I am a total sucker for a good muffin. I love them chock-a-block full of fruit and golden on top with a sprinkle of sugar.

Makes 12 muffins

450 g (16 oz) plain flour
1 tablespoon baking powder
1 cup (220 g) caster sugar
1 teaspoon ground
   cinnamon myrtle
1½ cups (375 ml) buttermilk
1½ cups (375 ml) macadamia oil
2 large free-range eggs
1 teaspoon vanilla extract
½ cup (75 g) Illawarra plums,
   seeds removed, cut in half
½ cup (80 g) midyim berries
Raw or brown sugar, for sprinkling

Substitution options:

Cinnamon myrtle
→ ground cinnamon
Illawarra plums
→ plums
Midyim berries
→ blueberries

Preheat oven to 180°C (350°F). Line a 12-hole muffin tin with paper cases. Mix dry ingredients in a bowl, then add wet ingredients and fruit and fold together until a loose batter forms.

Divide evenly between muffin cases, sprinkle with sugar, then bake for 20 minutes or until a skewer inserted in the centre of a muffin comes out clean. Cool in tin. Muffins will keep in an airtight container at room temperature for 2 days.

Fruity

Fruity Flapjacks

Not the pancake kind, the muesli-bar kind. These are so good for the kids' (or grown-ups') lunchboxes, and this easy sub-in sub-out recipe lends itself to having all sorts of goodies mixed through, so use what you have and play around with your favourite flavours.

Serves 10

2 cups (190 g) rolled oats
1 cup (150 g) plain flour
¼ cup (45 g) lightly packed brown sugar
½ cup (35 g) shredded or desiccated coconut
½ cup (75 g) macadamia nuts, coarsely chopped
½ cup (85 g) bush tomatoes
¼ cup (80 g) muntries (dried or fresh)
½ cup (70 g) quandongs (dried or fresh), coarsely chopped
¼ cup (30 g) Davidson's plum, chopped, or 1 teaspoon powder
1 teaspoon ground cinnamon myrtle
150 g (5½ oz) butter
2 tablespoons raw honey
1 tablespoon golden syrup or maple syrup

Preheat oven to 180°C (350°F). Grease a 23 cm (9 in) square baking tin. Mix oats, flour, sugar, coconut, nuts, fruit and cinnamon myrtle together in a bowl.

Melt butter, honey and golden syrup in a saucepan over medium heat (or in the microwave), add to dry ingredients and mix well to combine. Transfer to tin and press down firmly, going to the edges. Bake for 15 minutes or until golden brown.

Remove from oven, turn out onto a wire rack and allow to cool, then cut into bars. Flapjacks will keep in an airtight container at room temperature for up to a week. Use up any crumbs on your yoghurt for brekkie.

Substitution options:

Macadamia nuts
→ sandalwood nuts
Bush tomatoes
→ midyim berries, sultanas or blueberries
Muntries
→ bush apple, apple or pear
Quandong
→ dried peach
Davidson's plum
→ goji berries

Plum Leather

Tart and moreish, these lunchbox snacks are like Roll-Ups, just much better. Give them a go with whatever fruit and spices you like.

Serves 8–10

400 g (14 oz) ooray, peeled, seeds removed, diced
½ cup (90 g) chopped Illawarra plums
50 g (1¾ oz) raw honey
Splash of Bush Flower Water (see page 149)
Pinch of ground cinnamon myrtle

Substitution options:

Ooray
→ plums
Illawarra plum
→ plums
Bush flower water
→ rosewater
Cinnamon myrtle
→ ground cinnamon

Preheat oven to 110°C (225°F) and line several large baking trays with baking paper. Put plums in a saucepan, cover with water, bring to a simmer and cook for 10–15 minutes or until just soft. Once cooked, press plums through muslin-lined sieve into a food processor. Add honey, bush flower water and cinnamon myrtle and process until smooth.

Spoon into small paper-thin circles on the lined baking trays, then bake for 1 hour, or until they're bendy (if you prefer them crisp, bake for a little longer). Remove from oven and leave to cool completely on the trays. Carefully peel each piece off the paper. Store in an airtight container at room temperature, with baking paper between each layer, for up to a week.

Strawberry Gum, Cherry and Riberry Tapioca Trifle

Kind of like a super-grown-up chia pudding, in trifle form. Give it a go for any festive occasion — the flavours are incredible. You can use chia in place of tapioca if you prefer, and any fruity liqueur or syrup will work for the sponge.

Serves 10

2 cups (275 g) fresh (or frozen and thawed) native cherries
3½ cups (480 g) fresh (or frozen and thawed) cherries
1¼ cups (200 g) riberries or lilly pillies
2 tablespoons caster sugar, plus extra to taste
6 strawberry gum leaves or 1 teaspoon powder
80 g (2¾ oz) tapioca (sago)
400 g (14 oz) packet ladyfinger or savoiardi biscuits, or ½ bought sponge cake
1–1½ cups (250–375 ml) Økar amaro (or other amaro) or Lilly Pilly Cordial (page 68) or Rosella Syrup (page 144)
Edible flowers, to serve

WATTLESEED CUSTARD
350 ml (12 fl oz) milk
3 free-range eggs
¼ cup (30 g) cornflour
⅓ cup (75 g) firmly packed brown sugar
1–2 teaspoons wattleseed extract (page 78)

CHERRY CREAM
⅔ cup (160 ml) pure cream
1 tablespoon pure icing sugar
½ teaspoon cherry or almond essence

For wattleseed custard, whisk milk, eggs and cornflour together in a saucepan over low-medium heat. Whisk constantly for 5 minutes, or until thick. Remove from heat and whisk in sugar and wattleseed extract until dissolved. Transfer to a small bowl, cover surface with plastic wrap and refrigerate until set.

Put cherries, riberries, sugar and strawberry gum leaves in a large saucepan and add enough water to cover by 2–3 cm (¾–1¼ in). Place over low-medium heat and bring to the boil, stirring constantly. Reduce heat to low and simmer, continuing to stir, for about 2 minutes or until cherries are soft. Remove from heat and remove strawberry gum leaves.

Cook tapioca using the instructions on the packet and rinse under cold water to remove starch.

For cherry cream, whip cream and icing sugar with an electric hand mixer until almost thick. Slowly drizzle in cherry essence and continue to whip until thick enough to hold the mixer up without it falling off.

To serve, arrange biscuits or sponge in the bottom of a large glass serving bowl. Pour Økar or cordial over to your preferred level of sogginess. Spoon most of the fruit on top, then pour in wattleseed custard. Spoon tapioca on top, then a layer of cherry cream. Decorate with remaining fruit, and garnish with edible flowers.

Substitution options:

Native cherries
→ cherries
Riberries or lilly pillies
→ blueberries
Wattleseed extract
→ ground coffee or vanilla extract

medicine garden

It's no secret that First Nations Foods are some of the world's most nutritious. But while there's a place for powders and superfood concoctions, we're firm believers in cultivating a garden that works as a pick-and-choose medicine cabinet, rather than getting everything out of a packet. These recipes are tried and tested by us, and while they may not be cure-alls, we've found them to be beneficial whenever we feel run-down or in need of a boost. Give them a try and see what works for you.

Medicine Garden

I've been fascinated by the power of plants for more than a decade — in fact I wrote a couple of books on the subject. The more I learn about the incredible power of native plants, the more I want to share about the benefits of growing your own.

After realising that medicine is part of nature, and that we're prepared to pay $30 for a bag of goji berries but not for Davidson's plum, which has similar health benefits, I started exploring the native pantry.

Damien's great-grandmother was one of the last of his people's healers, a knowledge keeper of traditional plants and a healer of community and Country. Finding this out gave me so much joy and really inspired me. I briefly studied herbal medicine and, coupled with my experience working in the food industry for nearly fifteen years, I wanted to share some simple recipes that can be made from a medicine garden. These are recipes that our elders (both mine and Damien's) would use instead of resorting to antibiotics at the first sign of a cough.

We are not doctors, nor are we telling you to ditch your doctor or that you'll be a pillar of health by using these recipes. But we're excited to share the joy you will experience by planting these plants, watching them grow and using them for the benefit of you and your family.

Foraging

First, a warning: please be respectful. These foods are often attached to cultural practice and hold great significance for communities. Some things should not be harvested or picked by anyone other than Indigenous people. Wherever possible, ask permission first.

Secondly, it's important to respect the environment, biodiversity and wildlife. Pick only what you need and always, always leave some behind. Be absolutely positive of your identification before you harvest any wild food or medicine. This is crucial, as some species of these plants are toxic. Be especially careful with plants in families that also contain deadly poisonous species. Positively ID three times, always. It's also a good idea to consult with local Indigenous peoples, herbalists, botanists and experts. But if in any doubt, the best advice is: do not pick!

When and where to grow herbs

- Native herbs are amazing because they belong in our soils. For those new to native herbs, I would suggest planting in pots with good soil.
- Native plants in pots do prefer a native potting mix and love, love, love pine-bark mulch.
- A good soak of Seasol or a seaweed supplement every season does wonders.
- Choose a variety of plants, and a mix of perennials and annuals, to keep you going all year round.
- Always plant your herb garden as close to your kitchen as possible to encourage regular use. This also leads to renewed growth and healthy plants.
- Whether you're growing from seed or seedlings will determine what you should grow and when and where to begin. Refer to planting calendars and ask for advice where possible, and check our ingredients guide.
- Remember, just because something is Indigenous doesn't mean it will thrive across the country. Check on your particular climate and what grows there before investing heavily.

Note on eating kangaroo apples

Kangaroo apples are a good source of vitamin C and beta-carotene. The small berries, which look a lot like orange cherry tomatoes (see photo below), contain phytochemicals called phenols, which are beneficial antioxidants that have been shown to protect against heart disease, stroke and cancer.

The fruit also contains important alkaloids and a type of steroid that helps the body produce cortisone and tryptophan, helping to keep skin and hair healthy. It has been used by First Nations people for centuries as a natural anti-inflammatory and antioxidant.

The other important thing to know about kangaroo apples is that the unripe fruit was made into a concoction traditionally taken as a female contraceptive. This is because the unripe fruit contains solasadine, which is a toxic alkaloid. Only eat kangaroo apples when they are orange and ripe; green ones are not ripe.

Sore Throat Spray

Don't wait for a scratchy throat to develop into a sore one. At the first sign of a tickle, treat your throat with this concoction. You'll need a small spray bottle.

Makes 1 small bottle

1 teaspoon dried native lemongrass
½ teaspoon ground peppermint gum
½ teaspoon powdered finger lime
1½ tablespoons raw honey

Combine lemongrass, peppermint gum and finger lime in a small heatproof bowl, pour in 100 ml (3½ fl oz) boiling water and leave for 5 minutes to infuse. Strain into a jug and once coolish (not cold), mix in the honey. Pour into a spray bottle. Use at the first sign of a sore throat by spraying the back of your mouth. Repeat as needed.

Ginger and Basil Digestion Candy

These fabulous little candies aren't just for digestion, they also work wonders for nausea and travel sickness, or indeed when you're feeling a little run-down. Ginger, particularly, is fabulous at fighting bugs and flus.

Makes about 12 candies

150 g (5½ oz) raw honey
1 small bunch native basil
100 g (3½ oz) native ginger, finely chopped

Warm honey in a frying pan over low heat with basil and ginger. Once it starts to bubble a little, remove basil. Increase heat to medium-high and cook until honey thickens slightly and becomes tacky. Scoop spoonfuls of honey mixture onto greaseproof paper and leave to cool and dry a little. They will still be sticky once dried but the honey will set further, making them easier to handle. Store in the fridge for up to 1 month.

Decongestant Rub for Colds and Flu

There's something wonderful about the smell of Vicks VapoRub, but in search of a traceable version we decided to give making our own a go, and it really does work. The other beauty here is that when you dab Vicks under your nose, it kind of burns, but this doesn't. It's also a great remedy for headaches — rub a little on your temples and where the pain is on your forehead.

Makes 1 small jar

150 g (5½ oz) coconut oil
4 cut-leaf mint sprigs, torn
4 native sage sprigs, torn
4 native thyme sprigs, torn
4 native basil sprigs, torn
15 drops thyme oil
15 drops eucalyptus oil
15 drops lavender oil
10 drops lemon oil

Put coconut oil and herbs in a heatproof bowl set over a saucepan of gently simmering water (don't let base of bowl touch water). Heat gently until oil begins to turn slightly green. Cool, strain and stir in essential oils. Transfer to a small jar and use liberally as needed.

Herby Chest Rub for Asthma

This one is for my little godson Charlie. The poor little monkey is in and out of hospital so often with his asthma. I am hoping that once he gets over this scary phase of his asthma that he'll be able to use this in addition to whatever else he needs. It is also great for colds, and makes for a fab steam.

Makes 1 small jar

15 g (½ oz) beeswax
10 drops thyme oil
10 drops eucalyptus oil
10 drops lavender oil
10 drops frankincense oil

Melt beeswax in a small heatproof bowl set over a saucepan of gently simmering water (don't let base of bowl touch water). Cool and stir in essential oils. Put into a small jar and use liberally as needed.

Flower and Leaf Stress Balls

Honestly, these make me so happy. Squeeze and smell: they really work. The essential oils are all chosen to reduce anxiety and induce calm. If you don't have essential oils, just use the fresh stuff and refresh it with new herbs and flowers weekly; you may also need to refresh it if you've squished the life out of it after a particularly stressful week!

Makes 1 ball

5 drops thyme oil
5 drops eucalyptus oil
5 drops lavender oil
5 drops rosemary oil
4 cotton-wool balls or pads
4 sprigs each native oregano, sage, thyme and basil, torn
4 lavender sprigs, torn
1 handful of rose petals, torn
1 piece of string

Drip each type of oil onto individual cotton balls. Stuff them, along with herbs and flowers, into a small square of muslin. Tie into a ball with string, and every time you're feeling a little stressed, squeeze and smell.

Garden Kefir

Like kombucha, kefir is a wondrous thing, but without any additional flavours it can be a little uninspiring. This recipe is a way to infuse this fermented drink with even more life. I love the combination of sage and lavender, but you can use this recipe as a base and make it your own with herbs that suit your tastes and needs.

Makes 1 litre (4 cups)

⅓ cup (75 g) caster sugar
1 litre (4 cups) coconut water
2 tablespoons water kefir grains (available from health food shops or online)
1 native thyme sprig
1 native lemongrass sprig
1 river mint sprig
1 finger lime, sliced

Stir sugar into coconut water until dissolved. Pour into a sterilised jar (see page 232) and add kefir grains and remaining ingredients. Cover with a piece of muslin, seal with a rubber band, and store in a cool, dark place to ferment for 2–3 days until it tastes nicely tangy. Strain through muslin into a sterilised bottle and keep in the fridge. Drink within 3 weeks.

Cough Medicine (Herbal Honey)

When the weather turns cold, the dreaded coughs and colds begin. A sore throat can mean sleepless nights, and one of the simplest solutions is honey. Honey has so many benefits: as well as being antibacterial and anti-inflammatory, it acts in a similar way to cough syrup by coating the throat. Add some herbs, and you have your very own natural cough syrup. Use it in your tea as a herbal sweetener or take 1 tablespoon before bed and as necessary. If possible, use manuka honey. This needs to infuse gently for around 6 hours, so set aside the time, and monitor it with a thermometer.

Makes 1 jar

200 g (7 oz) native herbs or spices (see below)
200 g (7 oz) raw honey

I would suggest any of the following to help ease a cough or sore throat:
Native elderberry
Pepperberries
Native lemongrass
Peppermint gum
Tea tree
Lemon-scented tea tree
White kunzea

Grind your chosen herbs or spices quite finely with a mortar and pestle or food processor.

Combine honey and herbs in a heatproof bowl set over a saucepan of very gently simmering water (don't let base of bowl touch water) and warm slowly for 6 hours, making sure that temperature of honey doesn't exceed 46°C (146°F). Make sure honey completely covers herbs. Top up water in pan occasionally and stir the mix every now and then so it infuses evenly.

Strain warm honey through muslin, pressing it through, then wringing out the muslin to extract as much honey as possible. Pour into a sterilised jar (see page 232); it will keep for up to 1 year.

Face Steam

For colds and flus. This baby is nature's decongestant. It also clears pores and generally relieves a little stress and anxiety. What's more, it also makes a great foot soak.

Makes enough for 6 bowls

1 tablespoon dried peppermint gum
1 teaspoon dried ground white kunzea
1 teaspoon dried lemon-scented gum
1 teaspoon dried native lemongrass

Combine all ingredients. When ready to use, place 1 heaped teaspoon in a heatproof bowl and cover with 5 cm (2 in) boiling water. Sit in a comfortable chair with the bowl on a table in front of you. Place your head over the bowl, with a towel over your head to keep the steam in. Breathe deeply and slowly in and out for 5 minutes.

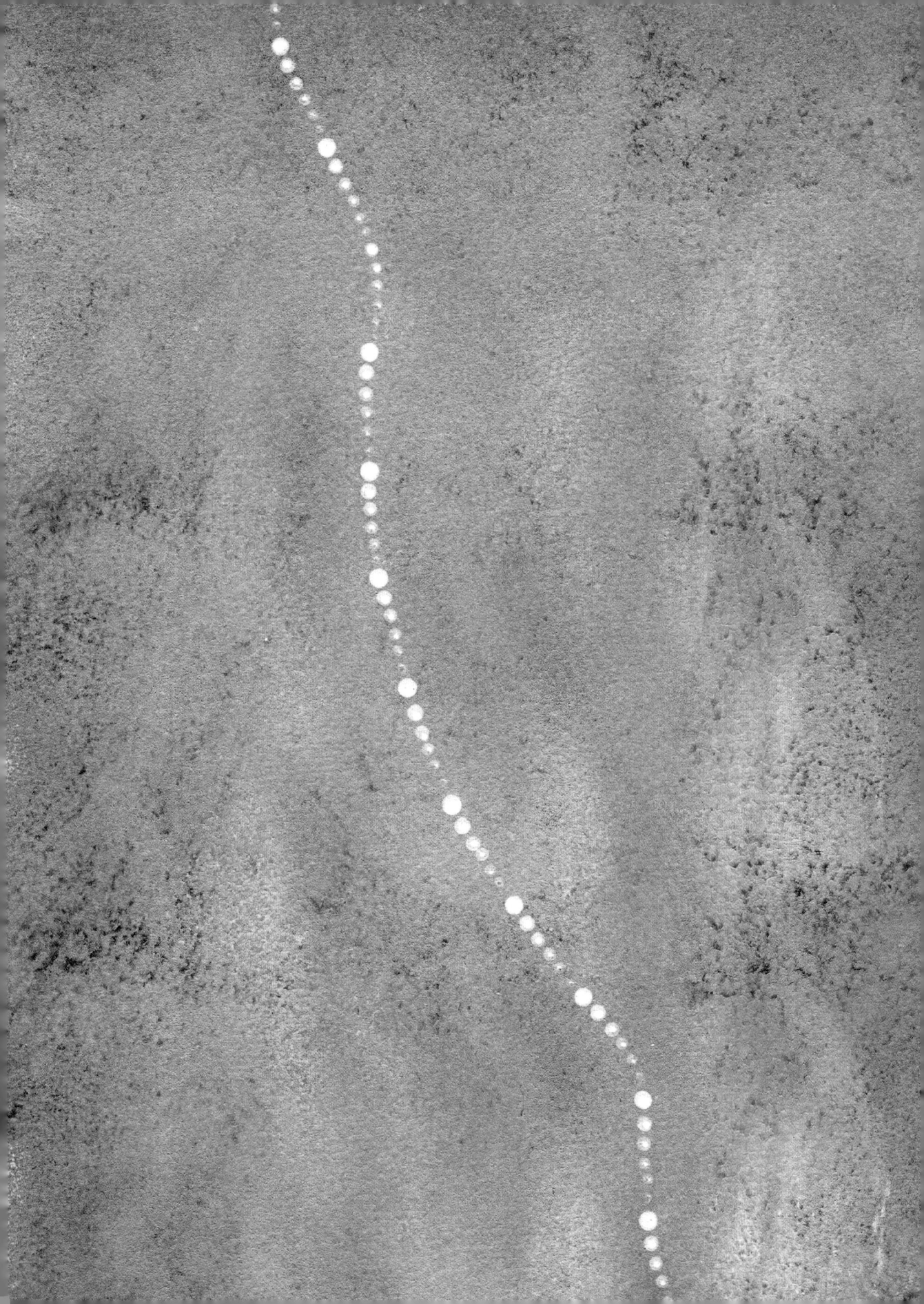

floral

These recipes feature flowers you've probably seen in vases for many years — like banksias, which are perfect for bitters and infusions. But it's not all about flowers. Some of our favourite floral-tasting ingredients of all time are the myrtles: cinnamon, anise and lemon. They come to the fore here in bright, fragrant recipes that'll have you reminiscing about long walks in the bush.

Rosella Syrup

This floral, slightly sour syrup (see image, page 147) can be used for anything from cocktails to mocktails, and kids' drinks to desserts. The sweetness can be adjusted to your liking. Make a batch and keep it in the pantry, or give it as a gift. You'll need a sterilised 2 cup (500 ml) jar or bottle (see page 232).

Makes 2 cups (500 ml)

40 g (1¾ oz) caster sugar
1 cup (40 g) dried whole rosella flowers (or 2 cups fresh)
4 finger limes, pearls squeezed
2 lemon, cinnamon or anise myrtle leaves (optional)

Substitution options:

Rosella flowers
→ sliced fresh rhubarb
Finger limes
→ lemon juice

Add sugar to a saucepan with 2 cups (500 ml) water and bring to the boil, stirring to dissolve sugar. Remove from heat, add rosella flowers (you can also add some rosella leaves, if you choose), then stir in finger lime and myrtle, if using. Leave at room temperature for 30 minutes to steep.

Strain into a sterilised jar, seal and cool. Label and store in a cool, dark place for up to 6 months. Once opened, store in the fridge. Use in cocktails or dilute with soda water.

Bush Botanical Bitters

A most wonderful addition to any cocktail that calls for bitters, but also a wonderful tonic. The herbs and flowers in these bitters have so many medicinal benefits, and if you can sneak in a tablespoonful per day when you're run-down, it acts as a wonderful pick-me-up. You'll need two sterilised 2 cup (500 ml) jars or bottles (see page 232).

Makes 2 cups (500 ml)

6 finger limes, sliced into rounds (or 1 tablespoon freeze-dried finger lime chips, available online)
1 orange, sliced into rounds, then cut into rough squares
40 g (1½ oz) native juniper
½ cup (20 g) dried whole hibiscus flowers
½ cup (20 g) dried banksia or bottlebrush petals
1 tablespoon dried elderflower or elderberry (native if possible)
8 anise myrtle leaves
2 tablespoons dried quandong
2 tablespoons dried river mint
2 teaspoons pepperberries
2 tablespoons raw honey
1 cup (250 ml) brandy, whiskey, bourbon or vodka

Put all ingredients in a sterilised jar or bottle, seal and shake well. Label and store in a cool, dark place for up to 6 weeks to infuse.

Strain into a sterilised jar or bottle and use 1–2 tablespoons per glass as a bitter flavouring. Label and store in a cool, dark place for up to 2 years.

Substitution options:

Finger limes
→ lime leaves
Native juniper
→ juniper berries
Hibiscus
→ dried rhubarb
Banksia
→ rose petals
Anise myrtle
→ star anise
Quandong
→ dried peach or apricot
River mint
→ mint
Pepperberries
→ peppercorns

From left to right: banksia, hibiscus, Geraldton wax, sorrel and native basil Bush Flower Waters (page 149); Rosella Syrup (page 144), Native Lily Syrup (page 148, neat on left and more diluted on right).

Native Lily Syrup

Never before have we been so excited by a flower as we were when we first tried our native vanilla and chocolate lilies. These perfect mini lilies, which fortunately grow in abundance on our property, are edible and smell (as their names suggest) like vanilla or chocolate. This syrup locks in their flavour and makes it something you can infuse into drinks in a snap. You'll need a sterilised 1 litre (4 cup) jar or bottle (see page 232).

Makes 1 litre (4 cups)

60 fresh native lilies (chocolate, vanilla or both)
4 cups (1 litre) boiling water
750 g (1 lb 10 oz) caster sugar
5 lemon myrtle leaves

Substitution options:

Native lilies
→ edible lily flowers
Lemon myrtle
→ lemon juice

Place lilies in a large heatproof bowl, then pour boiling water over the top. Cover with a clean tea towel and leave overnight at room temperature to steep.

The next day, strain into a saucepan over medium heat. Stir in sugar and lemon myrtle until the sugar has dissolved. Bring to a simmer and simmer for 2–3 minutes.

Strain into a sterilised jar or bottle, seal and cool. Label and store in a cool, dark place for up to 6 months. Once opened, store in the fridge. Use in cocktails or dilute with soda water.

Bush Flower Waters

The stunning nectar from our native flowers has traditionally been drunk as a refreshing sweet drink. Not only do these nectar-infused flower waters smell delightful, but they're also a great addition to many desserts — try drizzling them over ice cream or custard, or use anywhere you'd otherwise use rosewater or orange blossom water. They make a lovely little face spritz too. Feel free to play around with the flower combinations and add more flowers if you have an abundance. You'll need a sterilised 1 cup (250 ml) jar or bottle (see page 232).

Makes 1 cup (250 ml)

6 tablespoons fresh edible native flowers (such as banksia, hibiscus, bottlebrush, grevillea, wattle or native daisies)
250 ml (7 fl oz) boiling filtered water

Substitution options:

Native flowers
→ any edible flower that has nectar, such as honeysuckle

Place flowers in a heatproof bowl. Pour boiling water over the top and cover with a plate to weigh flowers down. Leave at room temperature overnight to infuse.

The next day, strain into a sterilised jar or bottle, then seal and store in the fridge for up to 6 months.

Fermented Banksia Fizz

Nothing says summer like this cold flowery banksia fizz. It also makes you feel as though you're having a cheeky glass of bubbles when you're not! The temperature during fermentation will change the amount of bubbles you get, so don't worry too much if you don't have a massive amount of carbonation, a light spritz is still very pleasant. You'll need two sterilised 1 litre (4 cup) bottles or jars (see page 232).

Makes 2 litres (8 cups)

6 large banksia flower heads
400 g (14 oz) caster sugar
2 lemons, sliced into rounds
1 tablespoon apple cider vinegar

Put all ingredients in a large ceramic bowl, pour in 2 litres (8 cups) water, then stir until sugar has dissolved. Cover with a clean tea towel, and leave somewhere warm and dry (not too hot) for 7–14 days to ferment.

Start tasting it after a week, if you like the flavour, stop fermentation by pouring through a strainer into sterilised glass bottles, then sealing and storing in the fridge. This fizz will keep for up to 2 weeks.

Substitution options:

Banksia
→ grevillea, bottlebrush or any edible flower that contains nectar, such as honeysuckle

Petal Powders

Use the dried petals of any edible flower for this recipe. You need to ensure that the petals are crisp-dry: we like to dry ours by picking them, shaking out any critters, and then leaving them on a clean sheet in a warm, dry place out of direct sunlight until dried. Petal powders can be used in cakes, bliss balls, smoothies or anything that needs some vibrancy.

Great petals to use are:
Grevillea
Banksia
Rosella
Bottlebrush
Native daisies
Native lilac

Place dried petals into a spice grinder in small batches and blitz until you get a fine powder. Store in airtight containers for up to 6 months.

Macadamia, Green Ant, Rose and Pepperberry Latte

This is the absolute dream-boat of all fancypants lattes!

Makes 1

1 cup (250 ml) macadamia milk
3 cm (1¼ in) piece fresh turmeric, grated, or 1 teaspoon turmeric powder
1 teaspoon green ants (see page 74)
Pinch ground pepperberry, plus another pinch to serve
1–2 tablespoons Bush Flower Water (page 149) or rosewater, to taste
1 teaspoon macadamia oil
1 teaspoon raw honey or maple syrup

> **Substitution options:**
>
> Green ants
> → crushed cardamom pods
> Pepperberry
> → ground pink peppercorns
> Macadamia oil
> → coconut oil

Add macadamia milk to a blender with turmeric, green ants, pepperberry, Bush Flower Water and macadamia oil and blend to combine. Transfer to a small saucepan and bring to a light simmer over medium-high heat. Turn off heat and sweeten with honey. Drink cold or warm. If you like your latte to be extra-peppery, serve with another pinch of pepperberry.

If you want to increase the quantities and make a large batch to drink throughout the week, you can keep it in a covered jug in the fridge for 4–5 days.

Native Sorrel and Kangaroo Apple Baked Eggs

Baked eggs are a perfect breakfast, lunch or dinner. Please follow the instructions for using kangaroo apples in the first part of the book (see pages 30 and 137). If you can't get them, cherry tomatoes make a fine alternative.

Serves 1

1 tablespoon olive oil
2 handfuls native sorrel
8 kangaroo apples, seeds removed, halved
1 large free-range egg
¼ cup (25 g) grated parmesan

Preheat oven grill to high. Heat oil in a small frying pan over low heat, add sorrel and kangaroo apple and stir until greens are wilted and apple is tender. Season with salt and ground pepperberry to taste, then transfer to an ovenproof ramekin, crack egg on top, cover with cheese and place under grill until egg is cooked to your liking.

Substitution options:

Native sorrel
→ lemon sorrel or warrigal greens
Kangaroo apples
→ cherry tomatoes

Anise Myrtle Rice

A simple spiced coconut rice that's as versatile as it is delicious. Try it with lemon myrtle leaves, too.

Serves 4

1 cup (200 g) jasmine or basmati rice
8 anise myrtle leaves
½ cup (125 ml) coconut cream

Put rice, anise myrtle leaves and 2 cups (500 ml) water in a saucepan and bring to the boil. Reduce heat to low, cover with a lid and simmer for 10 minutes until rice is nearly cooked and liquid is almost absorbed. Remove from heat, stir in coconut cream and a pinch of salt, cover, and leave for 5 minutes to absorb. Remove myrtle leaves before serving.

Substitution options:

Anise myrtle
→ lemon myrtle or fennel fronds

Rosella Leaf Crisps

Rosella leaves have been a revelation thanks in large part to a trip to Newchurch farm in South Australia. We took a bunch of chefs there for an event we organised for the Adelaide Festival called Narku'adlu (Let's Eat). We decided to eat the leaves fresh from the bush, and they're divine — just like fresh rhubarb. Now we use them in everything from herbal teas to pies and salads, but this is probably the most common way we prepare them. No more kale chips in our house!

Serves 2–4

2 handfuls rosella leaves
Macadamia oil, for brushing
Large pinch dried saltbush, crumbled
Dried chilli flakes or ground pepperberry leaf (optional), to taste

Preheat oven to 160°C (315°F). Line a baking tray with baking paper. With a pastry brush, lightly brush rosella leaves with oil, then spread them out on tray in a single layer. Sprinkle with saltbush and chilli and bake for 10 minutes or until crisp.

Remove from oven and cool completely on baking tray. Store in an airtight container at room temperature — they'll keep for a couple of days, if you can keep your hands off them.

Substitution options:

Rosella leaves
→ fig or vine leaves
Saltbush
→ salt

Anise Myrtle and Macadamia Poached Chicken

This is undoubtedly a very easy place to start if you are using First Nations ingredients for the first time. It will have you hooked on their flavours and visibility.

Serves 4

2 tablespoons macadamia oil
2 eschalots, finely diced
1 litre (4 cups) macadamia milk
Finely grated zest and juice of 3 lemons
3 garlic cloves, bruised
2 tablespoons island sea celery leaves
10 fennel flowers or fronds
2 anise myrtle leaves
1 lemon myrtle leaf
½ teaspoon pepperberries
4 skinless chicken thighs or breasts
Roasted macadamia nuts, seasonal greens and steamed rice, to serve

Substitution options:

Macadamia oil
→ olive oil
Macadamia milk
→ milk or dairy-free milk
Island sea celery
→ celery stalks or leaves
Anise myrtle
→ ground fennel seed
Lemon myrtle
→ lime leaves
Pepperberries
→ ground pepper

Heat 1 tablespoon oil in a large saucepan over low heat. Add eschalot and cook, stirring, for 3–4 minutes or until softened. Stir in macadamia milk, lemon zest and juice, garlic, celery leaves, fennel flowers, anise myrtle, lemon myrtle and pepperberries and season to taste with salt and ground pepperberry. Increase heat to medium and bring to a simmer.

Meanwhile, heat 1 tablespoon oil in a frying pan over medium-high heat. Season chicken all over with salt and ground pepperberry and fry, turning halfway, for 3–4 minutes or until browned on both sides.

Add chicken to macadamia milk, cover with a lid and simmer gently for 20 minutes or until chicken is just cooked through. Remove from heat and stand, covered, for 15 minutes, then remove chicken from pan.

Strain poaching liquid, discarding solids, then serve chicken in a little poaching liquid topped with macadamia nuts, with some fresh seasonal greens and rice on the side.

Strawberry Gum and Emu Bush Sleepy Milk

Both strawberry gum and emu bush have amazing sleep-aiding qualities. The addition of hops makes for a perfect after-dinner, before-bedtime drink, as hops also help assist rest. Strawberry gum has the added benefit of nurturing our microbiome to promote gut health, making this a great all-rounder for both gut and mental health.

Serves 2

2 cups (500 ml) whole milk or macadamia nut milk
1½ teaspoons finely chopped fresh turmeric (or ground turmeric)
Pinch of ground pepperberry
1 teaspoon ground cinnamon myrtle
1 teaspoon vanilla extract
1 teaspoon dried hops (from select health food shops or online)
2 teaspoons raw honey
1 teaspoon ground or flaked strawberry gum leaves, plus 1 strawberry gum leaf to serve
1 teaspoon ground or flaked emu bush leaves (from warndu.com)

Substitution options:

Cinnamon myrtle
→ ground cinnamon
Strawberry gum
→ bay leaves
Emu bush
→ ginger

Place all ingredients except honey, strawberry gum and emu bush into a saucepan over low heat and bring to a simmer. Simmer for 5 minutes, then turn off the heat. Stir in honey until dissolved, then add strawberry gum and emu bush and leave for 1 minute to steep. Strain into mugs or cups and serve topped with a strawberry gum leaf.

Rosella and Tamarind Pie

Since our last book, which has our quandong pie in it, we've been trying to top that recipe. Tamarind is very much like rhubarb, and rosella complements it like nobody's business. The great thing about both tamarind and rosella is they are available frozen and can be used straight from the freezer.

Serves 8

300 g (10½ oz) rosella flowers
300 g (10½ oz) small-leaved tamarind fruit or quandongs
Handful of muntries (optional)
4–6 tablespoons coconut sugar (to taste), plus extra for sprinkling
Finely grated zest of 1 orange, juice of 2
1¼ tablespoons rosewater
Whipped cream and native fruit, to serve

PIE CRUST

1¼ cups (185 g) plain flour
½ teaspoon ground lemon or anise myrtle (optional)
1 teaspoons caster sugar, or more to taste
110 g (3¾ oz) cold butter, cut into large dice, plus extra for greasing
1½ tablespoons iced water, plus 2–4 teaspoons extra
1 egg, beaten, for brushing

Substitution options:

Rosella flowers
→ rhubarb
Small-leaved tamarind
→ tamarind
Lemon or anise myrtle
→ ground fennel seed

For pie crust, place flour, lemon myrtle, sugar and 1 teaspoon salt in a food processor and pulse for 2 seconds. Add half the butter and pulse about 8 times, then add remaining butter and pulse another 6 times. By now your mix should have small pea-sized clumps of flour and butter. Add iced water evenly over the mix. Pulse again and begin adding extra teaspoons of iced water, one at a time and pulsing between additions, until the dough begins to hold together. You may need a little extra, but go slowly as too much liquid makes the pastry tough. The dough is ready when it resembles crumbs and holds together if you pinch it.

Turn out dough onto a dry surface. Gather it into a pile and push it down with the palm of your hand a few times to bring it together (do not overwork as kneading develops gluten and will toughen the dough). Form into a disc and sprinkle with a tiny bit of flour, then wrap in plastic wrap and chill for 1 hour to rest.

While dough is resting, make the filling. Combine all ingredients except rosewater in a saucepan and bring to just below boiling point, stirring to dissolve sugar. Reduce heat to low and simmer for 5 minutes or until fruit begins to soften and liquid has evaporated by half. Stir in rosewater. If you like a sweeter pie, add a little more sugar to taste. Remove from heat and cool for 10 minutes.

Preheat oven to 180°C (350°F). Scoop filling and most of the liquid into a 23 cm (9 in) pie dish. Dust bench lightly with flour, then roll out dough to a 30 cm (12 in) circle, about 1 cm (½ in) thick. Cut into strips around 25 cm (10 in) long and 3 cm (1¼ in) wide, then lay them in a lattice pattern on top of the filling. Brush pastry with egg wash and sprinkle with a little coconut sugar. Bake for 20–25 minutes or until pastry is cooked and golden brown.

Serve with whipped cream and native fruit.

Rosella and Native Raspberry Swiss Roll

Nothing recalls school days more than a Swiss roll — although it used to be filled with shop-bought sugar-filled jam and that fake cream. This one, on the other hand, is very lady-like and is filled with handmade perfumed jam and very much not-fake cream. What a gorgeous birthday cake this makes!

Serves 6–8

50 g (1¾ oz) butter, melted, plus extra for greasing
4 free-range eggs
115 g (4 oz) caster sugar, plus extra for sprinkling
130 g (4¾ oz) self-raising flour, sifted
2 cups (500 ml) thickened cream
¼ cup (30 g) pure icing sugar
1 teaspoon rosella petal powder (page 150)
1 cup (320 g) native jam (such as Native Raspberry Jam or Quandong Jam, page 178)
Edible flowers, to decorate

Substitution options:

Hibiscus powder
→ raspberry powder
Native jam
→ any jam

Preheat oven to 180°C (350°F). Grease a Swiss roll tin about 30 cm x 21 cm (12 in x 8¼ in) with a little butter and line it with baking paper.

Whisk eggs and sugar in a bowl until thick, pale and light. Add melted butter and whisk it in, then add flour, gently folding it in to form a batter. Pour batter into tin, smoothing it out evenly. Bake for 10 minutes or until sponge is lightly browned and coming away from edges of tin.

Lay a sheet of baking paper bigger than the sponge onto your bench and sprinkle it with a layer of caster sugar. Turn sponge out onto sugared paper, then carefully peel paper off base of sponge. Trim off any loose edges, then transfer sponge to a wire rack (still on the sugared paper) and leave to cool completely.

Whip cream and icing sugar in a stand mixer or with electric beaters until stiff. Divide in two, folding rosella powder into one half. Refrigerate this rosella cream for later.

Spread top of sponge with a thick layer of jam, then a layer of the unflavoured whipped cream, going right to the edge. Score sponge lightly about 2.5 cm (1 in) from one short end. With scored end nearest you, roll it up carefully away from you, using the paper to help you, then neaten up the ends with a knife. Decorate with a thick layer of rosella cream and finish with edible flowers.

Buttermilk and Lemon Myrtle Set Cream with Muscat Quandongs

A creamy, sweet, luscious dessert with tart fruit that cuts through the richness of the cream. This one has a high fat content, so when it sets, you may see a little fat on the top (depending on where you get your cream and buttermilk) — this is perfectly edible and will be covered with quandongs anyway, so no need to worry. Start this recipe a day ahead.

Serves 4

400 ml (14 fl oz) pure cream (use good quality, with a high fat content)
1 cup (250 ml) buttermilk
3 lemon myrtle leaves
4 gold-strength gelatine leaves
130 g (4¾ oz) caster sugar
1 teaspoon wattleseed extract (page 78)
Oil spray, for greasing
River mint and native basil leaves, edible flowers and roasted macadamia nuts, to serve

MUSCAT QUANDONGS

3 cups (500 g) quandongs, halved, seeds removed (frozen or dried are fine, too)
Finely grated zest and juice of 1 orange
¼ cup (60 ml) grand muscat or other sweet wine

Substitution options:

Lemon myrtle
→ lemon zest
Wattleseed extract
→ vanilla extract
Quandongs
→ any tart fruit — unripe stone fruit, rhubarb, etc

Combine cream, buttermilk and lemon myrtle in a bowl. Cover and refrigerate overnight to infuse.

The next day, soak gelatine in a bowl of water until soft. Pour infused cream into a saucepan, add sugar and wattleseed and bring to just below boiling point, stirring to dissolve sugar. Squeeze excess water from gelatine, add to saucepan, then turn off heat and whisk until dissolved. Remove lemon myrtle leaves.

Spray four small 1 cup (250 ml) ramekins (or 1 large ramekin) with oil, then pour in cream mixture. Refrigerate for 6 hours to set.

For muscat quandongs, combine quandongs, orange zest and juice in a saucepan with just enough water to cover. Cook over low heat, stirring occasionally, for 15 minutes until thickened and quandongs are tender. Add muscat and cook for another 1–2 minutes to cook off alcohol. Cool.

Serve the set cream topped with muscat quandongs, mint and basil leaves, edible flowers and roasted macadamia nuts.

From left to right: Rustic Native Jam Tarts (page 165); Quandong Jam (page 178); muntrie jam; Rosella Jam (page 164).

Rosella Jam

This jam is delightful on toast and makes an ace relish to go with a cheeseboard too, and it's swell in jam tarts (see opposite, and page 163). You'll need four 1 cup (250 ml) sterilised jars (see page 232).

Makes 1 litre (4 cups)

2 kg (4 lb 8 oz) fresh rosella flowers
6 lemon myrtle leaves
1 cup (220 g) white sugar per cup of pulp

> **Substitution options:**
>
> Rosella flowers
> → rhubarb

Separate rosella petals from seed pods. Keeping them apart, wash and shake dry.

Place pods in a heavy-based saucepan and cover with around 2 litres (8 cups) water. Boil over medium-high heat for 30 minutes.

Place petals in another saucepan. Strain juice from boiled pods directly over the petals, then discard pods. Add lemon myrtle leaves, and bring slowly to the boil over medium heat, then boil for 20 minutes until reduced by one-third. Remove from heat.

Measure the petal pulp, and add 1 cup (220 g) sugar for every cup of pulp, stirring to dissolve. Place over high heat and boil for 20 minutes or until setting point is reached (see page 232). Cool briefly, then remove lemon myrtle leaves and transfer jam to sterilised jars. Seal and store in a cool, dark place for up to 2 years.

Rustic Native Jam Tarts

There's no need to be perfect here, because these fruit-flavoured tarts will be devoured in seconds. Since they're rustic, they also lend themselves to experimentation.

Makes 12

1 cup (150 g) plain flour
1 tablespoon cocoa powder
75 g (2¾ oz) butter, diced
1 teaspoon ground lemon myrtle
¾ cup (250 g) native jams (such as Rosella Jam (opposite), Quandong Jam or Native Raspberry Jam (page 178)
Edible flowers and herbs, to serve

Preheat oven to 180°C (350°F) and grease a 12-hole muffin tin. Put flour, cocoa powder, butter, lemon myrtle and a pinch of salt in a bowl and rub together with your fingertips until it resembles fine breadcrumbs. Add cold water a tablespoon at a time, working it in to form a dough — about 4 tablespoons. Wrap in plastic wrap and refrigerate for 1 hour to chill.

Divide into 12 pieces and push one into each hole of a muffin tin, shaping to form a little cup. Fill with jam and bake for 20 minutes or until dark brown on the edges. Lift out and top with edible flowers and herbs to serve.

Substitution options:

Lemon myrtle
→ lemon zest
Native jams
→ any jam

Strawberry Gum and Geraldton Wax Cupcakes

The perfect fluffy, moist cupcake, with a perfumed and elegant icing.

Makes 10–12

2 cups (300 g) plain flour
2½ teaspoons baking powder
3 teaspoons ground strawberry gum leaves
125 g butter
1 cup (250 ml) milk
4 large free-range eggs, room temperature
1½ cups (165 g) caster sugar
1 tablespoon macadamia oil
Edible flowers and leaves, to decorate

STRAWBERRY GUM ICING

⅓ cup (80 ml) milk
3 teaspoons ground strawberry gum leaves (or 6 whole leaves)
1 sprig Geraldton wax, leaves picked
220 g (7¾ oz) butter, melted
½ cup (60 g) pure icing sugar, sifted

> **Substitution options:**
>
> Macadamia oil
> → olive oil or light nut oil
> Strawberry gum
> → freeze dried fruit powder
> Geraldton wax
> → lemon zest

Preheat oven to 180°C (350°F) and line a 12-hole muffin tray with paper liners. Put flour, baking powder, strawberry gum leaves and a pinch of salt in a large bowl and mix to combine. Melt the butter and milk together in a small saucepan over medium heat (or in a microwave).

Whisk eggs in a stand mixer until fluffy. With the motor running, slowly pour in sugar and keep whisking until mixture doubles in size and turns pale, almost white, in colour. Mix in the flour mixture bit by bit with a rubber spatula or wooden spoon until fully combined. Slowly add milk mixture, then the oil, stirring until combined. The batter should be pourable; if not, add a bit more oil.

Pour batter into paper liners, filling them two-thirds of the way up. Bake for 20 minutes or until golden brown and a skewer inserted into the centre of a muffin comes out clean.

For icing, heat milk in a small saucepan until just below boiling point. Remove from heat, add strawberry gum leaves and Geraldton wax and leave to infuse and cool.

Pour melted butter into a stand mixer fitted with the paddle attachment and beat briefly until smooth, then add icing sugar, a tablespoon at a time, beating until very light and fluffy. Add infused milk a tablespoon at a time, beating between additions until fully incorporated. Beat until icing is thick enough to pipe or spread.

Pipe or spread icing onto cooled cupcakes and decorate with edible flowers or leaves to serve.

Rose and Pepper Leaf Chocolate Tart with Honeyed Macadamias

Pepperberry leaf has a subtle sweetness to it, but the extra kick of spice (much like a chilli heat) makes the taste of this tart a little like Mexican-style chilli chocolate. The addition of rose brings out the floral element of the pepper leaf, too. The honeyed macadamias, used to blind-bake, then for garnish, are another bonus. Next-level delicious.

Serves 6–8

600 ml (21 fl oz) double cream
2 teaspoons ground pepperberry leaves (or 4–6 fresh or dried leaves)
1 tablespoon dried rose petals
1 tablespoon rosewater
400 g (14 oz) dark chocolate (at least 70% cocoa solids), coarsely chopped
Candied flowers, or dried or fresh unsprayed rose petals, to serve

TART CRUST

150 g (5½ oz) butter, softened, plus extra for greasing
½ cup (100 g) coconut sugar (or brown sugar)
1 teaspoon toasted ground wattleseed
2 cups (200 g) raw cacao powder
2 teaspoons raw honey, plus extra for drizzling
1⅔ cups (250 g) plain flour, plus extra for dusting
½ cup (75 g) macadamia nuts, coarsely chopped

Substitution options:

Wattleseed
→ ground coffee
Pepperberry leaves
→ bay leaves

For tart crust, cream butter, sugar and wattleseed in a stand mixer fitted with the whisk attachment until light, fluffy and pale, then add cacao powder and honey and whisk for 1 minute more. Add flour and a pinch of salt and mix to form a dough. Wrap in greaseproof paper and refrigerate for 1 hour to chill.

Preheat oven to 200°C (400°F). Grease a 23 cm (9 in) loose-bottomed tart tin. Dust a bench with a little flour, then roll out dough and use it to line tin. Prick base all over with a fork, then line with greaseproof paper, fill with macadamia nuts in a single layer, drizzle with extra honey and sprinkle with salt. This is blind-baking at its best, done with edible 'baking beans' that can be used for decorating later.

Bake for 20 minutes, or until crust looks set, then remove paper and nuts and bake for a further 5 minutes or until crust is cooked through and golden. Remove from oven and leave to cool completely.

Meanwhile, combine cream, pepperberry leaves, rose petals and rosewater in a saucepan over low heat and simmer gently for 20 minutes or until infused to your liking — taste it occasionally to see when it's spicy enough for your palate. Strain through a fine sieve into a bowl, discarding solids.

Add chocolate to warmed cream, then gently whisk until melted, glossy and smooth. Chill for 5–10 minutes to cool and thicken. Once cool, spoon into tart crust and spread out evenly, then transfer tart to fridge and chill for at least 1 hour before serving. Decorate with flowers and honeyed nuts just before serving.

Geraldton Wax Shortbread with Kunzea Sugar Sprinkle

In my family, we all fight over shortbread at Christmas time. My nan spends weeks baking batches for the whole family (28 of us) and packing them into recycled tins and jars. It's a bit of a contentious issue because if someone gets a bigger tin or jar, the squabbles begin immediately. Nan, this recipe is for you.

Makes 10-12

⅓ cup (75 g) caster sugar, plus extra for sprinkling
2 teaspoons finely grated lemon zest, plus extra for sprinkling
125 g (4½ oz) butter, softened
1 cup (150 g) plain flour
2 teaspoons Geraldton wax leaves (or powder)
1 teaspoon dried ground white kunzea flower

Substitution options:

Geraldton wax
→ dried lemon verbena or lemon balm
White kunzea
→ dried lemon thyme

Line a large baking tray with baking paper. Place sugar, lemon zest and butter in the bowl of a stand mixer and beat until light and fluffy. Add flour, Geraldton wax and a pinch of salt and mix on low until just combined. Place dough onto baking tray in a loose ball, then chill for 10 minutes.

Roll dough into a log about 20 cm (8 in) in length. Wrap in baking paper and chill again for 1 hour.

Preheat oven to 180°C (350°F). Remove dough from fridge, slice into 10-12 thin rounds, then place rounds on lined baking tray, leaving a little space between. Sprinkle with kunzea, and extra lemon zest and sugar.

Bake for 15-18 minutes or until edges are golden. Cool on tray briefly, then transfer to a wire rack and leave to cool completely. Store in an airtight container at room temperature for up to a week, ensuring you don't give one family member more than the other!

Wattlemisu

This dessert is decadent to the max. Wattleseed gives the same rich, chocolaty flavour you'd get with coffee, but with an extra hint of nuttiness and without the caffeine that makes tiramisu so dangerous after dinner. Begin this recipe 24 hours ahead.

Serves 6-8

40 g (1½ oz) ground roasted wattleseed
2 egg yolks
½ cup (110 g) caster sugar
1⅔ cups (400 g) mascarpone
2 egg whites
400 g (14 oz) packet savoiardi or ladyfinger biscuits
2 cups (500 ml) wattleseed extract (page 78)
1 tablespoon roasted wattleseed sprinkle (optional, available from warndu.com), to serve

SYRUP

1½ tablespoons Lilly Pilly Cordial (page 68) or Rosella Syrup (page 144)
1 cup (185 g) lightly packed brown sugar
15 g (½ oz) wattleseed

Substitution options:

Wattleseed
→ ground coffee
Lilly Pilly Cordial or Rosella Syrup
→ raspberry cordial

Add wattleseed to a saucepan with coffee or water and bring to a simmer, stirring to dissolve. Allow to cool.

Beat egg yolks and sugar with an electric mixer or with a stand mixer fitted with the whisk attachment until fluffy. Add mascarpone and fold through by hand until combined.

In a separate bowl, whisk egg whites until soft peaks form, then gently fold into mascarpone mixture.

Layer biscuits in the base of one large or a few small serving glasses. Cover with wattleseed extract. Layer and swirl mascarpone mixture thickly on top. Refrigerate for 24 hours to meld.

Next day, combine all syrup ingredients with 1 cup (250 ml) water and a pinch of salt in a small saucepan over medium heat. Bring to a simmer and cook, stirring occasionally, for about 20–30 minutes until it thickens. Allow to cool completely before using.

Drizzle wattlemisu with syrup, top with wattleseed sprinkle and devour.

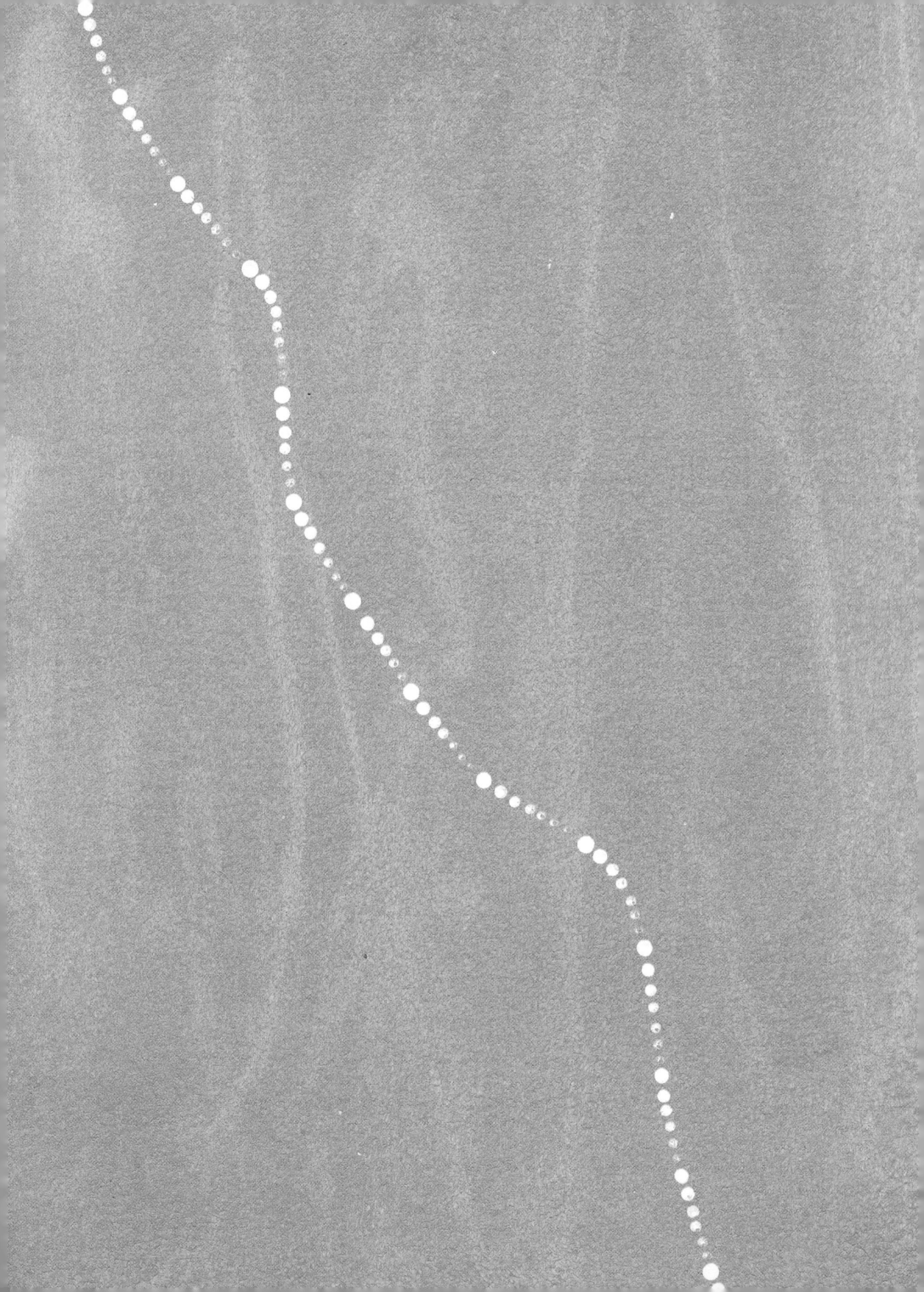

citrusy

Native citrus is so versatile and varied. Along with finger and desert limes, lots of plants have citrus notes too, from lemon myrtle to Geraldton wax. Then there's the acidic fruits in the First Nations pantry — think Davidson's plum or native tamarind. Sweet, savoury or in between, there's always room for these incredible ingredients.

Honey-Fermented Cherries 'n' Berries

We love to ferment cherries for Christmas time, when they're perfect with a ham or turkey. These are also great on cheeseboards; and the honey has an amazing flavour too. We've used cherries, riberries and quandongs here, but you can do this with any fruit, really. You'll need a 2 cup (500 ml) sterilised jar (see page 232).

Makes 2 cups (500 ml)

⅔ cup (100 g) native cherries (Ballarat or rainforest), pricked with a fork
2 tablespoons quandongs
2 tablespoons riberries
2 tablespoons rosella flowers
3 slices native ginger
6 pepperberries
Juice of 1 orange
150 g (5½ oz) runny honey

Substitution options:

Native cherries
→ cherries or other stone fruit
Quandongs, riberries and rosella flowers
→ any berries
Native ginger
→ ginger
Pepperberries
→ peppercorns

Fill sterilised jar with fruit, ginger, pepperberries and orange juice. Pour honey over the fruit: be patient, it will take a while to get to the bottom. Seal with the lid, then roll the jar around to coat the fruit.

Loosen the lid a little, then leave the jar in a cool, dark place, sat in a bowl in case you get a little leakage (totally normal with fermentation) for 2–3 months before using.

Eat the fruit and use the honey however you like. Once jar has been opened, keep in fridge and use within 1–2 weeks.

Bush Botanical Sugars

Such a great pantry staple for baking, and a great way to add some native flavours without the need for fresh ingredients. Plus, this is just so, so easy.

For every cup of sugar, try any of these:

- 1 tablespoon ground sea rosemary, plus a couple of extra sprigs
- Dried zest of 4 finger limes
- 10 pepperberries, lightly crushed
- 4 lemon, anise or cinnamon myrtle leaves
- 6 strawberry, peppermint or lemon-scented gum leaves
- 2 banksia flowers
- 1 small handful dried quandongs
- 2 teaspoons dried or powdered Davidson's plum
- 1 tablespoon dried ground white kunzea flower
- 1 sprig ruby saltbush
- 6 bush tomatoes

There are actually two approaches to try here. The first version involves immersing whole ingredients in sugar, while the second version is done by blending the dried ingredients with sugar. Infusion takes longer than blending but gives a more subtle result.

It's up to you which approach you take, but generally infusion works well with dried leaves and the like, which you can add as you accumulate them, while blending is good for delicate ingredients such as petals or extracts. The blended sugar should be ready to use within a week, and infused sugar a couple of weeks after that — but both take on more flavour the longer you leave them. Sprinkle on baked treats, use them to rim glasses, or give away in jars as a gift.

Native Fig and Vanilla Jam

Use whichever native figs you can get hold of (we like sandpaper figs), but feel free to mix them with European figs if you can't quite get enough. Start this recipe a day ahead.

Makes 1 litre (4 cups)

1 kg (2 lb 4 oz) sandpaper figs or other native figs, quartered, any hard tops removed
Finely grated zest and juice of 1 lemon
2¼ cups (500 g) caster sugar (or brown for richer flavour)
1 vanilla pod, split
6 cinnamon myrtle leaves (or anise or lemon myrtle)

Substitution options:

Sandpaper figs
→ any fig
Cinnamon myrtle
→ ground cinnamon

Add all ingredients to a large saucepan, stir, then cover with a clean tea towel and leave overnight.

Next day, place saucepan over low heat and stir until sugar dissolves, then increase heat and bring to the boil. Reduce heat to low, and simmer for 20 minutes or until thick.

Remove vanilla and leaves. (Don't waste these; rinse, dry and pack into a jar of sugar to make flavoured sugar, see opposite). Cool for 5–10 minutes, then pour into sterilised jars (see page 232). Jam will keep, sealed, in a cool, dark place for a year. Refrigerate after opening.

Native Raspberry Jam

Mix the berries up or stick to a single flavour. Best to put in some under-ripe ones to improve the set as berries are the lowest in pectin of the fruits. Try adding a small handful of chopped river mint or a tablespoon of rosewater for extra flavour. You'll need 4 x 1 cup (250 ml) sterilised jars (see page 232).

Makes 1 litre (4 cups)

1 kg (2 lb 4 oz) Atherton raspberries
900 g (2 lb) caster sugar
Finely grated zest and juice of 1 lemon

Substitution options:

Native raspberry
→ raspberry

Wash raspberries and pat dry. Place in a wide, heavy-based saucepan, add sugar and lemon zest and juice, then stir well. If you have time, let this sit for a few hours, loosely covered with a clean tea towel.

Place saucepan over very low heat and cook, stirring occasionally, until sugar has completely dissolved. Increase heat to high and stir occasionally until the jam is at a rolling boil and begins to froth. Boil, stirring every couple of minutes or so to prevent burning, for about 20 minutes or until jam reaches setting point (see page 232).

Once jam has reached setting point, cool for a few minutes, then transfer to sterilised jars. Label and store in a cool, dark place for up to 2 years. Refrigerate after opening.

Quandong Jam

This recipe (pictured on page 163) is easy and can be made with dried, fresh or frozen fruit. If you're using dried fruit, we would recommend soaking it in water for a few hours beforehand to rehydrate it. For frozen fruit, you won't need as much liquid in the pan as it will thaw out as you cook. If you prefer a sweeter jam, use the same weight of sugar as fruit. Feel free to add some native spices like lemon, cinnamon or anise myrtle leaves (about 4–6); remove before pouring into jars.

Makes 1 litre (4 cups)

1 kg (2 lb 4 oz) quandongs, halved, seeds removed and reserved
2 cups (500 ml) orange juice
750 g (1 lb 10 oz) caster sugar

Substitution options:

Quandongs
→ peaches or other stone fruit

Place quandong in a wide, heavy-based saucepan, cover with orange juice (top up with water if juice isn't covering all the fruit) and leave to sit for up to an hour.

Heat sugar in a microwave or low oven until warm to the touch. Once the fruit has begun to soften, transfer into a saucepan with juice and place over low heat. Add sugar slowly, stirring to dissolve. Bring to a rapid boil and boil, stirring often to stop it sticking, for 10 minutes.

Allow to cool for 10 minutes before pouring into sterilised jars (see page 232). Store in a cool dark place for up to a year. You can wash the reserved seeds and keep for propagating.

Boonjie Tamarind and Macadamia Noodle Salad

A midweek meal that's our take on a noodle salad using our rainforest favourite, the boonjie (or small-leaved) tamarind. Feel free to use any kind of noodle that you enjoy.

Serves 2

200 g (7 oz) bean noodles or soba noodles
¼ cup (50 g) karkalla or other native greens, chopped
2 carrots, cut into matchsticks
1 red capsicum, seeds removed, thinly sliced
1 cup (75 g) finely shredded white cabbage
100 g (3½ oz) snow peas, trimmed and thinly sliced lengthways
1 tablespoon island sea celery leaves
¼ cup (40 g) small-leaved tamarind, finely chopped
1 tablespoon ground roasted wattleseed (optional)
1 cup (60 g) wild basil leaves, chopped, to serve
Chopped macadamia nuts, to serve

DRESSING

1 garlic clove, crushed
¼ cup (40 g) macadamia butter (see page 108)
3 finger limes, pearls squeezed
¼ cup (60 ml) maple syrup
½ teaspoon sesame oil
1 teaspoon grated ginger

For dressing, place all ingredients in a blender with 1–2 tablespoons water and whiz to combine. Season to taste with salt and ground pepperberry.

Place vegetables in a bowl, add tamarind and wattleseed, then pour in dressing, tossing to combine and coat. Serve topped with basil and macadamia nuts.

Substitution options:

Karkalla
→ swiss chard or borage flowers
Island sea celery
→ celery stalks
Small-leaved tamarind
→ tamarind or unripe pineapple
Wild basil
→ holy basil
Finger limes
→ lime juice

Limey Lime Drizzle Cake

A hit of native limes in one fell swoop, with finger and desert lime combining in a delightful, zesty cake that's even better than lemon drizzle. You can use frozen fruit here, or freeze-dried powders if that is all you can get, but do use fresh if you have the chance.

Serves 8

225 g (8 oz) unsalted butter, softened
1 cup (220 g) caster sugar
4 free-range eggs
1½ cups (225 g) self-raising flour
Finely grated zest and pearls of 6 finger limes (or 2-3 teaspoons powdered)
10 desert limes, chopped (or 2-3 teaspoons powdered)
1 tablespoon finger lime chips (optional), to serve

LIME DRIZZLE
Juice of 1½ lemons
2 finger limes, pearls squeezed, plus extra to serve
¼ cup (40 g) desert limes, plus extra to serve
85 g (3 oz) caster sugar

Substitution options:

Finger lime
→ lime juice
Desert lime
→ lime juice and zest

Preheat oven to 180°C (350°F). Grease and line a 21 cm x 8 cm (8¼ in x 3¼ in) loaf tin with baking paper. Beat butter and sugar in a stand mixer fitted with the whisk attachment until pale and creamy. With the motor running, add eggs one at a time, making sure each one is fully incorporated before adding the next. Sift in flour, then add finger lime zest, pearls and desert lime. Mix until well combined.

Spoon batter into loaf tin and bake for 45-50 minutes or until risen, golden and a skewer inserted in the centre comes out clean. Remove and allow to cool briefly in tin.

Meanwhile, for lime drizzle, mix lemon juice, finger limes, desert limes and sugar together until smooth. Prick warm cake all over with a skewer, then pour lime drizzle over the top — the juice will sink in and the sugar will form a lovely, crisp topping.

Leave to cool completely in tin, then remove and serve topped with finger lime chips, if using.

Desert Lime Shortbread

Zesty, buttery, creamy sweet and tangy. Try these with finger limes, sunrise limes, Davidson's plums or actually just about any citrus or sour fruit in place of desert limes.

Makes 10-12

⅓ cup (75 g) caster sugar, plus extra for sprinkling
1 teaspoon desert lime powder
10 desert limes, coarsely chopped (or 1 tablespoon powdered)
1 cup (150 g) plain flour
125 g (4½ oz) butter

Substitution options:

Desert lime powder
→ lime zest
Desert lime
→ lime juice and zest

Put sugar and lime powder into a stand mixer fitted with the whisk attachment, then beat on medium speed until combined. Add desert limes, flour, butter and 1 teaspoon salt, reduce speed to low and beat until well combined. Transfer to a baking tray lined with baking paper and chill for 20 minutes.

Remove from fridge and roll into a 10 cm-long (4 in) log, then chill for a further 45 minutes.

Preheat oven to 170°C (325°F). Cut dough into 10-12 thin rounds and spread out on a baking tray lined with baking paper, leaving 5 cm (2 in) between. Bake for 20-25 minutes until golden around the edges. Cool briefly, then transfer to a wire rack and cool for a further 10 minutes or so before serving.

Shortbread will keep in an airtight container at room temperature for up to a week.

Citrusy

Kunzea and Illawarra Plum Jelly

This jelly is so pretty and delicate. It has a very grown-up feel to it, and is made even more wonderful with the addition of native flowers and herbs. If you don't want to make this cordial, you can use any other kind for the jelly (try the Lilly Pilly Cordial on page 68) so long as you stick to the measurements. You'll need a sterilised 1 litre (4 cup) bottle (see page 232).

Serves 4

100 g (3½ oz) caster sugar
4 gelatine leaves
Edible flowers and herbs, to serve

KUNZEA AND ILLAWARRA PLUM CORDIAL

2 cups (300 g) Illawarra plums (or Davidson's plums), halved, seeds removed
1 teaspoon dried ground white kunzea flower
2 cups (440 g) caster sugar
1 teaspoon tartaric acid
Juice of 2 lemons

Substitution options:

Illawarra plums
→ any plum
White kunzea
→ lemon thyme

For cordial, combine all ingredients with 4 cups (1 litre) water in a saucepan. Bring to the boil, and boil for 5 minutes or until fruit is just starting to soften. Remove from heat, mash fruit coarsely, then strain through a fine sieve into a jug, then pour into a sterilised bottle. (You can use this like any cordial — put a splash in a glass and add water to taste.)

To make jelly, put sugar and 400 ml (14 fl oz) water in a saucepan and bring to the boil, stirring to dissolve sugar. Remove from heat.

Soak gelatine leaves in cold water for 5 minutes to soften. Squeeze excess water from gelatine, then add to hot syrup and stir until dissolved. Add 100 ml (3½ fl oz) cordial and stir to combine.

Pour into four small bowls or moulds and refrigerate overnight to set. Turn out onto plates, or serve in bowls, topped with flowers and herbs.

Davidson's Plum Lamington

A true Australian classic, made even more so with Davidson's plum jam layered between the sponge, and a pink coconut coating. You'll need sterilised jars for the jam (see page 232).

Serves 4

190 g (6¾ oz) butter, grated
1 cup (220 g) caster sugar
1 teaspoon wattleseed extract (page 78)
3 free-range eggs
2⅓ cups (350 g) self-raising flour, sifted
1 cup (250 ml) milk
220 g (7¾ oz) dark chocolate (at least 80% cocoa solids)
1 cup (250 ml) thickened cream
1 teaspoon vanilla paste
⅓ cup (35 g) Davidson's plum powder
1 cup (90 g) desiccated or shredded coconut

DAVIDSON'S PLUM JAM

1.5 kg (3 lb 5 oz) Davidson's plums
300 ml (10½ fl oz) orange juice
1 teaspoon ground cinnamon
1 teaspoon mixed spice
1.25 kg (2 lb 12 oz) caster sugar (brown for more depth)

Substitution options:

Davidson's plum
→ plum or raspberry

For Davidson's plum jam, wash, rinse and halve the plums, reserving stones for their pectin (place them in a square of muslin and tie it closed with kitchen string). Add plums to a wide-based saucepan with orange juice, cinnamon and mixed spice. Add muslin bag of stones and bring to the boil, then simmer over medium-low heat until the skin falls away from the plums. This should take around 20 minutes.

Reduce heat to low, add sugar and stir rapidly until it dissolves. Bring back to the boil and once it reaches a rolling boil, cook for a further 10–15 minutes or until it has reached setting point (see page 232).

Remove from heat. Discard muslin bag and contents, then pour jam into hot sterilised jars, seal and allow to cool. Store in a cool, dark place for up to 2 years; refrigerate after opening. Makes 2.5 litres (10 cups).

For Lamingtons, preheat oven to 170°C (325°F). Grease and line a 20 cm (8 in) square cake tin with baking paper.

Put butter and sugar in a stand mixer fitted with the whisk attachment and beat for 2 minutes until light and fluffy. Add wattleseed extract and, with the motor running, add eggs one at a time, making sure each one is fully incorporated before adding the next. Add flour and milk in batches, alternating between the two and beating in bursts to combine.

Pour batter into tin and bake for 50–60 minutes until a skewer inserted in the centre comes out clean. Cool for 5 minutes, then turn out onto a wire rack to cool completely. Slice in half lengthways, then cut into squares.

Place chocolate, cream and vanilla in a heatproof bowl set over a saucepan of simmering water (don't let base of bowl touch water) and stir until smooth.

Toss Davidson's plum powder with coconut to combine.

Dip sponge squares in melted chocolate, then quickly roll in coconut mix to coat. Spread a third of the sponge squares with jam, top with another sponge square, followed by more jam and one more sponge square, gently squeezing together.

Baked Bush Apples

These apples are tart and chewy when fresh. Baked with a delicious macadamia and bush tomato stuffing, they make a magnificent dessert.

Serves 4–6

1 teaspoon lemon juice
8 bush apples, halved, seeds removed
¼ cup (45 g) bush tomatoes
¼ cup (40 g) macadamia nuts, coarsely chopped
2 tablespoons brown sugar
2 teaspoons vanilla extract
1 teaspoon each ground cinnamon myrtle, anise myrtle and lemon myrtle
Custard, cream or ice cream, to serve

Preheat oven to 180°C (350°F). Drizzle lemon juice into apple cavities. Place apples, cut-side up, in a baking dish. Combine remaining ingredients in a bowl, mix well, then scoop into cavities of the apples.

Cover dish tightly with foil and bake for 10 minutes, then remove foil and bake for a further 10 minutes or until apples are tender. Serve warm with custard, cream or ice cream.

Substitution options:

Bush apples
→ Granny Smith apples
Bush tomatoes
→ chopped sundried tomatoes
Macadamia nuts
→ cashews
Cinnamon myrtle
→ ground cinnamon
Anise myrtle
→ ground fennel seed
Lemon myrtle
→ lemon zest

Lemon Myrtle Ricotta Cake with Pickled Native Cherries

Pickled cherries cut through this thick lemony, creamy cheesecake. We can't get enough of it.

Serves 8

60 g (2¼ oz) macadamia nuts, roasted
1⅓ cups (200 g) plain flour
50 g (1¾ oz) caster sugar
120 g (4¼ oz) butter, diced
½ lightly beaten egg

PICKLED NATIVE CHERRIES

1 kg (2 lb 4 oz) native cherries
350 g (12 oz) caster sugar
2 cups (500 ml) white wine vinegar
2 cm (¾ in) piece ginger, bruised
2 cinnamon quills
10 cloves
6 cardamom pods, bruised
6 strips orange zest
1 teaspoon ground lemon myrtle, or 4 leaves

RICOTTA FILLING

4⅓ cups (1 kg) ricotta
1 cup (240 g) mascarpone
3 free-range eggs
⅓ cup (115 g) raw honey
¼ cup (20 g) ground lemon myrtle
1 teaspoon vanilla paste
1 tablespoon Warndu wattleseed balsamic or other balsamic glaze

---

Substitution options:

Macadamia nuts
→ cashews
Native cherries
→ cherries
Lemon myrtle
→ lemon zest

For pickled native cherries, wash cherries and remove pips and stems, keeping cherries as intact as possible. Combine all ingredients except cherries with ¾ cup (180 ml) water in a saucepan, bring to the boil, then reduce heat to medium and simmer for 20 minutes. Add cherries and cook for 1–2 minutes or until tender. Strain and cool before using. Pickled native cherries will keep, refrigerated, for 3 months if covered in their liquid and stored in an airtight container.

Blitz macadamia nuts in a food processor until coarsely chopped, then add flour and sugar and pulse to combine. Add butter and process until incorporated, then add egg, pulsing until it just comes together. Turn dough out onto a bench, bring together with your hands and wrap in plastic wrap. Chill for at least 1 hour.

Preheat oven to 180°C (350°F). Roll out pastry on a lightly floured bench to about 5 mm (¼ in) thick. Use the base of a 23 cm (9 in) non-stick springform tin to measure out a circle of pastry, cutting around the tin. Cut out a circle of baking paper the same size and place it on the base of tin (but don't attach the sides of the tin yet), then carefully place pastry disc on top and prick with a fork.

Bake for 15–20 minutes or until light golden, then remove from oven and allow to cool. When cool, remove pastry and baking paper. Attach sides of tin to base, then place cooked disc of pastry into the assembled tin. Reduce oven temperature to 160°C (315°F).

For ricotta filling, place all ingredients in a food processor and blitz until smooth. Spoon filling on top of pastry base, smoothing out the top with a spatula. Bake for 1–1¼ hours until golden and set. Allow to cool completely, then refrigerate for 1 hour to chill.

Cover with pickled native cherries and slice to serve. Cheesecake will keep refrigerated for up to 5 days.

Citrusy

Quandong and Davidson's Plum Iced VoVos

Childhood memories galore here. This version of the popular biscuit is made super-Aussie with the addition of quandong jam and Davidson's plum marshmallows. If you don't feel like making the marshmallows yourself, you can always replace them with bought ones.

Makes 10

60 g (2¼ oz) butter, softened
½ cup (110 g) caster sugar
1 free-range egg
⅔ cup (100 g) self-raising flour, sifted
⅔ cup (100 g) plain flour, sifted
⅓ cup (115 g) Quandong Jam (page 178)
½ cup (45 g) desiccated coconut
Davidson's plum powder, for sprinkling

DAVIDSON'S PLUM ICING

100 g (3½ oz) Davidson's plum marshmallows (see page 120)
30 g (1 oz) butter
¼ cup (30 g) pure icing sugar

> **Substitution options:**
>
> Davidson's plum powder
> → goji berry powder
> Quandong jam
> → plum jam

Preheat oven to 180°C (350°F) and line two baking trays with baking paper. Beat butter and sugar in a stand mixer fitted with the paddle attachment until pale and fluffy. Beat in egg, then gently fold in flours. Turn out onto a lightly floured bench and knead lightly to bring dough together. Wrap in plastic wrap and chill for 10 minutes.

Roll out dough between two sheets of baking paper to about 5 mm (¼ in) thick. Cut into 7 cm x 4 cm (2¾ in x 1½ in) rectangles, then spread on baking trays, leaving 2 cm (¾ in) between each biccie. Bake for 10 minutes or until golden, then transfer to a wire rack to cool.

For icing, melt marshmallow and butter in a small saucepan over low heat, then stir in icing sugar.

To decorate, spread two strips of icing across the top of each biscuit, leaving a gap in the centre. Fill the gap with jam, then sprinkle with coconut. Sprinkle with Davidson's plum powder to finish.

Muntrie and Quandong Jelly Slice

This is Aunty Daphne's recipe and it is the best. She suggests making it at least a day before eating, and you can change up the filling or topping flavour if you like.

Serves 8

1 packet Nice biscuits or YoYos
170 g (6 oz) butter, melted
Mint or basil sprigs, to serve

QUANDONG FILLING

1 cup (150 g) quandongs
3 level teaspoons powdered gelatine
¼ cup (60 ml) boiling water
400 g (14 oz) tin condensed milk
Juice of 2 lemons

MUNTRIE TOPPING

2 cups (500 ml) cranberry juice
12 g (½ oz) sachet powdered gelatine
250 g (9 oz) muntries

Substitution options:

Quandongs
→ any stewed fruit
Muntries
→ Granny Smith apple

Crush biscuits by blitzing in a food processor or smashing in a bag. Stir crushed biscuits with melted butter to combine, then press firmly into a 20 cm (8 in) square tin. Refrigerate until cold and set.

For quandong filling, place quandongs in a small saucepan over low heat, cover with water, and simmer for 5 minutes or until soft. In a heatproof bowl, stir gelatine into boiling water until dissolved. Add condensed milk and lemon juice, stir to combine, then spread onto biscuit base in tin. Spread stewed quandongs over the top and refrigerate until set.

For muntrie topping, place cranberry juice in a saucepan over medium heat and bring to a simmer, then whisk in gelatine until dissolved. Cool to room temperature. Scatter muntries onto stewed quandong in tin, then pour cranberry jelly mixture over the top. Refrigerate for 4 hours or until set.

Cut into rectangles and decorate with mint or basil to serve.

marine

This is the connection many of us will have probably already made with First Nations foods, as most of the seafood available in Australia is native. Because there is so much variety, here we've focused on some of those lesser-seen species, such as pipis and even crocodile — although you'll find recipes with prawns and barramundi too. Then there's the native coastal plants, which have an amazing array of marine notes. Bursting with juicy, salty and sometimes bitter qualities, these make worthy accompaniments.

Pipi Mornay

We serve this in old-school vols-au-vent, which you can find in supermarkets, but you could serve it on rice, with pasta, or even on its own.

Serves 2–4

4 cups (1 litre) chicken or vegetable stock
2 garlic cloves, bruised
1 kg (2 lb 4 oz) pipis, cleaned
60 g (2¼ oz) butter
¼ cup (35 g) plain flour
⅓ cup (80 ml) dry white wine
1⅔ cups (410 ml) milk, warmed
½ cup (45 g) grated tasty or cheddar cheese
1 handful samphire, chopped, plus extra samphire to serve
1 handful karkalla, chopped
1 small handful seablite, chopped
1 teaspoon ground saltbush, plus extra to serve
4 vols-au-vent, to serve
Sea parsley and desert limes, to serve

Substitution options:

Pipis
→ mussels or oysters
Samphire
→ blanched asparagus
Karkalla
→ cooked green beans
Seablite
→ cooked green beans
Saltbush
→ capers or caper leaves
Pepperberry
→ pepper

Put stock and garlic in a saucepan and bring to a simmer over medium-high heat. Add pipis and simmer until they open up, removing them to a separate bowl as they pop open. Cool, then remove pipis from shells. Set aside until needed. Discard stock.

Melt butter in a saucepan over medium heat and swirl until it starts to foam. Add flour and stir constantly until the mixture bubbles and begins to come away from the sides of the pan. Remove from heat. Gradually whisk in wine until smooth, then slowly add milk, whisking constantly until smooth and combined.

Place over medium heat and cook, stirring constantly with a wooden spoon, for 3–4 minutes or until sauce boils, thickens and coats the back of the spoon. Add cheese, stir to melt, then add samphire, karkalla, seablite, saltbush and pipis (reserve a few for garnish) and stir to combine. Season to taste with salt and ground pepperberry.

Meanwhile, heat vols-au-vent in a 160°C (320°F) oven for 2 minutes.

Serve mornay in vols-au-vent, topped with sea parsley, desert lime, extra samphire and reserved pipis. Sprinkle with ground pepperberry and extra ground saltbush to serve.

Fish Pie

Comfort food at its best. You can use any seafood you like for this, but it's always best to go with local and ethically sourced. Make double and freeze the extra for quick midweek meals.

Serves 4–6

½ brown onion, finely diced
1 carrot, finely diced
4 sea parsley sprigs
Small handful of island sea celery leaves, chopped
125 g (4½ oz) frozen peas
300 g (10½ oz) skinless barramundi fillets, cut into bite-sized pieces
300 g (10½ oz) other skinless fish (such as Murray cod or garfish), cut into bite-sized pieces
200 g (7 oz) king prawns, peeled and cut into bite-sized pieces
Finely grated zest and juice of 1 lemon
1 tablespoon olive oil
Pinch of ground saltbush
3 cups (750 ml) mashed potato (you can use the below recipe)
150 g (5½ oz) cheddar, grated

Preheat oven to 200°C (400°F). Combine onion, carrot, herbs, peas, fish and prawns in a deep baking dish. Add lemon zest and juice, drizzle with oil and season with saltbush, salt and ground pepperberry. Toss to coat and combine.

Add mashed potato to seafood mix and stir until combined. Cover tightly with foil and bake for 30 minutes, then remove foil, sprinkle with cheese and bake for a further 5 minutes until golden. Serve hot.

Substitution options:

Island sea celery
→ celery
Sea parsley
→ parsley
Barramundi
→ any white flaky fish

The Epic Mash

We call this epic for the cheese, but also because it's overloaded with spring onion and karkalla.

1 kg (2 lb 4 oz) floury potatoes (such as sebago), peeled and cut into chunks
30 g (1 oz) butter
¼ cup (60 ml) pure cream
1 teaspoon seeded mustard
30 g (1 oz) parmesan or cheddar
1 handful of karkalla, chopped
2 spring onions, thinly sliced

Place potatoes in a large saucepan of salted water and bring to the boil. Boil until soft enough to mash, about 15 minutes. Drain, return to saucepan, then add butter and cream. Place over low heat and stir a few times to warm through. Remove from heat, add mustard, cheese, karkalla and spring onion and mash to your liking. Season to taste with salt and ground pepperberry.

Substitution options:

Karkalla
→ Swiss chard

Green Ant and Crocodile Curry

Crocodile is so easy to cook, it should always be in your freezer. Treat it like a minute steak and cook it quickly, being careful not to let it overcook. The best part is that because croc is low in fat and cholesterol and high in protein, it's good for you too.

Serves 4-6

2½ tablespoons macadamia oil
1 brown onion, diced
2 garlic cloves, crushed
2 cm (¾ in) piece ginger, finely chopped
6 curry leaves or 1 tablespoon chopped curry bush (if you can find it)
10 g (¼ oz) native lemongrass, chopped
400 g (14 oz) tin tomatoes
2 cardamom pods, bruised
2 teaspoons paprika
1 teaspoon ground cinnamon myrtle
1 teaspoon fenugreek seeds
1 teaspoon ground turmeric
½ teaspoon chilli powder
1 teaspoon green ants (page 74), plus extra to serve
500 g (1 lb 2 oz) crocodile meat (from select butchers), sliced
200 ml (7 fl oz) coconut milk
1 finger lime, pearls squeezed, plus extra to serve
Steamed rice, to serve

Substitution options:

Green ants
→ crushed coriander seeds
Crocodile
→ prawns
Finger lime
→ lime juice

Heat oil in a large saucepan or wok over medium-high heat. Add onion, garlic, ginger, curry leaves and lemongrass and cook, stirring, for about 2 minutes or until softened and the curry leaves start to release their oils.

Add tomatoes, remaining spices and green ants, stir to combine, then add crocodile meat and cook, stirring occasionally, for 2 minutes. Pour in coconut milk and simmer for about 15 minutes or until crocodile is just cooked through.

Season to taste with salt and ground pepperberry, top with finger lime and extra green ants and serve with steamed rice.

Barra Burger with Bush Tartare Sauce

The key here is to never overcook the fish. Keep it just under so it stays super-juicy.

Serves 2

2 barramundi fillets, pin-boned
Extra-virgin olive oil, for brushing
2 burger buns or white rolls, cut in half
¼ cup (10 g) mixed greens, such as bower spinach, warrigal greens, karkalla and ice plant
1 large pickle, sliced

TARTARE SAUCE
1 cup (235 g) mayonnaise
2 finger limes, pearls squeezed (or 1 teaspoon powdered)
2 teaspoons finely chopped karkalla
1 teaspoon finely chopped seablite
2 gherkins, finely chopped
1 teaspoon chopped sea parsley leaves

For the tartare sauce, stir all ingredients together in a small bowl. Season to taste.

Brush the barramundi lightly with oil and season with salt. In a hot frying pan, lay the barramundi skin-side down and fry for 2–3 minutes until crisp. Flip and cook for 3–4 minutes, or until the flesh flakes easily. Spread top and base of rolls with tartare. Add the greens, then the barra and pickle. Top with lids and serve.

Substitution options:

Finger limes
→ lime zest or lemon zest
Karkalla
→ capers
Seablite
→ capers
Sea parsley
→ curly parsley
Barramundi
→ any fish of your choice
Native greens
→ rocket or spinach

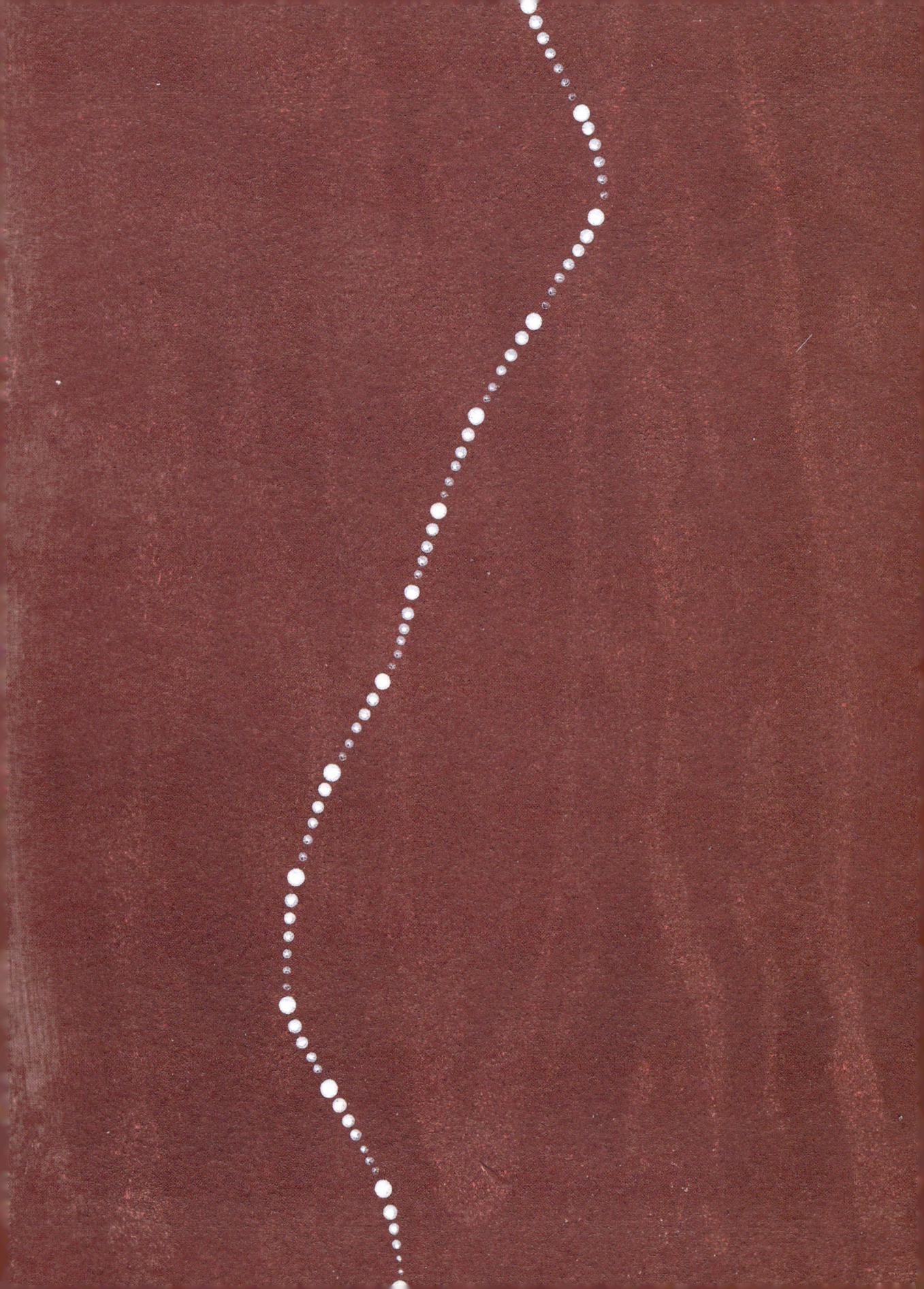

earthy

This section celebrates the deeper, stronger flavours of the native pantry, with breads, pickles, brews and some heartier dishes featuring native meats such as kangaroo and emu (plus there's an addictive macadamia pumpkin pie in the mix). We love these recipes because not only are they good for you, they're better for the planet too.

Pickled Bush Onions

These tiny pops of goodness are like a cocktail onion, just as moreish and just a little nuttier. Bush onions are admittedly not the easiest to find, but if you can source them, they truly are wonderful. You'll need four sterilised 2 cup (500 ml) jars (see page 232). Start this recipe a day ahead.

Makes 1 loaf

500 g (1 lb 2 oz) bush onions
¼ cup (70 g) fine salt
2 litres (8 cups) white vinegar
2 litres (8 cups) brown malt vinegar
⅓ cup (75 g) firmly packed brown sugar
4 garlic cloves, bruised
2 cm (¾ in) piece of ginger, bruised
Small handful curry bush
6 pepperberries
4 cinnamon myrtle leaves

JAR SPICES

1 teaspoon yellow mustard seeds
1 teaspoon brown mustard seeds
1 teaspoon fresh or dried lemon myrtle leaves
4 cinnamon myrtle leaves

> **Substitution options:**
>
> Bush onions
> → pickling onions
> Curry bush
> → curry leaves
> Pepperberries
> → peppercorns
> Lemon myrtle leaves
> → bay leaves
> Cinnamon myrtle leaves
> → cinnamon

Simmer onions in a large saucepan of water for 1 hour to loosen skins, then drain and peel.

Place onions in a large bowl and add salt and 1 litre (4 cups) water. Cover with a clean tea towel and leave for 24 hours. Next day, wash and dry onions and set aside.

Combine vinegars, sugar, garlic, ginger, curry bush, pepperberries and cinnamon in a large saucepan. Bring to the boil, then boil for 10 minutes.

Spoon onions into sterilised jars, then add half the jar spices. Strain pickling liquid into a jug then pour into jars to cover onions. Add remaining jar spices, then seal. Store in a cool, dark place for up to a year.

For the best flavour, let the onions mature for at least 3 months before eating. Refrigerate after opening and use within 1–2 months.

Caramelised Bush Onions

A beautiful spin on caramelised onions, which is rich and sweet from dark beer and maple syrup. Try this with an emu steak, or on a Barra Burger (see page 200).

2 tablespoons olive oil
½ cup (75 g) bush onions, peeled
½ cup (125 ml) Dark Emu Beer by Sailors Grave
2 tablespoons maple syrup
3 native thyme sprigs, leaves picked

Heat oil in a large saucepan over low heat. Add onions and a pinch of salt, cover and cook, stirring occasionally, for 5 minutes or until onions begin to soften. Increase heat to medium, add remaining ingredients, bring to a simmer, then cook, stirring occasionally, until thick and reduced by half. Season to taste with salt and ground pepperberry before serving.

Substitution options:

Bush onions
→ red onions
Dark emu beer
→ any dark beer
Native thyme
→ thyme

Kangaroo Grass Brew Bread

This is a recipe for Uncle Bruce Pascoe. His inspiring work with kangaroo grass, along with the people at Black Duck Foods, is important both culturally and environmentally, and soon we hope we'll all be using kangaroo grass flour everyday. Kangaroo grass can be bought from some specialist nurseries, and comes as a dried seed.

Makes 1 loaf

290 ml (10 fl oz) boiling water
Handful unhulled kangaroo grass, or 1 tablespoon kangaroo grass seeds
170 g (6 oz) wholemeal self-raising flour
170 g (6 oz) plain flour
1½ teaspoons ground saltbush
½ teaspoon bicarbonate of soda
1 sea rosemary sprig, finely chopped
Macadamia oil, for brushing
1 tablespoon whole wattleseeds
1 tablespoon roasted kangaroo grass

Substitution options:

Kangaroo grass brew
→ strong black tea
Wattleseeds
→ poppy seeds or black sesame seeds
Sea rosemary
→ rosemary
Roasted kangaroo grass
→ sesame seeds

For the kangaroo grass brew, pour boiling water over kangaroo grass or kangaroo grass seeds in a heatproof jug or bowl and steep for 1 hour.

Preheat oven to 200°C (400°F) and line a baking tray with baking paper. Put flours, saltbush, bicarb and a small pinch of salt in a large bowl and stir to combine. Make a well in the centre and pour in kangaroo grass brew. Add rosemary, and mix quickly with a fork to form a soft dough. Add a little water if it feels too dry, or more flour if too sticky.

Turn out onto a lightly floured surface and knead briefly (don't over-knead or it will be as hard as a rock). Form into a round loaf, flatten slightly and place on baking tray. Score the top a couple of times, brush lightly with macadamia oil and sprinkle with wattleseed and roasted kangaroo grass.

Bake for 30 minutes or until the loaf sounds hollow when you knock the bottom. Eat fresh or toasted.

Dark Emu Beer and
Ant Pickle (page 208)

Dark Emu Beer and Ant Pickle

This is another recipe dedicated to our mate Bruce Pascoe, an inspiring man who we admire immensely. We use cauliflower, but this pickle can equally be made with eschalots or pickling onions. Also, a huge shoutout to Sailors Grave Brewing, exceptionally connected brewers based on Gunai land in Orbost, Victoria, who make the beer. You'll need three sterilised 2 cup (500 ml) jars (see page 232).

Makes 1.5 litres (6 cups)

1 kg (2 lb 4 oz) cauliflower, cut into florets
2 tins (800 ml) Dark Emu Beer by Sailors Grave (or another dark, malty, grassy beer)
400 ml (14 fl oz) white vinegar or malt vinegar
¼ cup (70 g) fine salt
1 tablespoon bush honey
1 teaspoon green ants (see page 74)
1 teaspoon black ants (available online from select suppliers)
4 anise myrtle leaves
3 lemon myrtle leaves
3 garlic cloves, peeled and pricked with a fork
1 teaspoon pepperberries

Blanch cauliflower in a large saucepan of boiling water for 2–3 minutes until just beginning to soften. Drain.

Place beer in a saucepan with 400 ml (14 fl oz) water, bring to the boil and boil rapidly for 5 minutes to get rid of some of the alcohol. Reduce heat to medium, add vinegar, salt and honey, stir to dissolve, then simmer for another 5 minutes. Simmer for 10 minutes, then adjust to taste: if it's too tangy, add a little more honey to soften it. Remove pickling liquid from heat.

Spoon cauliflower into sterilised jars, add green and black ants, then tuck in anise and lemon myrtle leaves, as well as garlic and pepperberries. Pour in pickling liquid while it's still hot.

Seal jars and allow to mature in a cool, dark place for at least 1 week before eating. Try these on charcuterie boards, in toasties or with slow-roasted meats. Refrigerate once opened and use within 2 months.

Substitution options:

Green ants
→ coriander seeds
Black ants
→ mustard seeds
Anise myrtle leaves
→ fennel seeds
Lemon myrtle leaves
→ bay leaves
Pepperberries
→ long red chilli

Buttermilk Pickles

These slightly fermented, crunchy pickles are really, truly delicious, whatever you use — we like root vegetables, yam daisy and bush apples for starters. Feel free to experiment with a variety of vegetables or fruits. You can also add aromatics such as dried rosemary and thyme or peeled garlic cloves into the pickle for extra flavour.

Makes 3 litres (12 cups)

2 kg (4 lb 8 oz) root vegetables or fruit (such as yam daisy and youlk or bush pears and bush apples), sliced
6 anise myrtle leaves (or cinnamon or lemon myrtle)
8 pepperberries
6 dried bush tomatoes
1 litre (4 cups) buttermilk

Substitution options:

Yam daisy and youlk
→ carrots, turnips, radish, daikon, parsnip
Bush pears and apples
→ apples or pears
Anise myrtle
→ star anise
Pepperberries
→ peppercorns
Bush tomatoes
→ raisins

Place vegetables, leaves, pepperberries and bush tomatoes into a large, clean, sealable glass jar or ceramic container. Pour in buttermilk and mix vegetables or fruits through the liquid. Place a heavy weight (like a smaller jar filled with water) directly onto them, so that they are compressed and just covered with the liquid. Seal and leave to ferment in a warm place for 12 hours.

After 12 hours, if contents aren't fully submerged, top up with salt water; use a ratio of 3 teaspoons salt dissolved in 1 litre (4 cups) water. Place weight on vegetables and seal again.

Leave in the same warm place to ferment for 3 days this time. After this, you can seal the pickles and liquid in sterilised jars as you like and refrigerate or keep in a cool place. These just improve with time! Eat as a side with almost anything.

Earthy

Kangaroo Apple and Bush Tomato Chutney

This chutney hits both sweet and savoury notes, and is great in sandwiches or with cold meats. Kangaroo apples are a member of the nightshade family and take well to being cooked like tomatoes — see pages 30 and 137 for important information on them. They are really special and actually easy to grow at home, but can be bought frozen too. You'll need several sterilised jars (see page 232).

Makes 3 kg (6 lb 12 oz)

1 tablespoon olive oil
500 g (1 lb 2 oz) brown onions, very finely diced
500 g (1 lb 2 oz) red onions, very finely diced
500 g (1 lb 2 oz) apples, very finely diced
250 g (9 oz) kangaroo apples, seeds removed, coarsely diced
2 kg (4 lb 8 oz) tomatoes (preferably Roma or vine), coarsely diced
50 g (1¾ oz) ground bush tomato
275 g (9¾ oz) raisins
60 g (2¼ oz) fine salt
1¾ cups (385 g) white sugar
125 g lightly packed soft brown sugar
1½ cups (375 ml) apple cider vinegar
3 garlic cloves, crushed
40 g (1½ oz) ginger, crushed
1 teaspoon ground anise myrtle
1 teaspoon ground cinnamon myrtle
Small pinch of chilli flakes
4 cardamom pods, bruised
Finely grated zest of 1 lemon

Heat oil in a large, heavy-based saucepan over medium heat, add brown and red onion, apples, kangaroo apples and tomatoes and cook, stirring, for 10 minutes or until softened.

Add remaining ingredients and simmer gently, stirring occasionally to prevent catching, for 2–3 hours. Season to taste with salt and ground pepperberry.

Drain any excess liquid into a smaller saucepan, reduce it over high heat until thickened and syrupy, then return it to mixture and heat again over medium heat. (If you prefer you can actually just bottle the liquid separately for use in sauces, or have a looser or thicker chutney.)

Transfer chutney to sterilised jars, seal and allow to cool. Label and store in a cool, dark place for up to 3 years. For the best flavour, let the chutney mature for at least 3 months before eating it.

Substitution options:

Kangaroo apples
→ cherry tomatoes
Bush tomato
→ sun dried tomato
Anise myrtle
→ ground fennel seed
Cinnamon myrtle
→ ground cinnamon

Coffee and Anise Beetroot Chutney

We love beetroot, and this is a wonderful way to use up the summer glut making them into something a little more interesting than pickled beets. This really is an everything chutney, as perfect on a cheeseboard as it is in a sandwich. If you prefer fewer spices, just leave out any that don't take your fancy. You'll need three sterilised 2 cups (500 ml) jars (see page 232).

Makes 1.5 kg (6 cups)

1 teaspoon olive oil
3 teaspoons fennel seeds
3 teaspoons yellow mustard seeds
750 g (1 lb 10 oz) beetroot, peeled and cut into large dice
1 brown onion, finely diced
500 g (1 lb 2 oz) brown sugar
2 cups (500 ml) Warndu wattleseed balsamic (or other balsamic glaze)
Finely grated zest and juice of 1 orange, plus 5 cm (2 in) strip orange zest
6 anise myrtle leaves
1 teaspoon ground coffee
2 cloves

> **Substitution options:**
>
> Anise myrtle leaves
> → ground fennel seed

Heat olive oil in a frying pan over medium-high heat. Add fennel and mustard seeds and fry for about 30 seconds, just until the flavours are released.

Put all ingredients and 1 cup (250 ml) water in a large, heavy-based saucepan and bring to the boil over medium heat. Reduce heat to low and simmer for 30 minutes or until beetroot is soft and the liquid has reduced and thickened. Season to taste with salt and ground pepperberry.

Pour into sterilised jars, seal and allow to cool. Label and store in a cool, dry place for up to a year. Refrigerate after opening.

Bush Tomato Scones with Green Ant Butter

Our mate Billie Cornthwaite is an ace human who runs an amazing bush food catering company, Meez on Plus, and she inspired these fabulous scones. If you have some ground wattleseed, you could add a little for extra nuttiness.

Makes 16–20 scones

3½ cups (525 g) self-raising flour, plus extra for dusting
1 teaspoon baking powder
2 tablespoons ground bush tomato
¾ cup (180 ml) milk
¾ cup (180 ml) pure cream

GREEN ANT BUTTER
1 cup (250 ml) organic pure cream, at room temperature
10 g (¼ oz) green ants (see page 74)

Substitution options:

Bush tomato
→ sun-dried tomato
Green ants
→ crushed coriander seeds

For green ant butter, put cream, half the ants and a pinch of salt in a 1 litre (35 fl oz) jar and add a marble. Prepare a large bowl of iced water. Shake jar for 3 minutes or until cream looks softly whipped, then stiff; you should no longer be able to hear the marble. Keep shaking until you hear the marble again, as the cream separates into solids and buttermilk. Strain off buttermilk (reserve it for another use such as pancakes or smoothies; keep refrigerated).

Transfer solids to bowl of iced water and massage out remaining buttermilk with your hands (you need to remove it all, or it will sour the butter). Rinse butter a couple of times in a fresh bowl of iced water, then mould it into whatever shape you like and roll in remaining green ants. Place butter in an airtight container or wrap in plastic wrap and keep refrigerated. Butter will keep for 2–3 weeks. Makes 250 g (9 oz).

Preheat oven to 190°C (370°F) and line a baking tray with baking paper. Sift flour and baking powder into a large bowl. Add bush tomato, milk, cream and 1 cup (250 ml) cold water and gently fold mixture together with a butter knife until flour is incorporated and a loose dough forms. It should feel quite wet; don't be tempted to overmix.

Turn out dough onto a lightly floured surface and knead very lightly with your fingertips a few times to bring it together, adding just a touch more flour if necessary. Only knead until you can pat out dough with your hands. Pat out to about 2.5 cm (1 in) thick.

With a floured round cookie cutter or glass, cut out 16–20 scones and place on baking tray. Dust with extra flour and bake for 15–20 minutes or until golden on top. Serve with lashings of green ant butter.

Mushroom and Native Herb Broth

This savoury broth is a perfect alternative to meat broth because of its richness and umami qualities. Drink it on its own or use it as a soup base.

Serves 2

1 teaspoon olive oil
1 brown onion, halved
4 garlic cloves, halved
500 g (1 lb 2 oz) button mushrooms
2 carrots, coarsely chopped
10 island sea celery leaves
2 native thyme sprigs
1 cut-leaf mint sprig
2 lemon myrtle leaves
1 teaspoon tamari

Substitution options:

Cut-leaf mint
→ oregano
Island sea celery
→ celery
Native thyme
→ thyme
Lemon myrtle
→ lemon zest

Heat oil in a small frying pan over high heat. Add onion and garlic, cut-side down, and char until dark golden.

Transfer to a large saucepan and add remaining ingredients, then add 3 litres (12 cups) water. Bring to a low simmer and cook for 1½ hours until fragrant. Season with salt and ground pepperberry to taste.

Strain through a fine sieve, pushing down on mushrooms to extract as much broth as possible. Serve the broth alone or with noodles.

'Roo Bourguignon

Boeuf Bourguignon used to be one of our go-to red meat dishes, until we tried it with kangaroo. Now it's 'roo all the way. Make sure you check the important information about kangaroo apples on pages 30 and 137.

Serves 6

2 tablespoons olive oil
100 g (3½ oz) bacon rashers, cut into strips
1 kg (2 lb 4 oz) kangaroo stewing steak, cut into large dice
1 brown onion, sliced
1 carrot, sliced
⅓ cup (50 g) plain flour
2 cups (500 ml) red wine
1 cup (250 ml) beef stock
10 kangaroo apples, halved, seeds removed
1 garlic clove, crushed
1 teaspoon native thyme (fresh or dried)
4 pepperberry leaves (fresh or dried)
25 g (1 oz) butter
10 small pearl onions or eschalots
350 g (12 oz) small button mushrooms
The Epic Mash (page 198) and steamed asparagus, to serve
Seablite and native thyme, to serve

Substitution options:

Kangaroo
→ beef
Kangaroo apples
→ tomato paste
Native thyme
→ thyme
Pepperberry leaves
→ bay or curry leaves

Preheat oven to 230°C (450°F). Heat 1 tablespoon oil in a large casserole dish over medium heat, add bacon and cook, stirring, until lightly browned. Transfer to a bowl with a slotted spoon (leaving behind as much oil as possible), then cover and set aside.

Reheat casserole until the oil is very hot, almost smoking. Working in batches, add kangaroo and fry, turning occasionally, for 6–8 minutes until browned on all sides. Remove with a slotted spoon and add to the bowl with the bacon.

Add onion and carrot to casserole and cook, stirring, for 1–2 minutes until lightly browned. Pour or spoon out any excess fat, then return kangaroo and bacon to casserole. Season generously with salt and ground pepperberry, then sprinkle with flour and shake to coat everything. Cook, uncovered, on the middle shelf of the oven for 4 minutes, then give everything a stir and return to oven for another 4 minutes.

Reduce oven temperature to 160°C (315°F). Stir wine and stock into casserole, then add kangaroo apples, garlic, thyme and pepperberry leaves. Place over high heat on stovetop and bring to the boil, then cover and cook in oven for at least 2–3 hours, or longer if you like, until kangaroo is tender and sauce is thick and rich.

Heat butter and 1 tablespoon oil in a saucepan over medium heat. When it starts to bubble, add onions and cook, swirling pan occasionally, for 10 minutes or until softened. Remove with a slotted spoon, then repeat the process with the mushrooms.

When Bourguignon is ready, add onions and mushrooms and stir to combine. Serve with mashed potatoes and steamed asparagus, and garnish with seablite and native thyme.

Outback Burger with the Lot

OK, this is 'Straya on a plate. Especially if you use 'roo. You will need two hands to eat this baby.

Makes 4

500 g (1 lb 2 oz) minced kangaroo
1 brown onion, finely diced
1 tablespoon barbecue sauce
8 dried bush tomatoes, grated
¼ cup (35 g) plain flour
1 teaspoon ground saltbush
2 tablespoons olive oil
4 slices cheddar or Swiss cheese
4 free-range eggs
4 burger buns (we like brioche or white rolls), cut in half
½ cup (20 g) warrigal greens
4 slices tinned beetroot
Pickled Quandongs (page 66), Kangaroo Apple and Bush Tomato Chutney (page 210), or tomato sauce, to serve

---

Substitution options:

Minced kangaroo
→ minced beef or pork
Bush tomatoes
→ Vegemite or sun-dried tomato
Saltbush
→ salt
Warrigal greens
→ baby spinach

Place mince, onion, barbecue sauce and bush tomato in a large bowl and season with salt and ground pepperberry. With clean hands, mix until well combined.

Divide into 4 large balls (or 8 small balls if you want a double burger). Flatten between the palms of your hands to form patties. Place on a baking tray lined with baking paper and chill for 30 minutes to firm up.

Place flour on a large plate and mix saltbush through. Press patties into flour, turning to coat lightly and shaking off any excess.

Heat 2 teaspoons oil in a frying pan over medium-high heat. Add half the patties and cook, turning carefully, for 2–3 minutes each side (1–2 minutes for smaller patties) or until cooked through. Transfer to a plate, top with a slice of cheese and cover with foil to keep warm. Repeat with remaining patties and another 2 teaspoons oil.

Meanwhile, fry eggs to your liking in remaining 1 tablespoon oil. Load the buns with the greens, beetroot and pickles, chutney or sauce, add one or two patties and an egg and serve hot.

Kangaroo Lasagne

A sumptuous lasagne with mushrooms, ricotta and warrigal greens. You wouldn't even know it was 'roo, so it's a great starting point for those who haven't tried it yet. While making your own wattleseed-infused pasta is totally worth it, you can replace it with store-bought fresh lasagne sheets. Try the pasta with ground pepperberry or lemon myrtle instead of wattleseed for different flavour journeys.

Makes 4

2 tablespoons olive oil, plus extra for greasing
½ small brown onion, diced
800 g (1 lb 12 oz) minced kangaroo
200 g (7 oz) mushrooms, sliced
2 garlic cloves, grated or crushed
1 teaspoon Vegemite
Splash of red wine (optional)
600 g (1 lb 5 oz) tomato passata
2 native thyme sprigs, leaves picked
2 native basil sprigs, leaves torn
2 cup (90 g) warrigal greens
200 g (7 oz) ricotta
1 cup (100 g) grated cheddar
½ cup (50 g) grated parmesan

WHITE SAUCE
1 litre (4 cups) milk
⅓ cup (40 g) cornflour
1 cups (100 g) grated cheddar

WATTLESEED PASTA
140 g (5 oz) '00' flour
140 g (5 oz) fine semolina
1 tablespoon ground wattleseed
2 large free-range eggs

Substitution options:

Minced kangaroo
→ minced beef, pork or lamb
Warrigal greens
→ baby spinach
Native thyme
→ thyme or oregano
Native basil
→ basil
Wattleseed
→ ground coffee

Heat oil in a large non-stick frying pan over medium-high heat. Add onion and a pinch of salt and cook, stirring, for 5 minutes or until softened. Add mince — working in two batches if necessary — and cook, stirring, for 10 minutes or until browned all over. Add mushrooms, garlic, Vegemite and a splash of red wine, stir to combine, then add passata and simmer for 5 minutes. Stir in the thyme and basil, then remove from heat and allow to cool.

For white sauce, heat milk in a saucepan over medium heat until just simmering. Mix cornflour with 2–3 tablespoons water to make a paste, then whisk it into milk and stir over medium heat until sauce has thickened and coats the back of the spoon. Add cheddar and stir until melted, then season with salt and ground pepperberry to taste.

For wattleseed pasta, mix flour, semolina and wattleseed in a bowl with your hands. Make a well in the centre, crack in eggs, then add a pinch of salt. Mix into a dough with a fork, then turn out onto a lightly floured bench and knead for up to 5 minutes until smooth. If it feels too dry, add a few drops of water as necessary; if it's too wet, add a little more flour. Cover with a clean tea towel and leave for 30 minutes to rest. If you have a pasta machine, follow the instructions to make lasagne sheets, if not, use a rolling pin to roll into very thin sheets and cut into 30 cm x 20 cm (12 in x 8 in) strips. Blanch in boiling salted water for 1–2 minutes, then spread out on a clean tea towel to drain.

Preheat oven to 180°C (350°F). Grease the base of a 30 cm x 20 cm (12 in x 8 in) baking dish with olive oil. Assemble the lasagne with a layer of wattleseed pasta, followed by a thin layer of meat mixture, white sauce, warrigal greens and ricotta. Continue alternating layers until all sauce and meat mixture is used. Finish with a layer of pasta and remaining ricotta. Top with grated cheddar and parmesan.

Bake for 30 minutes until cooked through and cheese is melted and golden (if the top gets too brown, cover with foil). Allow to cool briefly before serving.

Kangaroo Chilli Con Carne

One for the campfire or the stovetop. This is wonderful with rice, jacket potatoes or in toasties — and it takes on even more flavour the next day. See pages 30 and 137 for important information about kangaroo apples.

Serves 8

1 tablespoon olive oil
½ brown onion, diced
1 tablespoon cumin seeds
2 tablespoons dried bush tomatoes, chopped
6 cinnamon myrtle leaves (or 1 teaspoon ground)
3 garlic cloves, crushed
1 long red chilli, finely diced (optional)
1 kg (2 lb 4 oz) minced kangaroo
2 red capsicums, finely chopped
400 g (14 oz) kangaroo apples, seeds removed
100 ml (3½ fl oz) Native Worcestershire Sauce (page 73)
2½ tablespoons Warndu wattleseed balsamic (or other balsamic glaze)
1 tablespoon barbecue sauce
1 tablespoon caster sugar
750 g (1 lb 10 oz) tinned kidney beans, drained
Baby spinach and guacamole (optional), to serve

Heat 1 tablespoon oil in a large heavy-based saucepan over medium heat. Add onion and a pinch of salt and cook, stirring occasionally, for 3–4 minutes until softened. Add cumin seeds, bush tomato and cinnamon myrtle, stir for 1 minute, then add garlic and chilli (if using) and cook, stirring, for another 1 minute or until softened.

Increase heat to high, add mince and fry, stirring occasionally, for 5–10 minutes until browned. Add capsicum and season with salt. Stir in kangaroo apples, Worcestershire sauce, wattleseed balsamic, barbecue sauce and sugar, then bring to the boil. Reduce heat to medium and simmer, stirring occasionally, for 10 minutes or until flavours have melded. Stir in beans and simmer for another 5 minutes or until heated through.

Season to taste with salt and ground pepperberry. Serve on a bed of baby spinach with guacamole on the side, if you like.

Substitution options:

Minced kangaroo
→ minced beef or lamb
Bush tomato
→ sun-dried tomato
Cinnamon myrtle
→ ground cinnamon
Kangaroo apples
→ tinned tomatoes
Native Worcestershire
→ Worcestershire sauce

'Roo Steak Sangas

A steak sanga reminds us of footy on Saturdays: white bread, a thin piece of steak and onions to boot. We have pimped this one up with a few additions and our favourite sustainable meat. You can buy 'roo steaks pre-marinated, or feel free to marinate them yourself with your favourite native spices.

Serves 2

2 marinated kangaroo steaks
2 teaspoons olive oil
1½ tablespoons Japanese mayonnaise
4 thin slices white bread (or if you insist, fancy sliced sourdough), fresh or toasted
2 teaspoons Kangaroo Apple and Bush Tomato Chutney (page 210)
2 tomatoes, sliced
1 cup (45 g) wilted warrigal greens

Substitution options:

Kangaroo
→ beef steaks
Chutney
→ tomato chutney
Warrigal greens
→ baby spinach

Heat a barbecue to medium-high heat. Rub steaks with olive oil, season generously with salt, then grill for 3–4 minutes a side (depending on thickness) for medium-rare. Transfer to a plate, cover loosely with foil and leave to rest for 5 minutes.

To assemble steak sangas, spread mayonnaise over half the bread slices. Thinly slice steaks, then pile on top, followed by chutney, slices of tomato and warrigal greens. Top with remaining bread and serve.

Emu Steak with Pepperberry and Mushroom Sauce

There is a misconception that emu is tough and rubbery, but like all meat it just depends on the cut and how you cook it. Get yourself a fillet and cook it the same way you would beef fillet and hey presto! Emu has a slightly gamy, ducky, beefy flavour — yes, that is a thing — and it's very lean, so it's good for you too.

Serves 4

25 g (1 oz) butter
1 tablespoon olive oil, plus extra for drizzling
400 g (14 oz) button mushrooms, sliced
Splash of red wine
1 cup (250 ml) beef stock
1¼ tablespoons pure cream
3 garlic cloves, crushed
1 native thyme sprig
1½ teaspoons pepperberries, bruised
½ teaspoon ground pepperberry leaf
3 tablespoons Native Worcestershire Sauce (page 73)
4 emu steaks (order from specialty butchers)

Substitution options:

Native thyme
→ thyme
Pepperberries
→ peppercorns
Pepperberry leaf
→ bay leaf
Native Worcestershire
→ Worcestershire sauce

Melt butter and oil in a saucepan over medium heat, add mushrooms and cook, stirring, for 3–4 minutes or until tender. Remove mushrooms from pan, then deglaze pan with wine, scraping base of pan. Add stock, cream, garlic, thyme, spices and Worcestershire sauce. Bring to the boil, then reduce heat to medium and simmer, stirring, for 5 minutes or until thick.

Season emu steaks with salt and ground pepperberry, drizzle with oil and cook in a pan or on a barbecue, turning halfway, for about 4–5 minutes for medium-rare or cooked to your liking.

Pour sauce over steaks and serve with any sides you like.

Macadamia and Pumpkin Pie

This is a darn-good pumpkin pie that just so happens to be gluten free. The native spices give it an awesome fragrant bite and the macadamia crust provides a sweet, buttery crunch. You can make the crust with any nuts, and for the filling, you could use a combination of pumpkins and sweet potatoes if you don't have enough of either to go around. For a savoury pie, leave out the sugar and add some savoury spices, such as paprika or sumac, and some fresh herbs. Serve cold in your lunchbox.

Serves 8

750 g (1 lb 10 oz) roasted butternut pumpkin, skin removed
120 g (4¼ oz) caster sugar
1 teaspoon ground cinnamon myrtle
½ teaspoon ground nutmeg
½ teaspoon mixed spice
1 sea rosemary sprig, leaves very finely chopped
2 free-range eggs, beaten
⅔ cup (160 ml) milk
25 g (1 oz) butter, melted
Bunya nuts, rosella flowers and lilly pillies (frozen and thawed), to serve (all optional)

MACADAMIA PIE CRUST

Oil, for greasing
2½ cups (250 g) macadamia nut meal
2 tablespoons buckwheat flour
1 teaspoon ground cinnamon myrtle
1 free-range egg
1 teaspoon ground Geraldton wax leaves

Preheat oven to 175°C (350°F). For pie crust, grease a 20 cm (8 in) pie tin with oil (if you have one, use a springform or loose-bottomed tin). Put all ingredients in a small bowl and stir until well combined. Transfer to pie tin and push evenly up the sides and across the base with your fingers.

Bake for 10–12 minutes until set (oil will begin to froth from the crust but there's no need to worry, it will subside as the crust cools). Remove from oven, blot with paper towel and leave to cool. Crust will keep in an airtight container for up to 3 days.

To make the filling, push roasted pumpkin through a sieve into a bowl. In a separate bowl, mix sugar with spices, rosemary and a pinch of salt. Add eggs, milk and butter and stir well.

Preheat oven to 200°C (400°F). Spoon filling into crust, bake for 10 minutes, then reduce oven temperature to 180°C (350°F) and cook for a further 30 minutes until filling has just set.

Just before serving, decorate with bunya nuts, rosella flowers and lilly pillies, if using. Serve in slices.

Substitution options:

Cinnamon myrtle
→ ground cinnamon
Sea rosemary
→ rosemary
Macadamia nut meal
→ almond meal
Geraldton wax
→ ground juniper berries and lemon zest

Beetroot, Chocolate and Wattleseed Cake

Beetroot, you say? Yes absolutely. It keeps the cake beautifully moist and gives it an earthy scent and flavour that complements the wattleseed. If you don't have any beetroot, you could use leftover mashed potato. It sounds crazy, but it has the same moisture-locking ability as beetroot. The cake batter here is enough to make a single cake, which you can ice and serve with the cream and munties alongside. If you want to make a two-layer cake like in the picture, double the recipe and make two cakes, filling the centre with the muntrie cream.

Serves 8

125 g (4½ oz) butter, softened
1⅓ cups (300 g) firmly packed brown sugar
2 teaspoons roasted ground wattleseed
3 large free-range eggs
75 g (2¾ oz) dark chocolate, melted
1½ cups (225 g) self-raising flour
⅔ cup (50 g) raw cacao powder, sifted
250 g (9 oz) cooked beetroot, peeled and grated

MUNTRIE CREAM
2 cups (500 ml) thickened cream
1 tablespoon pure icing sugar
1 cup (155 g) muntries

ICING
150 g (5½ oz) dark chocolate, chopped
135 g (4¾ oz) sour cream
¼ cup (30 g/1 oz) pure icing sugar, sifted
1 teaspoon roasted ground wattleseed
Davidson's plum powder, to serve

Preheat oven to 180°C (350°F). Line a 20 cm (8 in) cake tin with baking paper (or two tins if you are making a two-layer cake). Cream butter, sugar, wattleseed and eggs in a stand mixer fitted with the whisk attachment until pale and fluffy, then add melted chocolate and beat to combine. Gently fold in flour, cacao powder and a pinch of salt, then stir in beetroot.

Pour into tin(s) and bake for 45 minutes or until a skewer inserted into the centre comes out clean. Cool for 5 minutes, then turn out onto a wire rack to cool completely.

For muntrie cream, whip cream and icing sugar together until thick.

For icing, put all ingredients into a heatproof bowl set over a saucepan of simmering water (don't let base of bowl touch water) and stir until melted and combined. Remove from heat and keep stirring until glossy. Allow both cake and icing to cool.

For a single cake, transfer to a serving plate and ice the cake, serving with cream and muntries. For a two-layer cake, transfer one of the cakes to a plate, spread the cream across the top and scatter with muntries. Carefully place the second cake on top and spread with icing. Devour.

Substitution options:

Wattleseed
→ ground coffee
Muntries
→ raspberries or blueberries
Davidson's plum powder
→ goji berry powder

*On our farm: Mallee & Myrtle Farm,
Ngadjuri Country, Clare Valley,
South Australia.*

Tips on preserving and pickling

When it comes to jam, there are three things that contribute to the perfect set: sugar, acid and pectin. For chutneys, pickles and relishes, you typically need salt or sugar plus vinegar to prevent the formation of pathogens that may cause spoilage.

The basic method for jams, chutneys or relishes is to simmer the fruit or vegetables until soft, then add sugar or vinegar, boil until it reaches setting point (for jam) or is tender (for chutneys and relishes), then bottle. The fact that we're using First Nations ingredients means it pays to bear in mind the bitterness, astringency and acidity of the ingredients you're using — the flavours can be quite different to what you might be used to, so always try them raw to get an idea first.

The golden rules are:

CHOOSE YOUR FRUIT CAREFULLY

Always use just-ripe or slightly under-ripe fruit for jam. Over-ripe fruit won't set properly and takes a really long time to cook; use this fruit for stewing. You can use frozen fruit for jam, too, just make sure you thaw it out or use less liquid than the recipe says, as water will leach from the fruit as it cooks.

FOR A GOOD CRISP PICKLE, USE FRESH INGREDIENTS

Pickles are always best left for at least a month or two before eating so the flavours can really infuse. They will normally keep for up to two years, but make sure you check the recipe, as some pickles only last a few weeks in the fridge.

Jam is ready to eat as soon as it's cooled, and can be kept for up to two years if the jars are properly sterilised.

It's best to use a large, wide, heavy-based pan; this allows the preserving mixture to only come halfway up the sides of the pan and not spill over when it boils. Special preserving pans are best, but any large saucepan will suffice.

How to sterilise jars and lids

Preheat oven to 100°C (200°F). Wash jars in hot soapy water and rinse with hot water (or wash them in the dishwasher). I like to handle them with jar tongs (these are special wide tongs that make it easier to handle jars), as you need the water to be really hot. Stand jars upright on baking trays and put them in the oven while your jam is cooking. Remove them from the oven one by one as needed.

To sterilise lids, funnels and ladles, boil them in a saucepan and remove as needed. Place onto paper towel. Use the paper towel to wipe them totally dry and use them straight away.

How to jar and bottle jams and pickles

Don't introduce water to cooked preserves or mould will form. For jams, jellies and chutneys, fill the warm jars to the top and wipe the rims with a clean, damp cloth, then cover surface with a disc of wax paper (waxed-side down) while still hot. Allow to cool, then cover with cellophane jam covers, securing with a rubber band; for long-term storage, secure the jar with a screw-top lid.

For pickles and preserved fruits or vegetables, fill the warm jars to within 2.5 cm (1 in) of the top, pour in the preserving liquid to within 1 cm (½ in) of the top, making sure the fruit or vegetables are completely covered. Immediately cover with a disc of wax paper (waxed-side down). Seal with a screw-top lid.

For vinegars, fill the warm bottles or jars to within 2.5 cm (1 in) of the top then seal with a non-corrodible screw-top or a cork.

Always store preserves in a cool, dark place unless the recipe says otherwise.

How to test for setting point

If you want to be absolutely spot on, the easiest thing to do is buy a jam thermometer and when it reads 105°C (220°F), your jam will set. Or you could try the saucer test. To do so, place a few saucers in the fridge before you make your jam. When jam has been cooking for the time stated in the recipe, drop less than a teaspoon on a cold saucer, leave for a minute and then gently push your finger through the middle. If the jam crinkles, it's reached setting point. If it doesn't, boil for 5 minutes more, then test again with another cold saucer.

Useful equipment for your pickling and preserving

- Preserving pan or other large, wide, heavy-based saucepan
- Silicone mixing spoon
- Slotted spoon for skimming scum from the surface of jams
- Jar tongs
- Jars and lids
- Paper towel
- Kitchen string
- Funnel or jug for pouring jam into jars
- Sugar thermometer
- Oven mitts
- Baking tray
- Heatproof chopping board
- Labels and a marker pen

Stockists

Grocers and larger independent retailers such as Harris Farm and The Essential Ingredient have begun to stock a small selection of First Nations ingredients, such as fresh finger limes, freeze-dried fruit, and herbs and spices. The big supermarkets, meanwhile, stock some native meats and an array of native seafood.

HARRIS FARM
Stocks some native meats, and occasionally finger lime and coastal greens.
harrisfarm.com.au

THE ESSENTIAL INGREDIENT
Has a variety of largely dried fruit powders and herbs and spices.
essentialingredient.com.au

To stock up your pantry further, try these spice and produce shops where you'll find a wider variety in fresh, dried or processed products.

AUSTRALIAN NATIVE FOOD CO
Stocks value-added products made with native ingredients, as well as herbs, spices and fruit powders.
australiannativefoodco.com.au

AUSTRALIAN SUPERFOOD CO
Stocks a wide range of nuts, spices, dried fruits, extracts, syrups and powders.
austsuperfoods.com.au

BENT SHED PRODUCE
Specialises in dried herbs, spices and blends.
bentshedproduce.com.au

BUSH FOOD SHOP
Stocks an array of herbs, nuts and spices as well as value-added products.
bushfoodshop.com.au

BUSH LOLLY
Planning to stock a variety of fresh and dried native products on their website. Check for updates.
bushlolly.com

INDIGIEARTH
Specialises in native chutneys, teas and native herbs and spices, as well as catering and running a café.
indigiearth.com.au

KAIYU SUPERFOODS
Specialises in freeze-dried fruit, dried herbs and spices, nuts and processed products.
kaiyusuperfoods.com

KAKADU PLUM CO
Sells a small range of spices as well as processed products.
kakaduplumco.com

KUNGAS CAN COOK
Stocks a variety of fresh and dried products as well as offering catering; email for stock list.
kungkascancook.business.site

MAYI HARVEST
Specialises in fresh, dried and frozen produce, with an emphasis on fruit and greens.
mayiharvests.com.au

MELBOURNE BUSHFOOD
A one-stop shop that specialises in hard-to-find native food plants and stocks an array of products, including spices, fruit powders, teas and syrups.
melbournebushfood.com.au

MY DILLY BAG
Specialises in fresh and dried produce and bush food products, such as syrups, pasta and jam.
mydillybag.com.au

NATIF
Sells an array of herbs, spices and freeze-dried fruit powders.
natif.com.au

PLAYING WITH FIRE
Sells a small selection of fruits, spices and processed products to the public, with a larger range available wholesale.
playingwithfire.com.au

SALTBUSH KITCHEN
Stocks a variety of spices and flavoured salts.
saltbushkitchen.com.au

WARNDU
Our own shop, full of 100 per cent locally sourced seasonal and wild-harvested native produce.
warndu.com

For more specialty items, these shops specialise in particular categories, such as fresh plants, native meats or harder-to-find herbs and spices, such as coastal greens, muntries, crocodile or emu, and the likes of bush tomatoes and sandalwood nuts.

CREATIVE NATIVE
Sells a wide range of dried herbs, spices and fruit, plus frozen native fruit.
creativenativefoods.com.au

COOEE CAFÉ
Specialises in processed products as well as offering catering.
cooeecafeandcatering.com.au

CURRIE COUNTRY
Sells and wholesales an array of fresh bush foods, as well as playing an educational role in the community.
curriecountry.com

DIEMEN PEPPER
Specialises in native pepper, both fresh and dried.
diemenpepper.com

JALAJALA TREATS
Sells a range of processed products.
jalajala.com.au

MAALINUP
Western Australian gallery that also sells bush-tucker products, while its owner, Dale Tilbrook, sells fresh produce and runs food experiences.
**maalinup.com.au;
daletilbrookexperiences.com.au**

MABU MABU
A Melbourne restaurant that also does catering and sells sauces, spices, pickles and teas.
mabumabu.com.au

MACRO MEATS
Specialises in kangaroo meat.
macrogroupaustralia.com

MARVICK FARMS
Specialises in native citrus and citrus products, see website for stockists.
marvicknativefarms.com.au/

NEWCHURCH HORTICULTURE
Specialises in fresh and dried produce, get in touch on Facebook.
**facebook.com/
newchurchhorticulture/**

PUNDI PRODUCE
Currently specialises in river mint, with more greens, herbs and spices to come.
pundiproduce.com.au

RAINFOREST BOUNTY
Specialises in products made with rainforest fruit, ranging from curry bases to sauces and vinegars.
rainforestbounty.com.au

SOMETHING WILD
This Adelaide Central Market stall specialises in native meats, as well as fresh produce and value-added products; they also sell a limited range online.
somethingwild.com.au

TUMBEELA NATIVE FOODS
Specialises in myrtles and pepperberry, sold fresh and dried.
tumbeela.com.au

YAAMA FOODS
Specialises in value-added products, as well as education.
yaamafoods.com.au

These suppliers tend to sell only to wholesale customers, but many of them offer good resources for education, tours and training. They also are a good place to look for bush plants.

AUSSIE FOOD PLANTS
Mike and Gail Quarmby, previously of Outback Pride, now grow native food plants for educational purposes, as well as selling plants. Find them on Facebook for more.
facebook.com/Aussie-Food-Plants-111327267140716/

BLACK DUCK FOODS
Indigenous social enterprise overseeing Bruce Pascoe's kangaroo grass project and growing and harvesting other native grains and grasses; shop coming soon.
blackduckfoods.org

DALEYS FRUIT
Sells a variety of bush food plants.
daleysfruit.com.au

FINGER LIME CAVIAR
Specialises in finger lime products; wholesale only.
fingerlimecaviar.com.au

MIRRITYA MUNDYA
Specialises in native produce and education.
mmundya.com

NATIONAL INDIGENOUS CULINARY INSTITUTE
Specialises in training Indigenous chefs and educating people about native foods.
nici.org.au

TUCKER BUSH
Sells bush food plants to retailers (see website for stockists) and sells dried herbs to the public.
tuckerbush.com.au

Featured artists

These artists from Willie Weston provided artworks and props used throughout the book; Willie Weston is a profit-for-purpose business, based in Naarm (Melbourne), which works in partnership with First Nations artists.

JEAN BAPTISTE APUATIMI
Jean Baptiste Apuatimi (1940–2013) is internationally acclaimed as a painter, carver and printmaker. She was born at Pirlangimpi, Melville Island, Northern Territory, into the Japijapunga (March Fly) skin group. In 1991 she participated in her first exhibition; the next year the National Gallery of Victoria acquired eight of her bark paintings. Apuatimi exhibited widely and earned significant recognition as both an artist and a custodian of Tiwi culture. Her work is held in public and private collections around the world, including the British Museum (UK), the Seattle Museum of Art (USA) and the National Museum of Women in the Arts (USA).

Jilamara, by Jean Baptiste Apuatimi, is from our Tiwi Collection. Jilamara is a Tiwi word that refers to the ochre patterning traditionally painted on the bodies of dancers and on carved poles during Pukumani ceremonies. Jilamara is unique to the art and culture of Tiwi Islanders.

OSMOND KANTILLA
Osmond Kantilla (b.1966) is a master screen-printer. His country is Wurruranku and his skin group is Marntimapila (Stone). Kantilla has been selected for group exhibitions across Australia and internationally. His work is held in numerous public collections, including the National Museum of Australia, the Powerhouse Museum and the Art Gallery of South Australia.

Pandanus, by Osmond Kantilla, is from our Tiwi Collection. Pandanus represents the pointy leaves of the pandanus plant. Osmond Kantilla created this design in memory of his father.

APRIL JONES
April Jones spent many years teaching in Port Hedland, Broome and Fitzroy Crossing before arriving at the Marninwarntikura Women's Resource Centre, wanting to learn how to sew. Seven years later she began working with Marnin Studio, creating block and screen prints of local bush tucker, flora and fauna.

River Stones, by April Jones, is from our Fitzroy Crossing Collection and combines natural elements local to the Fitzroy River area. It depicts the leaves of a gum tree with large nuts found on the Kimberley coast, and the small, elongated shapes represent flat, pointy stones.

COLLEEN NGWARRAYE MORTON
Colleen Ngwarraye Morton was born in 1957 into the Ngwarraye skin group. She paints Arreth, which translates to 'strong bush medicine', paying homage to the significance of traditional bush medicine. Morton often depicts her grandfather's country, where her mother and grandmother taught her the importance of seasonal medicines and plants. She was part of the batik movement that emerged in Utopia, Central Australia, in the 1980s. Recent exhibitions include the Florence Biennale, Italy (2015), ReDot Gallery, Singapore (2012) and Batiks of the Desert, National Gallery of Victoria (2008).

Singing Bush Medicine, by Colleen Ngwarraye Morton is from our Ampilatwatja Collection and represents a ceremony performed by women to celebrate bush medicine through dancing, singing and painting the body in ochre. This design is about singing to country, singing the bush medicine and edible seeds into existence, and sourcing and maintaining them.

ROSIE NGWARRAYE ROSS

Rosie Ngwarraye Ross was born in 1951 near Amaroo Station, Northern Territory. Her skin group is Ngwarraye. In her paintings Ross depicts bush medicine plants and wild flowers from around her country. She has a bold, expressive style and often omits the sky from her compositions, combining both aerial and frontal views. Ross has exhibited widely, including as part of Fragrant Lands: Exhibition of Australian and Chinese Indigenous Art at Tandanya National Aboriginal Cultural Institute, Adelaide, which toured to Shanghai (2014), Flinders Lane Gallery, Melbourne (2014) and at Booker-Lowe Gallery, Texas (2015).

Sugarbag Dreaming, by Rosie Ngwarraye Ross, is from our Ampilatwatja Collection. Sugarbag is a name used for both the honey made by native bees and also for the sweet nectar that comes from the big yellow flowers of the 'tarrkarr' trees. Rosie Ngwarraye Ross and her family often gather Sugarbag out in the sandy country around Ampilatwatja.

ELIZABETH KANDABUMA

Elizabeth Kandabuma (deceased) was born near Bulgay on Yirritjinga Country. She depicted the natural world in a distinctive, lyrical and painterly style. Kandabuma worked with Bábbarra Designs, an art centre in Maningrida, from the early 1990s, and exhibited across Australia, including at Tandanya National Aboriginal Cultural Institute, Adelaide, the Australian National University, Canberra, and in multiple Darwin Aboriginal Art Fairs.

Mud Ripples, by Elizabeth Kandabuma, is from our Bábbarra Collection and depicts the patterns of freshwater mud ripples which emerge after monsoonal wet seasons on the Arnhem Land flood plains. These ripples form on the earth's surface in delicate, repetitive and shifting patterns, and they move, crack, disappear and re-emerge in response to the changing wind, rains and light.

LEE-ANNE WILLIAMS

Lee-Anne Williams, of the Bunuba and Wangkatjunka language groups, began her career painting boab nuts, moving onto screen and lino printing on textiles before becoming a founding member of the 2017 Design Within Country fashion project. Williams aspires to run her own fashion business in order to support her community.

Water Levels, by Lee-Anne Williams, is from our Fitzroy Crossing Collection and references the marks that remain on the rocks of the Fitzroy River after flood waters rise and fall.

Acknowledgements

To our parents, Sunny and Elson Coulthard, and Mandy and Andrew Sullivan. Without them, we would never have arrived at this journey. You are undoubtedly our inspiration and support, always along with our brothers and sisters, aunties, uncles and cousins aplenty. And our Warndu partner in crime, who is family (albeit a tall Irish one), thank you for always supporting our crazy dreams, Siobhan. To the extended Coulthard family and Nepabunna community, who have shared everything with us, from Adnyamathanha words to uses of ingredients, taken us foraging or shared valuable knowledge with us, thank you. As well as our own Nation, we have been particularly lucky to meet more and more First Nations peoples, who have shared with us invaluable cultural and plant knowledge.

Our industry is brimming with amazing people doing incredible things. Some have been in this industry longer than we have walked the earth, and to them we owe immense gratitude. Collaboration is the key to longevity and sustainability for us all. To the extended Australian native food industry, a huge, giant thank you to you all. You are a big bunch of small and large businesses and leaders, too many to thank on these pages: Indigenous knowledge holders, farmers, growers, harvesters, chefs, value-adders, politicians, writers, activists.

Uncle Bruce Pascoe and Aunty Daphne Rickett, thanks for your inspired forewords to our book. Bruce, your words in *Dark Emu* changed our trajectory for the better and we thank you for everything you do. Getting to know you in person has been the highlight of our work. Your generosity and passion is unwavering, and we thank you for your support. Daniel and Raquel Newchurch, you might be new to this industry but you have grown up on the shoulders of a giant (your pop, Ron Newchurch), and we thank you and your family for your ongoing support. Neville Bonney, thanks for being the greatest fount of knowledge about these amazing ingredients and their botanical names, true editorial eyes. Gayle and Mike Quarmby, thank you for always being generous with your knowledge, fantastic produce and love for this industry. Mark at Tucker Bush, your plants have taught us so much about growing, and your business is such a great addition to this industry.

To the amazing Willie Weston, the artists whose stunning work adorns the photographs, thank you (check out page 236 for more on them and their work). We are grateful for the pottery from Clay Beehive and Leap and Wander, always magic and made especially for us.

Books are not just made by authors. Jane Morrow, our publisher, and the whole Murdoch team are really bloody brilliant at this stuff. Jane, we can't really put into words how much we appreciate you and your honesty, guidance and love from afar (Covid!). Thanks to Justin Wolfers, our editorial manager, as fabulously patient as it gets! Big thanks to the legendary Kristy Allen, our design manager, as well as our wonderful designer Jenna Lee and beautiful illustrator Charlotte Allingham. Our A-team on set: photographer Josh Geelen and stylist Duy Dash. You guys were an absolute dream to work with, bringing these recipes to life through the lens; Billie Cornthwaite and Aunty Daphne on the pans were the best cooks on the block.

Last, but not at all least, for those of you amazing home cooks who bought our book and are now using these beautiful ingredients, there are so many people here for you to buy from and support! Thank you for growing this vital industry with us, and more importantly, enjoy the journey, just as we are.

Index

A
almonds: Breakkie muffins 110
anise myrtle 16
  Anise myrtle and macadamia poached chicken 156
  Anise myrtle rice 154
  Baked bush apples 188
  Barb and Lil's Christmas pudding 82
  Barramundi poached in Geraldton wax, kunzea flower and lemon-scented gum 96
  Bush botanical bitters 145
  Bush botanical sugars 176
  Buttermilk pickles 209
  Coffee and anise beetroot chutney 211
  Dark emu beer and ant pickle 208
  Kangaroo apple and bush tomato chutney 210
  marinade 70
  Myrtle tea cake 80
  Native fig and vanilla jam 177
  Pepperberry cookies with lemon aspen 78
  Pickled quandongs 66
  pie crust 158
  Spiced bush apple cider 72
ants
  Bush tomato scones with green ant butter 212
  Dark emu beer and ant pickle 208
  Green ant and crocodile curry 199
  green ant butter 212
  Green ant curry paste 74
  Macadamia, green ant, rose and pepperberry latte 152
  soda water pops 100
  yoghurt pops 100
apple
  Barb and Lil's Christmas pudding 82
  Kangaroo apple and bush tomato chutney 210
  see also apple, bush; kangaroo apple; muntries; Tanami apple
apple, bush 17
  Baked bush apples 188
  Buttermilk pickles 209
  Spiced bush apple cider 72
apricot, native 17
Atherton raspberry 18
  Native raspberry jam 178
  Rosella and native raspberry Swiss roll 160
  Rustic native jam tarts 165
Aussie olives 70

B
Baked bush apples 188
banksias 18
  Bush botanical bitters 145
  Bush botanical sugars 176
  Bush flower waters 149
  Fermented banksia fizz 150
Barb and Lil's Christmas pudding 82
barbed wire grass 54
barilla see bower spinach
Barra burger with bush tartare sauce 200
Barramundi poached in Geraldton wax, kunzea flower and lemon-scented gum 96
basil, native 19
  Bunya nut rice paper rolls with macadamia dipping sauce 116
  bush green pesto 114
  Buttermilk and lemon myrtle set cream with muscat quandongs 161
  Decongestant rub for colds and flu 139
  Ginger and basil digestion candy 138
  Green ant curry paste 74
  Kangaroo lasagne 220
  yoghurt pops 100
basil, wild 20
  Boonjie tamarind and macadamia noodle salad 180
Native watercress and lentil soup 94
  beach flax lily 54
beans: Kangaroo chilli con carne 222
beetroot
  Beetroot, chocolate and wattleseed cake 228
  Coffee and anise beetroot chutney 211
  Outback burger with the lot 218
bitters, Bush botanical 145
black ants see ants
bloodroot 20
blue flax lily 54
blue quandong 43
  see also quandong
blue trumpet 54
blue yam 54
boab 21
boobialla see juniper, native

boonjie see tamarind, small-leaved
bottlebrush 21
  Bush botanical bitters 145
  Bush flower waters 149
bourguignon, 'Roo 216
bower spinach 19
  Barra burger with bush tartare sauce 200
  Green garden soup 92
bread, Kangaroo grass brew 206
Breakkie muffins 110
broad-leaved paperbark 54
broth, Mushroom and native herb 214
brownies, Davidson's plum and sandalwood nut 124
bunya pine 22
  Breakkie muffins 110
  bunya nut butter 114
  Bunya nut rice paper rolls with macadamia dipping sauce 116
  Bunya nut risotto with bush green pesto 114
  bush green pesto 114
  macadamia and bunya nut dipping sauce 116
burgers
  Barra burger with bush tartare sauce 200
  Outback burger with the lot 218
bush apple see apple, bush
Bush botanical bitters 145
Bush botanical sugars 176
Bush flower waters 149
bush green pesto 114
bush onion see onion, bush
bush pears see pear, bush
bush tomato see tomato, bush
butter
  bunya nut 114
  green ant 212
  Macadamia 108
Buttermilk and lemon myrtle set cream with muscat quandongs 161
Buttermilk pickles 209

C
cabbage: Boonjie tamarind and macadamia noodle salad 180
cakes
  Beetroot, chocolate and wattleseed cake 228
  Davidson's plum and sandalwood nut brownies 124

Lemon myrtle ricotta cake with pickled native cherries 189
Limey lime drizzle cake 182
Macadamia blondies 110
Myrtle tea cake 80
Sandalwood and custard cake with Tanami apples and bush pears 118
Strawberry gum and Geraldton wax cupcakes 166
Campfire s'mores with Davidson's plum 120
Cape Barren tea 54

capsicum
Boonjie tamarind and macadamia noodle salad 180
Kangaroo chilli con carne 222
Caramelised bush onions 205

carrot
Boonjie tamarind and macadamia noodle salad 180
Bunya nut rice paper rolls with macadamia dipping sauce 116
Dolmades with river mint yoghurt 88
Fish pie 198
Macadamia lentil curry 113
Mushroom and native herb broth 214
'Roo bourguignon 216

cauliflower
Dark emu beer and ant pickle 208
Macadamia, finger lime, native lemongrass and cauliflower soup 112

celery, island sea 29
Anise myrtle and macadamia poached chicken 156
Boonjie tamarind and macadamia noodle salad 180
Dolmades with river mint yoghurt 88
Fish pie 198
Green garden soup 92
Herb powders 66
Macadamia lentil curry 113
Mushroom and native herb broth 214
Native watercress and lentil soup 94

cheese
Bunya nut risotto with bush green pesto 114
bush green pesto 114
Bush tomato cheese on toast 64
Fish pie 198
Green baked eggs 90
Kangaroo lasagne 220
Lemon myrtle ricotta cake with pickled native cherries 189
Native sorrel and kangaroo apple baked eggs 154
Outback burger with the lot 218
Pipi mornay 196
The epic mash 198
Warrigal greens and saltbush cob 86
Wattlemisu 170
white sauce 220
cherry: Strawberry gum, cherry and riberry tapioca trifle 132

cherry, native 22
Honey-fermented cherries 'n' berries 174
Lemon myrtle ricotta cake with pickled native cherries 189
pickled native cherries 189
Strawberry gum, cherry and riberry tapioca trifle 132
cherry cream 132
chest rub, Herby, for asthma 139

chicken
Anise myrtle and macadamia poached chicken 156
Bunya nut rice paper rolls with macadamia dipping sauce 116

chilli
Green ant curry paste 74
Herby salt rub 103
Kangaroo chilli con carne 222
Macadamia lentil curry 113
Macadamia, finger lime, native lemongrass and cauliflower soup 112
chilli con carne, Kangaroo 222

chocolate
Beetroot, chocolate and wattleseed cake 228
Campfire s'mores with Davidson's plum 120
Davidson's plum and sandalwood nut brownies 124
Davidson's plum lamington 186
icing 228
Macadamia blondies 110
Macadamia butter cups 108
pastry 168
Peppermint gum slice 98
Rose and pepper leaf chocolate tart with honeyed macadamias 168
Rustic native jam tarts 165
Wattella 106
White chocolate quandong truffles 126
chocolate lily 35

Christmas pudding, Barb and Lil's 82

chutneys
Coffee and anise beetroot chutney 211
Kangaroo apple and bush tomato chutney 210
cider, Spiced bush apple 72

cinnamon myrtle 23
Baked bush apples 188
Barb and Lil's Christmas pudding 82
Bush botanical sugars 176
Cinnamon myrtle and maple popcorn 76
Fruity flapjacks 130
Green ant and crocodile curry 199
Kangaroo apple and bush tomato chutney 210
Kangaroo chilli con carne 222
Macadamia and pumpkin pie 226
macadamia pie crust 226
Myrtle tea cake 80
Native fig and vanilla jam 177
Native Worcestershire sauce 73
Not-quite-blueberry muffin with Illawarra plum and midyim berry 129
Pepperberry cookies with lemon aspen 78
Plum leather 131
Sandalwood and custard cake with Tanami apples and bush pears 118
Spiced bush apple cider 72
Strawberry gum and emu bush sleepy milk 157
Strawberry gum rice pudding 128
Wattella 106
White chocolate quandong truffles 126
coastal wattle 54
cob, Warrigal greens and saltbush 86

coconut
Anise myrtle rice 154
Davidson's plum lamington 186
Fragrant coconut rice 90
Fruity flapjacks 130
Garden kefir 140
Green ant and crocodile curry 199
Green ant curry paste 74
macadamia and bunya nut dipping sauce 116
Quandong and Davidson's plum iced VoVos 190

coffee
Coffee and anise beetroot chutney 211

Index

Wattlemisu 170
compote, quandong 128
cookies, Pepperberry, with lemon aspen 78
coral pea 54
cordials
   kunzea and Illawarra plum cordial 184
   Lilly pilly cordial 68
corn *see* popcorn
cottonwood 54
Cough medicine (herbal honey) 141
cream, Buttermilk and lemon myrtle set, with muscat quandongs 161
cream, cherry 132
crisps, Rosella leaf 155
crocodile: Green ant and crocodile curry 199
cupcakes, Strawberry gum and Geraldton wax 166
cups, Macadamia butter 108
currant, native 23
curries
   Green ant and crocodile curry 199
   Green ant curry paste 74
   Macadamia lentil curry 113
curry bush
   Herb powders 66
   Pickled bush onions 204
custard, wattleseed 118, 132
cut-leaf mint *see* oregano, native

D

dandelion: Green garden soup 92
Dark emu beer and ant pickle 208
dates: Wattella 106
Davidson's plum 25
   Bush botanical sugars 176
   Campfire s'mores with Davidson's plum 120
   Davidson's plum and sandalwood nut brownies 124
   Davidson's plum icing 124, 190
   Davidson's plum jam 186
   Davidson's plum lamington 186
   Davidson's plum marshmallows 120
   Fruity flapjacks 130
   Quandong and Davidson's plum iced VoVos 190
Decongestant rub for colds and flu 139
deeringia 54
desert fig 54
desert lime
   Barramundi poached in Geraldton wax, kunzea flower and lemon-scented gum 96
   bush green pesto 114
   desert lime icing 80
   Desert lime shortbread 183
   lime drizzle 182
   'Lime'ade 68
   Limey lime drizzle cake 182
   Pipi mornay 196
desert raisin *see* tomato, bush
devil's marbles 54
digestion candy, Ginger and basil 138
dipping sauces *see* sauces
Dolmades with river mint yoghurt 88
dressings 180
   yoghurt dressing 88
drizzle, lime 182
drying herbs 102

E

edible flowers *see* banksia; bottlebrush; hibiscus; rosella; sorrel
eggs
   desert lime icing 80
   Green baked eggs 90
   Native sorrel and kangaroo apple baked eggs 154
   Outback burger with the lot 218
   wattleseed custard 132
emu: Emu steak with pepperberry and mushroom sauce 225
emu bush: Strawberry gum and emu bush sleepy milk 157
extract, wattleseed 78

F

Face steam 141
fennel: Barramundi poached in Geraldton wax, kunzea flower and lemon-scented gum 96
Fermented banksia fizz 150
figs, native 54
   Native fig and vanilla jam 177
finger lime 26
   Barb and Lil's Christmas pudding 82
   Barramundi poached in Geraldton wax, kunzea flower and lemon-scented gum 96
   Bush botanical bitters 145
   Bush botanical sugars 176
   bush green pesto 114
   dressing 180
   finger lime sauce 116
   Garden kefir 140
   Green ant and crocodile curry 199
   Green ant curry paste 74
   lime drizzle 182
   'Lime'ade 68
   Limey lime drizzle cake 182
   macadamia and bunya nut dipping sauce 116
   Macadamia, finger lime, native lemongrass and cauliflower soup 112
   Myrtle tea cake 80
   Pepperberry cookies with lemon aspen 78
   River mint granita 99
   Rosella syrup 144
   soda water pops 100
   Sore throat spray 138
   tartare 200
   White chocolate quandong truffles 126
First Nations flavour wheel 58–9
fish
   Barra burger with bush tartare sauce 200
   Barramundi poached in Geraldton wax, kunzea flower and lemon-scented gum 96
   Fish pie 198
   Native Worcestershire sauce 73
fizz, Fermented banksia 150
flapjacks, Fruity 130
flavour wheel 58–9
Flower and leaf stress balls 140
flowers, edible *see* banksia; bottlebrush; hibiscus; rosella; sorrel
foraging 16, 136
Fragrant coconut rice 90
freezing herbs in oil 102
Fruity flapjacks 130
fuchsia, native 54

G

Garden kefir 140
Geraldton wax 27
   Barramundi poached in Geraldton wax, kunzea flower and lemon-scented gum 96
   Bunya nut risotto with bush green pesto 114
   Geraldton wax shortbread with kunzea sugar sprinkle 169
   macadamia pie crust 226
   Strawberry gum and Geraldton wax cupcakes 166

strawberry gum icing 166
ginger, native
   Ginger and basil digestion candy 138
   Green ant curry paste 74
   Honey-fermented cherries 'n' berries 174
   Macadamia blondies 110
   Native Worcestershire sauce 73
granita, River mint 99
grape, native 54
green ants *see* ants
Green baked eggs 90
Green garden soup 92
guava, native 28, 54
gymea lily 54

H

Herb powders 66
herbal oil infusions 102
herbs
   Cough medicine (herbal honey) 141
   Flower and leaf stress balls 140
   preserving 102
   when and where to grow 136
   see also basil, native; celery, island sea; myrtle; oregano, native; parsley, sea; rosemary, sea; sage, native; thyme, native
Herby chest rub for asthma 139
Herby ice pops 100
Herby salt rub 103
hibiscus
   Bush botanical bitters 145
   Bush flower waters 149
   see also rosella
   Honey-fermented cherries 'n' berries 174

I

ice plant: Barra burger with bush tartare sauce 200
ice pops, Herby 100
icing 78, 228
   Davidson's plum icing 124, 190
   desert lime icing 80
   strawberry gum icing 166
Illawarra flame tree 54
Illawarra plum 28
   kunzea and Illawarra plum cordial 184
   Kunzea and Illawarra plum jelly 184
   Not-quite-blueberry muffin with Illawarra plum and midyim berry 129
   Plum leather 131
island sea celery *see* celery, island sea

J

jams
   Davidson's plum jam 186
   Native fig and vanilla jam 177
   Native raspberry jam 178
   Quandong jam 178
   Rosella jam 164
jar spices 204
jars, sterilising 232
jelly, Kunzea and Illawarra plum 184
jelly slice, Muntries and quandong 192
juniper, native 29
   Bush botanical bitters 145

K

kakadu plum 30
kale: Breakkie muffins 110
kangaroo
   Bunya nut rice paper rolls with macadamia dipping sauce 116
   Dolmades with river mint yoghurt 88
   Kangaroo chilli con carne 222
   Kangaroo lasagne 220
   Outback burger with the lot 218
   'Roo bourguignon 216
   'Roo steak sangas 224
kangaroo apple 30
   Bush tomato cheese on toast 64
   Kangaroo apple and bush tomato chutney 210
   Kangaroo chilli con carne 222
   Native sorrel and kangaroo apple baked eggs 154
   note on eating 137
   Outback burger with the lot 218
   'Roo bourguignon 216
   'Roo steak sangas 224
Kangaroo chilli con carne 222
kangaroo grass 54
   Kangaroo grass brew bread 206
kangaroo vine berry 54
karkalla 41
   Barra burger with bush tartare sauce 200
   Boonjie tamarind and macadamia noodle salad 180
   Pipi mornay 196
   tartare 200
   The epic mash 198
kefir, Garden 140
kunzea *see* white kunzea
kurrajong 54

L

lamington, Davidson's plum 186

lasagne, Kangaroo 220
leather, Plum 131
leek, native 31
lemon
   Anise myrtle and macadamia poached chicken 156
   Barb and Lil's Christmas pudding 82
   bush green pesto 114
   Fermented banksia fizz 150
   Fish pie 198
   Geraldton wax shortbread with kunzea sugar sprinkle 169
   Green garden soup 92
   Kangaroo apple and bush tomato chutney 210
   kunzea and Illawarra plum cordial 184
   Kunzea and Illawarra plum jelly 184
   Lilly pilly cordial 68
   lime drizzle 182
   Macadamia lentil curry 113
   marinade 70
   Muntries and quandong jelly slice 192
   Native fig and vanilla jam 177
   Native raspberry jam 178
   Pepperberry cookies with lemon aspen 78
   yoghurt dressing 88
lemon aspen 32
   icing 78
lemon myrtle 33
   Anise myrtle and macadamia poached chicken 156
   Baked bush apples 188
   Barb and Lil's Christmas pudding 82
   Bush botanical sugars 176
   Buttermilk and lemon myrtle set cream with muscat quandongs 161
   Dark emu beer and ant pickle 208
   Fragrant coconut rice 90
   Herby salt rub 103
   jar spices 204
   Lemon myrtle ricotta cake with pickled native cherries 189
   Macadamia, finger lime, native lemongrass and cauliflower soup 112
   marinade 70
   Mushroom and native herb broth 214
   Myrtle tea cake 80
   Native lily syrup 148
   Pepperberry cookies with lemon aspen 78

Index   243

pickled native cherries 189
quandong compote 128
Rosella jam 164
Rustic native jam tarts 165
Spiced bush apple cider 72
Spiced honey nuts 111
lemon-scented gum 32
    Barramundi poached in Geraldton wax, kunzea flower and lemon-scented gum 96
    Bush botanical sugars 176
    Face steam 141
lemongrass, native 31
    Face steam 141
    Garden kefir 140
    Green ant and crocodile curry 199
    Green ant curry paste 74
    Macadamia, finger lime, native lemongrass and cauliflower soup 112
    Sore throat spray 138
lentils
    Macadamia lentil curry 113
    Native watercress and lentil soup 94
lilly pilly 34
    Lilly pilly cordial 68
    Macadamia and pumpkin pie 226
    Strawberry gum, cherry and riberry tapioca trifle 132
    syrup 170
lily, native 54
    Native lily syrup 148
lime *see* desert lime; finger lime; sunrise lime
lime drizzle 182
'Lime'ade 68
Limey lime drizzle cake 182

M

macadamia 35
    Anise myrtle and macadamia poached chicken 156
    Baked bush apples 188
    Barb and Lil's Christmas pudding 82
    Barramundi poached in Geraldton wax, kunzea flower and lemon-scented gum 96
    Boonjie tamarind and macadamia noodle salad 180
    Breakkie muffins 110
    bush green pesto 114
    Buttermilk and lemon myrtle set cream with muscat quandongs 161
    Campfire s'mores with Davidson's plum 120
    dressing 180
    Fruity flapjacks 130
    Lemon myrtle ricotta cake with pickled native cherries 189
    macadamia and bunya nut dipping sauce 116
    Macadamia and pumpkin pie 226
    Macadamia blondies 110
    Macadamia butter 108
    Macadamia butter cups 108
    Macadamia lentil curry 113
    macadamia pie crust 226
    Macadamia, finger lime, native lemongrass and cauliflower soup 112
    Macadamia, green ant, rose and pepperberry latte 152
    pastry 168
    Pepperberry cookies with lemon aspen 78
    Peppermint gum slice 98
    Rose and pepper leaf chocolate tart with honeyed macadamias 168
    Spiced honey nuts 111
    Strawberry gum and emu bush sleepy milk 157
    Wattella 106
mangosteen, yellow 54
marinade 70
marshmallows, Davidson's plum 120
mash, The epic 198
meadow rice grass 54
medicine garden 136
midyim berry 36
    Not-quite-blueberry muffin with Illawarra plum and midyim berry 129
milk, Strawberry gum and emu bush sleepy 157
mint *see* river mint
muffins
    Breakkie muffins 110
    Not-quite-blueberry muffin with Illawarra plum and midyim berry 129
mulberry, native 36
muntries 37
    Barb and Lil's Christmas pudding 82
    Beetroot, chocolate and wattleseed cake 228
    Fruity flapjacks 130
    Muntries and quandong jelly slice 192
    Sandalwood and custard cake with Tanami apples and bush pears 118
    Spiced bush apple cider 72
murnong 54
muscat quandongs 161
mushrooms
    Dolmades with river mint yoghurt 88
    Emu steak with pepperberry and mushroom sauce 225
    Kangaroo lasagne 220
    Mushroom and native herb broth 214
    'Roo bourguignon 216
myrtle
    Herb powders 66
    see also anise myrtle; cinnamon myrtle; lemon myrtle; white feather honeymyrtle
Myrtle tea cake 80

N

native plants
    Please look under the relevant English name, e.g. 'native apricot' can be found under 'apricot, native'
nettle: Green garden soup 92
noodles
    Boonjie tamarind and macadamia noodle salad 180
    Bunya nut rice paper rolls with macadamia dipping sauce 116
    Not-quite-blueberry muffin with Illawarra plum and midyim berry 129
nuts, Spiced honey 111

O

olives: Aussie olives 70
onion, bush 39
    Caramelised bush onions 205
    Pickled bush onions 204
orange
    Barb and Lil's Christmas pudding 82
    Bush botanical bitters 145
    Coffee and anise beetroot chutney 211
    Davidson's plum jam 186
    Honey-fermented cherries 'n' berries 174
    muscat quandongs 161
    pickled native cherries 189
    quandong compote 128
    Quandong jam 178
    Rosella and tamarind pie 158
oregano, native 24
    Decongestant rub for colds and flu 139

marinade 70
Mushroom and native herb broth 214
Outback burger with the lot 218

P
palm lilly 54
pandanus 39
pantry 56–7
Parramatta wattle 54
parsley, sea 47
   bush green pesto 114
   Dolmades with river mint yoghurt 88
   Fish pie 198
   Herb powders 66
   Native watercress and lentil soup 94
   Pipi mornay 196
   tartare 200
pasta
   Kangaroo lasagne 220
   wattleseed pasta 220
pastry 168
peanut tree 40
pear, bush
   Buttermilk pickles 209
   Sandalwood and custard cake with Tanami apples and bush pears 118
peas
   Boonjie tamarind and macadamia noodle salad 180
   Fish pie 198
   Native watercress and lentil soup 94
pepperberry 40
   Anise myrtle and macadamia poached chicken 156
   Bush botanical bitters 145
   Bush botanical sugars 176
   Buttermilk pickles 209
   Cinnamon myrtle and maple popcorn 76
   Dark emu beer and ant pickle 208
   Emu steak with pepperberry and mushroom sauce 225
   Honey-fermented cherries 'n' berries 174
   Macadamia, green ant, rose and pepperberry latte 152
   marinade 70
   Native Worcestershire sauce 73
   Pepperberry cookies with lemon aspen 78
   Pickled bush onions 204
   Pickled quandongs 66
   Salt 'n' pepper popcorn 76
   Saltbush and pepper vinegar 72

Spiced honey nuts 111
Strawberry gum and emu bush sleepy milk 157
pepperberry leaves
   Barb and Lil's Christmas pudding 82
   Emu steak with pepperberry and mushroom sauce 225
   Native Worcestershire sauce 73
   'Roo bourguignon 216
   Rose and pepper leaf chocolate tart with honeyed macadamias 168
peppermint gum 49
   Bush botanical sugars 176
   Face steam 141
   Peppermint gum slice 98
   Sore throat spray 138
pesto, bush green 114
Petal powders 150
pickles
   Aussie olives 70
   Buttermilk pickles 209
   Dark emu beer and ant pickle 208
   Pickled bush onions 204
   Pickled quandongs 66
   pickled native cherries 189
   tips for pickling 232–3
pies
   Fish pie 198
   Macadamia and pumpkin pie 226
   macadamia pie crust 226
   pie crust 158
   Rosella and tamarind pie 158
pig face 41
pink-fruited lime berry 54
Pipi mornay 196
plum *see* Davidson's plum; Illawarra plum; Kakadu plum
Plum leather 131
popcorn
   Cinnamon myrtle and maple popcorn 76
   Salt 'n' pepper popcorn 76
pork
   Bunya nut rice paper rolls with macadamia dipping sauce 116
   Native watercress and lentil soup 94
   'Roo bourguignon 216
   Warrigal greens and saltbush cob 86
potato
   Fish pie 198
   The epic mash 198
powders
   Herb powders 66

Petal powders 150
prawns: Fish pie 198
preserving
   native herbs 102
   tips for 232–3
puddings
   Barb and Lil's Christmas pudding 82
   Strawberry gum rice pudding 128
pumpkin
   Macadamia and pumpkin pie 226
   Macadamia lentil curry 113
purslane: Green garden soup 92

Q
quandong 42
   Barb and Lil's Christmas pudding 82
   Bush botanical bitters 145
   Bush botanical sugars 176
   Buttermilk and lemon myrtle set cream with muscat quandongs 161
   Fruity flapjacks 130
   Honey-fermented cherries 'n' berries 174
   Muntries and quandong jelly slice 192
   muscat quandongs 161
   Outback burger with the lot 218
   Pickled quandongs 66
   Quandong and Davidson's plum iced VoVos 190
   quandong compote 128
   Quandong jam 178
   Rosella and native raspberry Swiss roll 160
   Rosella and tamarind pie 158
   Rustic native jam tarts 165
   White chocolate quandong truffles 126
Queensland bottle tree 54
quince, wild 54

R
raspberry *see* Atherton raspberry
raspberry jam wattle 43
red cottonwood 54
riberry 44
   Barb and Lil's Christmas pudding 82
   Honey-fermented cherries 'n' berries 174
   Strawberry gum, cherry and riberry tapioca trifle 132
rice
   Anise myrtle rice 154
   Bunya nut risotto with bush green pesto 114
   Dolmades with river mint yoghurt 88

Fragrant coconut rice 90
Strawberry gum rice pudding 128
rice pudding, Strawberry gum 128
risotto, Bunya nut, with bush green pesto 114

river mint 44
Bunya nut rice paper rolls with macadamia dipping sauce 116
Bush botanical bitters 145
Buttermilk and lemon myrtle set cream with muscat quandongs 161
Garden kefir 140
River mint granita 99
yoghurt dressing 88

rock fig 54
roll, Rosella and native raspberry Swiss 160
rolls, Bunya nut rice, with macadamia dipping sauce 116
'Roo bourguignon 216
'Roo steak sangas 224
Rose and pepper leaf chocolate tart with honeyed macadamias 168

rosella 45
Honey-fermented cherries 'n' berries 174
Macadamia and pumpkin pie 226
Rosella and native raspberry Swiss roll 160
Rosella and tamarind pie 158
Rosella jam 164
Rosella leaf crisps 155
Rustic native jam tarts 165
syrup 144, 170

rosemary, sea 47
Bush botanical sugars 176
Green garden soup 92
Herb powders 66
Herby salt rub 103
Kangaroo grass brew bread 206
Macadamia and pumpkin pie 226
Macadamia lentil curry 113
Spiced honey nuts 111

rubs
Decongestant rub for colds and flu 139
Herby chest rub for asthma 139
Herby salt rub 103

ruby saltbush 45
Rustic native jam tarts 165

S

sage, native: Decongestant rub for colds and flu 139
salt rub, Herby 103

saltbush 38
Bush botanical sugars 176
Dolmades with river mint yoghurt 88
Fish pie 198
Green garden soup 92
Herb powders 66
Kangaroo grass brew bread 206
Outback burger with the lot 218
Pipi mornay 196
Rosella leaf crisps 155
Salt 'n' pepper popcorn 76
Saltbush and pepper vinegar 72
Warrigal greens and saltbush cob 86
white sauce 220
see also ruby saltbush

Salt 'n' pepper popcorn 76

samphire 46
Pipi mornay 196

sandalwood, Australian 46
Breakkie muffins 110
Davidson's plum and sandalwood nut brownies 124
Sandalwood and custard cake with Tanami apples and bush pears 118
Spiced honey nuts 111
Strawberry gum rice pudding 128

sandpaper fig 54
sangas, 'Roo steak 224
sarsaparilla, false 54

sauces
finger lime sauce 116
macadamia and bunya nut dipping sauce 116
Native Worcestershire sauce 73
white sauce 220

scones, Bush tomato, with green ant butter 212
scrambling lily 54
sea celery *see* celery, island sea
sea parsley *see* parsley, sea

seablite 48
Pipi mornay 196
'Roo bourguignon 216
tartare 200

shortbread
Desert lime shortbread 183
Geraldton wax shortbread with kunzea sugar sprinkle 169

silver-leaved mountain gum 54

slice
Muntries and quandong jelly slice 192
Peppermint gum slice 98

small-leaved tamarind *see* tamarind, small-leaved
s'mores, Campfire, with Davidson's

plum 120
soda water pops 100
Sore throat spray 138

sorrel, native 48
Green baked eggs 90
Native sorrel and kangaroo apple baked eggs 154

soups
Green garden soup 92
Macadamia, finger lime, native lemongrass and cauliflower soup 112
Native watercress and lentil soup 94

spice mix
Green ant curry paste 74
Herb powders 66
Herby salt rub 103
jar spices 204
wattleseed extract 78

Spiced bush apple cider 72
Spiced honey nuts 111
spinach *see* bower spinach
spray, Sore throat 138

steaks
Emu steak with pepperberry and mushroom sauce 225
'Roo steak sangas 224

sterilising jars 232
stockists 234–5

strawberry gum 49
Bush botanical sugars 176
Strawberry gum and emu bush sleepy milk 157
Strawberry gum and Geraldton wax cupcakes 166
Strawberry gum, cherry and riberry tapioca trifle 132
strawberry gum icing 166
Strawberry gum rice pudding 128

stress balls, Flower and leaf 140
sugars, Bush botanical 176
sunrise lime: 'Lime'ade 68
sunshine wattle 54
sweet apple berry 49
sweet-scented wattle 54
Swiss roll, Rosella and native raspberry 160

syrups 170
Native lily syrup 148
Rosella syrup 144

T

tamarind, small-leaved 50
Boonjie tamarind and macadamia noodle salad 180

Native Worcestershire sauce 73
Rosella and tamarind pie 158

Tanami apple
Sandalwood and custard cake with Tanami apples and bush pears 118
Spiced bush apple cider 72

tartare 200

tarts
Rose and pepper leaf chocolate tart with honeyed macadamias 168
Rustic native jam tarts 165

ten corners fruit 54

The epic mash 198

thyme, native 50
Caramelised bush onions 205
Decongestant rub for colds and flu 139
Emu steak with pepperberry and mushroom sauce 225
Garden kefir 140
Herby salt rub 103
Kangaroo lasagne 220
Mushroom and native herb broth 214
'Roo bourguignon 216

toast, Bush tomato cheese on 64

tomato
Dolmades with river mint yoghurt 88
Green ant and crocodile curry 199
Kangaroo apple and bush tomato chutney 210
Kangaroo lasagne 220
'Roo steak sangas 224

tomato, bush 51
Baked bush apples 188
Bush botanical sugars 176
Bush tomato cheese on toast 64
Bush tomato scones with green ant butter 212
Buttermilk pickles 209
Fruity flapjacks 130
Kangaroo apple and bush tomato chutney 210
Kangaroo chilli con carne 222
Outback burger with the lot 218
'Roo steak sangas 224
Salt 'n' pepper popcorn 76

trifle, Strawberry gum, cherry and riberry tapioca 132

truffles, White chocolate quandong 126

V

vinegar, Saltbush and pepper 72

VoVos, Quandong and Davidson's plum iced 190

W

warrigal greens 51
Barra burger with bush tartare sauce 200
bush green pesto 114
Green baked eggs 90
Green garden soup 92
Kangaroo chilli con carne 222
Kangaroo lasagne 220
Outback burger with the lot 218
'Roo steak sangas 224
Warrigal greens and saltbush cob 86

watercress, native 52
Green baked eggs 90
Native watercress and lentil soup 94

Wattella 106

wattle *see* coastal wattle; Parramatta wattle; raspberry jam wattle; sunshine wattle; sweet-scented wattle; wattleseed

Wattlemisu 170

wattleseed 52
Barb and Lil's Christmas pudding 82
Beetroot, chocolate and wattleseed cake 228
Boonjie tamarind and macadamia noodle salad 180
Breakkie muffins 110
Buttermilk and lemon myrtle set cream with muscat quandongs 161
Campfire s'mores with Davidson's plum 120
coastal wattle 54
custard 118, 132
Davidson's plum and sandalwood nut brownies 124
Davidson's plum lamington 186
extract 78
icing 228
Parramatta wattle 54
pasta 220
pastry 168
Pepperberry cookies with lemon aspen 78
Peppermint gum slice 98
Sandalwood and custard cake with Tanami apples and bush pears 118
Spiced honey nuts 111
Strawberry gum, cherry and riberry tapioca trifle 132
sunshine wattle 54
sweet-scented wattle 54
syrup 170
Wattella 106
Wattlemisu 170
White chocolate quandong truffles 126

White chocolate quandong truffles 126

white feather honeymyrtle 54

white kunzea 53
Barramundi poached in Geraldton wax, kunzea flower and lemon-scented gum 96
Bush botanical sugars 176
Face steam 141
Geraldton wax shortbread with kunzea sugar sprinkle 169
kunzea and Illawarra plum cordial 184
Kunzea and Illawarra plum jelly 184

white sauce 220

wild basil *see* basil, wild

wild currant 24

wild onion 39

wild quince 54

Worcestershire sauce, Native 73

Y

yam, blue 54

yam daisy: Buttermilk pickles 209

yellow mangosteen 54

yoghurt dressing 88

yoghurt pops 100

youlk: Buttermilk pickles 209

Z

zucchini: Breakkie muffins 110

Published in 2022 by Murdoch Books, an imprint of Allen & Unwin

Murdoch Books Australia
83 Alexander Street
Crows Nest NSW 2065
Phone: +61 (0)2 8425 0100
murdochbooks.com.au
info@murdochbooks.com.au

Murdoch Books UK
Ormond House
26–27 Boswell Street
London WC1N 3JZ
Phone: +44 (0) 20 8785 5995
murdochbooks.co.uk
info@murdochbooks.co.uk

For corporate orders and custom publishing, contact our business development team at salesenquiries@murdochbooks.com.au

Publisher: Jane Morrow
Editorial Manager: Justin Wolfers
Design Manager: Kristy Allen
Designer: Jenna Lee
Editor: David Matthews
Photographer: Josh Geelen
Stylists: Duy Dash and Rebecca Sullivan
Illustrator: Charlotte Allingham
Production Director: Lou Playfair

Text © Damien Coulthard and Rebecca Sullivan 2022
The moral right of the authors has been asserted.
Design © Murdoch Books 2022
Photography © Josh Geelen 2022
Artworks on endpapers and pages 14, 62, 84, 104, 122, 134, 142, 172, 194, 202 © Damien Coulthard 2022
Artworks on pages 15, 63, 85, 105, 123, 135, 143, 173, 195, 203 © Jenna Lee 2022

We acknowledge that we meet and work on the traditional lands of the Cammeraygal people of the Eora Nation and pay our respects to their elders past, present and future.

All rights reserved. No part of this publication may be reproduced, stored in a retrieval system or transmitted in any form or by any means, electronic, mechanical, photocopying, recording or otherwise, without the prior written permission of the publisher.

ISBN 9 781 92235 188 3

 A catalogue record for this book is available from the National Library of Australia

A catalogue record for this book is available from the British Library

The information provided within this book is for general inspiration and informational purposes only. While we try to keep the information up-to-date and correct, the author and publisher do not assume and hereby disclaim any liability to any party for any loss, damage, or disruption caused by errors or omissions, whether such errors or omissions result from negligence, accident, or any other cause. Individuals using or consuming the plants listed in this book do so entirely at their own risk. Always check a reputable source to ensure that the plants you are using are non-toxic, organic, unsprayed and safe to be consumed. The author and/or publisher cannot be held responsible for any adverse reactions.

Oven guide:
You may find cooking times vary depending on the oven you are using. For fan-forced ovens, as a general rule, set the oven temperature to 20°C (35°F) lower than indicated in the recipe.

Tablespoon measures:
We have used 20 ml (4 teaspoon) tablespoon measures. If you are using a 15 ml (3 teaspoon) tablespoon, add an extra teaspoon of the ingredient for each tablespoon specified.

Colour reproduction by Splitting Image Colour Studio Pty Ltd, Clayton, Victoria

Printed by 1010 Printing International Limited, China

10 9 8 7 6 5

JENNA LEE is a Larrakia, Wardaman and Karajarri woman with mixed Asian (Chinese, Japanese and Filipino) and Anglo Australian ancestry. Formally trained as a graphic designer, Jenna Lee works as an independent designer specialising in culturally informed book cover design, exhibition identity design, catalogue design and arts sector design. Finding great joy in working collaboratively with other First Nations curators and artists allowing overlaying passions of typesetting, design and art to collide. Lee has designed for Redland City Council Art Gallery, Blaklash Creative, Aboriginal Art Co as well as The Institute of Modern Art. Lee's design exhibition identity and catalogue dean for 'Gathering Strands' received a Highly Commended award at the Museums & Gallery Design Publication Awards in 2016.
Insta: @jenna.mlee

CHARLOTTE ALLINGHAM is a 28-year-old Wiradjuri and Ngiyampaa, Queer Woman from central nsw, with family ties to Condobolin and Ivanhoe areas, currently living in Naarm (melbourne). Focusing on Blak excellence, she weaves through self-determination and Truth through her work. She tries to challenge the perception of her people through her own creative expression.